"Pastor Josh Moody takes us verse by verse through Paul's letter to the Galatians. Along the way, he exposes our tendency toward man-exalting 'gospels' and then focuses our attention on the good news that exalts Christ. *No Other Gospel* is a model of compelling biblical exposition and a timely reminder to the church of the unchanging good news."

Trevin Wax, author, *Counterfeit Gospels: Rediscovering the Good News in a World of False Hopes* and *Holy Subversion: Allegiance to Christ in an Age of Rivals*

"Paul's letter to the Galatians so strongly and passionately articulates the gospel of grace that it has proved transforming in many generations of preachers from Luther to Wesley and beyond. Here Josh Moody reinforces that heritage for the twenty-first century."

D. A. Carson, Research Professor of New Testament, Trinity Evangelical Divinity School

"These expositions are clear, well-organized, exegetically careful, and theologically faithful. They're also filled with good illustrations, personal application, and a proper dose of British wit. These qualities make for very good preaching and a very good book."

Kevin DeYoung, Senior Pastor, University Reformed Church, East Lansing, Michigan

"Josh Moody's *No Other Gospel* blends attention to the text, theological insight, and pastoral application in a model of scriptural exposition. His focus on Galatians is a great choice, since this letter addresses so clearly the nature and importance of the gospel—a critical matter in an age when so many Christians and so many churches are confused about the gospel and its centrality."

Douglas J. Moo, Blanchard Professor of New Testament, Wheaton College

no
other
gospel

31 Reasons
from Galatians
Why Justification
by Faith Alone Is
the Only Gospel

josh moody

CROSSWAY

WHEATON, ILLINOIS

Trade paperback ISBN: 978-1-4335-1567-5
PDF ISBN: 978-1-4335-1568-2
Mobipocket ISBN: 978-1-4335-1569-9
ePub ISBN: 978-1-4335-2489-9

Library of Congress Cataloging-in-Publication Data
Moody, Josh.
  No other gospel : 31 reasons from Galations why justification by faith alone is the only gospel / Josh Moody.
      p. cm.
  Includes index.
  ISBN 978-1-4335-1567-5 (tpb)   ISBN 978-1-4335-1568-2 (PDF)
  ISBN 978-1-4335-1569-9 (Mobipocket)   ISBN 978-1-4335-2489-9 (ePub)
  1. Bible, N.T. Galations—Commentaries. I. Title. II. Title: 31 reasons from Galatians why justification by faith alone is the only gospel. III. Title: Thirty one reasons from Galatians why justification by faith alone is the only gospel. IV. Thirty and one reasons from Galatians why justification by faith alone is the only gospel.
BS2685.53.M66   2011
227'.4077—dc22   2010032013

Crossway is a publishing ministry of Good News Publishers.
VP		21	20	19	18	17	16	15	14	13	12	11
15	14	13	12	11	10	9	8	7	6	5	4	3	2	1

To Rochelle
without whom none of this would be possible

Contents

Introduction

This book is born of a passionate conviction that large swathes of the church have grown used to a gospel that is no gospel. This was the conviction that fueled Paul's famous letter to the Galatians, and the more I have studied it, the more I have felt its relevance as never before. Yes, commentaries on this book outweigh its contents at a rate far exceeding a book per word in the original manuscript. But this is not another commentary; it is the text preached first in the context of a congregation and then in the wider context of the community, now the readers of these written words.

I make no bones about them originating as sermons. Lloyd-Jones felt that his sermons should be printed fairly close to the original as preached. I feel somewhat the same. Certainly there are references to time and specifics of place that need to be removed, as well as peculiarities of the spoken word that suit ill with the written. But like much of our Christian literature, this began as a dynamic oral tradition, and it is passed on now with that same gleam of ardor.

What do I mean by the many gospels that are not gospels of which the contemporary church has grown accustomed? I mean any gospel that is essentially human in its taste. That seems to be the defining issue for Paul. When Paul distinguishes his gospel as "not by man," he is far from merely making an intellectual argument that he is an apostle of Christ and got his doctrine by revelation. That is part of his case—at an intellectual level it is fundamental to it—but he is saying something far more profound than that. Why does he begin this way with this epistle designed to be read by all the church down through history? He does so because that is always the first issue and the root cause of our going astray. We tend toward human gospels. Their taste suits our palate. We prefer things that are perhaps masked in novel formulations or interesting speculations but which at the bottom line are basically human. They have the similar feel to all other gospels that are really no gospel at all.

That feel is one of humanness. It is one of looking to please other humans. The gospel of God is by its nature not designed to please humans. It is designed to please God. That is one sign of a false gospel, that somehow it tastes as we should have expected. If the gospel that we are used to is something that we could have made up, then we can be sure that it is not a gospel from God. The gospel requires revelation, and it requires divine illumination for us to see. Every other aspect of gospels that are really not gospels stems from this one basic error. That is why Paul starts there. It is the drumbeat throughout the letter. He is most passionate—throughout this passionate letter!—at any point that seems to diverge from the "God-ness" of the gospel.

So there is that. But then there are many gospels that are God-centered which are not Christian. That of course is obvious to any student of world religions, but it seems necessary to state, for Christians can sometimes feel that they have cornered the market on divine properties. There are other monotheisms. But no, Paul does not stop there, and at the very heart of the letter he identifies the central issue: the cross of Jesus Christ.

All true proclamations of the gospel center on Christ. They do not *start* there. Christ is the answer to a deep, profound, human problem. Some gospels seem to get God right but miss entirely the cross. Well, actually that too is a human-pleasing gospel, not a gospel of true divine origin. God has designed things to exalt his Son at the cross, and any gospel that does not center on the cross of Jesus Christ is not truly God-centered in a real sense. It is a distortion of God-centeredness. Paul makes all of this very clear at the end of Galatians 2. We are crucified with Christ. Any gospel that has no room for that stark message is no gospel that Paul (or more importantly the Bible or God himself) would recognize.

This brings us to one of the great oddities about Galatians, rarely mentioned if at all, which is its comparative silence on the matter of sin for long portions of its discussion. Of course, Paul here, as in Romans, understands the essential need of humanity in terms of our "sin," saying as much in verse 4 of the first chapter! Much of chapter 5 is also about living morally. Still, in the book of Romans (the best commentary on Galatians) sin is first declared as the universal sickness of humanity before the solution of Christ crucified is presented. But not here. We have an extended argument about Paul's credentials as someone who did get this gospel by revelation, and a display of how Paul was right in what had become a well-known disagreement with Peter, and then these statements that center upon the cross. Why no extended theology of sin?

The answer of course is that Paul is dealing with people who were beyond thinking of themselves as sinners. At least in Romans the separation of man from God was a live problem to which Paul presented the solution, but in Galatians they had moved beyond all that. Nothing displays the profound seriousness of the problem in which the Galatians found themselves more than that they seemed to have made themselves immune to the category of being sinners in need of salvation. I suspect that nothing shows the great sickness of much of our Western society more than the same thing.

These were Christians in danger of losing their authentic orthodox Christianity, but at this point still Christians nonetheless. And for our churches today nothing, I think, shows the seriousness of the situation we are in more than that we have birthed a generation that is not used to feeling humbled by the grandeur of the holiness of God and therefore not living in the profound joy of thankfulness to Christ. I speak to myself as much as to anyone. Perhaps the Western church is, above all, a complaining church. We harp on about our difficulties and problems, but rarely do we play the harp in praise to Christ our redeemer in consciousness of our own innate sinfulness.

What do we do with such a situation? We do what Paul did. Within our own context, we claim the divinity of our gospel message, we point to the necessity of the centrality of Christ, and we show how what we have been told is superior is really far inferior, and it is a perversion of the Bible that we hold dear. This gospel that is no gospel is far from breaking down barriers; it raises them up again. It is what caused Peter to separate himself from fellow believers. Why? Because it is human. And humans are tribal. And tribalism is divisive, for it's a play on endless shifting ground about who is superior.

We must grasp the universal nature of what Paul is talking about. Perhaps that is the key at a technical level for understanding Galatians today. The book of Galatians is really neither about first-century

Judaism nor about sixteenth-century Roman Catholicism. It is actually about our common human tendency to think we no longer need Jesus. We have moved on from the cross. We now have a bigger, better gospel—a gospel that is no gospel—that will divide us from God's people, and that is the common human tendency to self-righteousness.

Yes, sin is not expounded at great length in this letter but self-righteousness instead (even worse). That was the sin of the Galatians, and I suspect it is our sin too. So, as we survey all of Paul's argument about the right interpretation of the Old Testament in the middle part of the letter, we come to his other great theme, which is the work of the Spirit. Arguments innumerable abound about justification, as if for Paul this was "merely" a dry doctrine, a legal doctrine, a doctrine about position and status and declaration. In reality, it was for Paul a spiritual doctrine. It was connected to regeneration. So, far from being a confusing addition, as so many have thought, Paul's great treatise on the work of the Spirit in the Christian's life is inextricably connected to his teaching on justification.

Those three subjects form the heart of what is, and therefore what is not, the gospel. It is God-ness—in origin, subject, feel, taste, and honor—all to him and from him. It is cross-centered understanding of justification by faith alone. The cross is at the heart of all this, and then the work of the Holy Spirit, who breathes through the book and is inextricably connected with the one true gospel.

I suppose we should not be surprised that Paul's theology of the gospel is Trinitarian. Nor should we be surprised that his announced intention, the gospel of grace and peace, is what he provides through the atoning work of Christ on the cross—peace with God, according to the grace of Christ.

1

The God-ness of the Gospel

Paul, an apostle—not from men nor through man, but through Jesus Christ and God the Father, who raised him from the dead—and all the brothers who are with me, to the churches of Galatia.

GALATIANS 1:1–2

In the heart of everyone lies an atheist. Not perhaps the kind that thinks in a strict literal sense that God does not exist. There may be some in church like that. When Christians gather, we are never to assume that all believe; rather, we are to hope that those who do not believe come so that we might present the truth of God in word and deed.

There may be some reading these words who struggle with the reality of God when difficult things are happening and times are tough. But the kind of atheist I am talking about, which lies in my heart and in yours, is the kind which believes not that God does not exist but that God is not able. We are practical, not theoretical, atheists. We come to church. We are busy in God's work. We serve. We talk the talk; we even walk the walk. But we tend to act as if God and the gospel are not sufficient to achieve what needs to be achieved. We are people who have the gospel but for whom the gospel has become a starting point rather than the reference point for all our efforts. We are religious; we may call ourselves evangelicals, but the *evangel* (that is, the gospel) does not impregnate every aspect of our theology nor every part of our lives.

In short, we are tempted to believe that what happens in church on Sunday morning is a human event. That is why Paul begins his letter with such a fierce denial—"not from men nor through man" (v. 1). As we notice that, we realize that straight away, unlike many of his letters, Paul seems to feel the need to begin by establishing his authority. Why does he do that? It is just one of the many puzzles that Galatians presents to the Bible student. But for all its complexity, and we will gradually unravel some of those knots together, Galatians is a book of fire and ice. It reminds me of the story of the young man who was first being set aside for the ministry. He was asked whether he was zealous. He said that he was but that he was not the kind of person who set the Thames River on fire. The man interviewing him said, "I don't want you to set the river on fire. What I want to know is, when I throw you in will there be steam?"

Despite all the complexities in which Galatians has been tied up throughout the years of human interpretation, it still sets up steam whenever it is read. It, of course, was the book that really kicked off the Reformation. Martin Luther called it the love of his life; it was "Katherina Von Bora," his wife. He studied it repeatedly and found in it the release of the gospel to free him from his legalism. It has done that to many another since. It was John Wesley who, through the reading of Luther's preface to the book of Galatians, found that "his heart was strangely warmed."

In fact, I think we may take it as a rule that Galatians is one of those books of the Bible that the Devil loves to try to blunt. It is a sharp sword, and my suspicion is that today as never before it needs to be unleashed to our world and to our church, yet scholars know that there are many head-scratching moments that it produces and that people ponder over. Our task will not be to enjoy scratching our heads together over its difficult bits but to clarify and then unleash. Like any part of the Bible, it does not need defending. "Defend the Bible," Spurgeon said once, when asked about his approach to answering difficult questions of Scripture, "I'd sooner defend a lion." As no other, this is a lion, and together we simply need to study it carefully so that we can clearly listen to it roar.

In this chapter we are dealing with just two verses, so we don't need to tackle all the questions at once; these two verses will be quite enough for now. What I want us to learn here is that it is absolutely essential that we have our religious authority in the right place.

I'm a parent of three young children. Before I was a parent, there were certain things I thought I would never do as a parent. One was lick the corner of a handkerchief and wipe the face of my child. I remember seeing someone do that and thinking, *I'll never do that*. Another was resorting to the cop-out, "Because Daddy says so." Why are we going to do this, why that? "Because Daddy says so." But there are times when that assertion of parental authority is not only necessary but essential. "Don't cross the road. There's a car coming. Stop!"

That's what Paul is doing. *Not by man, but by God.* In fact, the whole first two chapters of this letter are really taken up with Paul's asserting his authority as an apostle. He interweaves complex doctrine, especially at the end of chapter 2, a long story about how he became an apostle, and about when he confronted Peter, and it's all saying, "Not by man but by God." Then in chapters 3 and 4 he outlines in more detail the message of the gospel as against those who had agitated the Galatian Christians with their message of the necessity of law. The agitators were saying that Jesus was not enough; you also needed lots of rules. Paul denies it there and explains why that is nonsense theologically as well as experientially. Then in chapters 5 and 6 he gets very practical and explains how his gospel (God's gospel) actually does what the agitators said the law could do. His gospel reconciles. His gospel produces moral fruit. His gospel has the power of the Spirit and frees people from the bondage of habits that self-destruct.

Paul is saying, "You're asking why. I've heard you're off on the wrong track. Okay, I'm going to explain, but you've got to get this first, partly *because the apostle says so.*" It's a straightforward, bold authority claim.

I want you to understand from these first two verses, as we begin to get into Galatians together, that it's very important that we have our religious authority in the right place. If we are crossing the road and about to get hit by a massive truck because we're looking the wrong way, we need to have that voice say, "stop," so he begins with this claim to his apostolic authority, "not." What we need to learn at the outset is this: believe the message of God's messenger. Paul gives us three reasons why we should do that.

Believe God's Messenger Because God Sent Him

First, *believe the message of God's messenger because God sent him.* "Paul, an apostle—not from men nor through man, but through Jesus Christ and God the Father" (v. 1). This looks like a traditional ancient greeting, but, like all of Paul's greetings, this is the summary of the message of his letter. It's like an e-mail heading: From, To, RE. This is what this letter is about. There are three practical implications for us.

1) *If God can use Paul, he can use you.* There is a unique aspect to Paul's sending, which we will get to, but Paul's conversion is also constantly used in Scripture as a model for what God can do. He was Saul. He was the religious terrorist. He was converted. He became a church planter and preacher, an evangelist and missionary. We are practical atheists if we limit God's usefulness of us to our personality. God did not so greatly use Paul because he thought Paul had all the right credentials. It was not "Oh, Paul, he knows the Bible and has good connections; let's get him." No, it was the religious terrorist. How unlikely is that? God delights to take unlikely people and use them because then the focus is on God, not on the unlikely people.

I've heard Billy Graham preach live two or three times. I was never impressed with his rhetorical skills, but I was deeply impressed with the power of the Spirit. I've met powerful religious leaders, and then I've met the dear old lady with the faraway prayerful look in her eye. I know that "the friendship of the LORD is for those who fear him" (Ps. 25:14), and that the lady is moving heaven and earth for the Billy Grahams of the Lord. She will be at the front of the line to the throne of heaven. There are lots of talented people around church today, and I don't despise that. We used to joke when I pastored near Yale that we were probably the Baptist church with the highest average IQ in America, and at the church where I worked in Cambridge, one practically needed a PhD to run the overhead projector. Fine, God can use our talents. He's given them to us. But as soon as we think our talents are why God chose us, rather than that God delighted to use us, the chief of sinners, I suspect that God may begin looking for another weeping widow or broken man, for God raises up the humble, and pride comes before a fall. It is the Sauls that God makes Pauls. That is a statement of practical theism, not practical atheism.

2) *If Paul was an apostle, we are not.* There are two kinds of apostles in the New Testament. There are the apostles of the churches, those sent by the churches for various tasks, and then there are the apostles of Christ, those sent by Jesus himself. Of course, Paul is claiming here to be the latter sort of an apostle of Christ. But where does this word

apostle come from? Some have said that it was a Jewish term used of an official position. That is possible, but the evidence for it is later than this, and those positions were different in some ways from this anyway. Others have said the word was just taken from the Greek, but in Greek it was rarely used in this way; sometimes it was used of a naval expedition or of a boat. The answer is that the word comes as used by Christ, and he is picking up on the word from the Old Testament, all of which is fulfilled in him. So Jesus said, "As the Father has sent me, even so I am sending you" (John 20:21). He called them to himself and designated some apostles. That word *apostle* in the Greek translation of the Old Testament is used repeatedly of Moses and his sending by God and of Isaiah and his sending by God. "Here I am, send me. . . . Go, I am sending you."

The apostles were God's sent people, uniquely authorized, as were the prophets in the Old Testament, specifically following on Christ's sending into the world by God the Father, carrying on that mission. This was a special sending, no longer in existence, that Paul had uniquely "as to one untimely born" (1 Cor. 15:8) through his Damascus road encounter with the risen Christ himself. Therefore, our authority must be, practically speaking, taken from Scripture, not from tradition or culture or what humans of any kind, dead or living, say. They can help, but they can never go toe-to-toe with Scripture, and when they do, the Bible must win. When preaching, I want people flicking through the pages, staring down at the Bible, believing the Word that comes through me, not just the human speech. When we plan, it is the Bible that must guide. Our worship must be Bible-centered in order to be God-centered.

3) *If Paul was not from man nor by man, we who minister God's Word must at least be not from man if we are also necessarily by man.* Ministers of the gospel are called by churches. They are "by man" in that sense, but they are also to be from God ultimately, that sending which the church confirms. No one is to be in the pulpit—ordained as a missionary, church planter, pastor, elder, or otherwise set aside by God for Word ministry—unless he is in an ultimate sense put there by God, even though that calling must be confirmed by the church in a regular and proper fashion to keep the lunatics out, and because there are no apostles in Paul's sense any more today.

No one in his right mind signs up for God's work for the fun of it. There are better ways to get beaten up. "Paul, you've got to go and do this, and let me show you how much you will suffer for my name."

"Moses, you want to go."

"Actually, no, I don't."

"Well, you've got to anyway.

"Isaiah, will you go?"

"Here I am, send me"

"Oh, and by the way, no one's going to listen."

"Jeremiah, you're on, but your ministry will have no impact, and the people will go into exile, and you'll be known as the weeping prophet."

"Thanks, God. *Sign me up.*"

First you'll be spit out, then you'll be beaten up. Some people will hate you. They'll twist your words. People like the Galatians, for whom you have given your heart and soul, will line up to get circumcised if you turn your back for five minutes. Sounds like fun. If God wants you, he'll get you, and you'll need this burden that you are there because God wants you there. Even Augustine was made a bishop against his initial desire. We should serve willingly but not willfully. God is real, and he gets his people where he wants them. That is practical theism.

Believe God's Messenger Because God Raised Jesus from the Dead

Second, believe the message of God's messenger *because God raised Jesus from the dead*. "Paul, an apostle—not from men nor through man, but through Jesus Christ and God the Father, *who raised him* [that is, Jesus] *from the dead*" (v. 1). People wonder why Paul mentions the resurrection at this point. They think it's strange that it comes before the cross, which we find in verse 4. The resurrection is mentioned here because it's part of Paul's establishing his authority. God raised Jesus from the dead, and Paul received his commission as an apostle by seeing the risen Jesus on the Damascus road. So we may guess that the Galatian agitators—those who were in one way or another causing difficulty in the churches in Galatia—were saying that Paul's experience was just a mystical one, a personal conversion experience. Paul is going to show that he received it all from Jesus, not from man, as he goes on throughout this first section of the letter. Right here at the beginning he includes that God raised Jesus from the dead. Paul is saying, "I did not have a personal mystical experience—I actually saw Jesus."

Why does that matter for practical atheists like us? It matters because Jesus is alive. We don't worship a dead hero; we worship a living Lord. Jesus rules the church, and he rules by his word. Prayer makes a difference. Private repentance is the bit of yeast that makes a difference to the whole batch of dough. So is the private sin. This is a spiritual reality. We are not playing at church. Heaven and hell stand on the brink, eternal decisions are being made in the secrets of all our hearts, and I want you to know that Jesus is alive. He has the power to rescue you. He breaks you that he might remake you. He has put you here reading for this very purpose, that your theft at work may stop, that your marriage may be healed, that your life may be turned around. The church is not a tomb for a dead Lord; it is a vehicle for a living Savior, vibrating with his Holy Spirit.

He is God. Notice how Paul just assumes Jesus' divinity here. It's not by men but by Jesus. Jesus is not just a man. He is God. He and God the Father are one. It's important to notice the internal logic of Scripture, as John Stott is said to have called it. Jesus is alive. He is God. He is Lord. He knows the secrets of your heart. He knows your pain. He knows all. He is not distant and dead; he is present by his Spirit, and there is a unique moment now when Christ, as you receive him by faith, can come and do his renewing work in your heart.

It seems to me that the great difference between practical theism and practical atheism is the church of the living God. Jesus is alive, and we can't keep that a secret. It is not okay to think, *When they get to know us, they'll realize that Jesus is alive.* It has to be front and center in our worship, our smiles, our greetings, our interaction, our preaching—in everything we do, Jesus is alive. Church is not an evangelical golf club. It is the church of the living God, and we need to indicate that. We don't want to give the impression that Jesus died and went to heaven in 1950. He's still alive and doing things today. A church that decides it has "arrived" is a breath away from dying. Pride becomes a fall. We need practical theism, a resurrection theology, the power of the Spirit through the Word of God.

Christ's resurrection confirms and establishes Paul's authority and therefore the authority of the Bible. Christ's resurrection means that he is alive today and here by his Spirit, and his Word is a living word. It means that preaching is not merely lecturing. Preaching is teaching, but preaching is to be logic on fire, as it's been called. It is to have what I call a "prophetic edge." One time when Charles Spurgeon was preaching, he looked up into the gallery and said, "There is a man there with a pair of gloves in his pocket that are not his." It was true, and the man was converted. This is not weird enthusiasm; it is the working of Christ by his Spirit through his Word. Another time Spurgeon was sounding out the acoustics in a building and said, "Behold, the Lamb of God who takes away the sin of the world." The janitor was converted on the spot.

I don't know what sadnesses you carry with you, but God does. Jesus does. Not man, but Christ. He is risen. He is here for you to take him and embrace him anew, to break down that brick wall of defense between you and the power of the Spirit and to be renewed in his likeness.

Believe the Messenger Because God's Family Agrees

Third, believe the message of God's messenger *because God's family agrees*. "And all the brothers who are with me, to the churches of Galatia . . . " (v. 2). First, notice that though Paul unashamedly asserts his authority, he is still humbly a part of the family. It is "all the brothers who are with me." He has a special calling as an apostle, but he is also one of the brothers. They are all mentioned here in general to indicate that they support this letter. Their support is not theologically required for Paul; all that's required is his authority as an apostle. But their support is noted. There may be times when, like Athanasius, we are to be against, it feels, the whole world in our support of the core message of the gospel, but, by and large, even the apostle, and especially servants such as we, are to be humbly aware of the support, the counsel, and the checks and balances of good brothers and sisters around us.

Notice also that Paul is not writing to the church of Galatia but to the *churches* of Galatia. There is a long, old debate about exactly which part of Galatia Paul means, and the answer to that debate doesn't matter as much as sometimes thought. (We will look at it when we get to those places in the text where it has some bearing on chronology.) But it is interesting that he does not talk of the church but of the church*es*. There are places in the New Testament where the church is mentioned as the universal church, but that same church always has a local manifestation. It is the constant assumption of Scripture that, to be a member of the universal church, one must be a member of a local church. Here were several local churches all alike affected by the confusion that Paul seeks to counter with the clarion call to the centrality of the gospel. Each of these churches is important, and every Christian is assumed to be a part of one of the local fellowships or congregations or churches.

Common in the Western world is the feeling that as long as we are Christians, we don't really need to be a part of a local church. Obviously some of the mechanics of the local church today are just part and parcel of life in the twentieth-first century, things we can't find in the text of the New Testament itself, any more than we can find church architecture explicitly discussed. Having said that, the New Testament knows nothing of a Christian who is not a part of a local church. So, if you're a Christian but not a part of a local church, find a biblical church where you can get involved in order to be securely and confidently a member of the universal church.

We have only just begun. As you can see, the book of Galatians is very relevant. The message of Galatians as a whole is simply that a "Jesus-plus" gospel is really a "Jesus-minus" gospel; if you add to Jesus, you are really detracting from Jesus, from his centrality, from his sufficiency, from his glory. Galatians is a call back to the centrality of the gospel in all things. It is a challenge to us to realize that the gospel itself makes us grow holy, not the law but the Spirit of the risen Christ. Chapter by chapter we are going to soak in these things.

In these first two verses, we have seen Paul set out his subject by means of a bold claim to his authority. He is watching the young Christians in Galatia enthusiastically embracing an addition to the gospel in order to become more mature, but that addition will be a subtraction and supplant their trust in Christ alone. Paul is worried for them. He is up late at night caring for them. He loves them. They are his children. He has fought battles for them. He is writing this letter at a frenetic pace. It's possible that he wrote this letter personally, not using a secretary, and wrote at great pace. As he did so his letters got larger

and larger as he wrote faster and faster over page after page. He longs
for them. He sees a sixteen-wheeler trailer truck bearing down the road,
and they are crossing into its path while looking the other way, misled,
smiling, but in real danger. He says, "Not by man but by God—by Jesus
Christ and God the Father—stop! Don't cross that road! Rest in Christ
alone." He is alive. He commissioned Paul. It is the Bible. It is the gospel.
There is no other way, and to this centrality of Christ and the gospel,
Paul is calling us.

This is what it's got to be. At the very heart of it is the gospel. If
you've come for anything else, you've come to the wrong book. Nothing
else do I have to offer. There is nothing else. You're going to read about
Christ, about faith in him, about the gospel of Jesus, and that is it.

2

The Gospel of Grace and Peace

Grace to you and peace from God our Father and the Lord Jesus Christ, who gave himself for our sins to deliver us from the present evil age, according to the will of our God and Father, to whom be the glory forever and ever. Amen.

GALATIANS 1:3–5

When you write a letter, you begin a certain way. Typically, letters in English begin with "Dear so-and-so." If you were instant-messaging on your Facebook page, it might just be "Hi." Other languages have different traditions. In French, a formal letter typically begins simply, "Monsieur," and the more intimate equivalent of "Dear" is reserved for someone one knows. We don't think of how affectionate our traditional greeting is in English. We don't normally go up to someone we hardly know and say, "My dear, let me talk to you about something." But it is the form to begin letters with "dear."

There was protocol in the ancient world too. Typically, letters in Greek began with "Greetings" or a wish for joy to the recipient. We find this traditional greeting at the beginning of James's letter in the New Testament. A common form of well-wishing among the Hebrew speakers was "Peace," or *shalom*. What we find in Paul's letters, and a few other places in the New Testament, is that the traditional greeting has been infused with Christian doctrine and pastoral application. So here we have, "Grace to you and peace" (v. 3).

Grace is very close to the traditional greeting, but here it is slightly changed, and it carries the weight of the Christian doctrine of grace. Peace is there as what grace achieves. So, at the very start of his letters, Paul says, "This is the gospel," grace and peace. Here, more than in any of his letters, Paul immediately feels the need to clarify that this greeting is not simply "Hi" on his instant-message Facebook, or

"Dear" in a letter. This grace and peace is about the one "who gave himself for our sins to deliver us from the present evil age" (v. 4). Right up front he puts forth what he is going to write about. This is it—grace and peace. Martin Luther said about grace and peace that they "embrace the whole of Christianity. Grace forgives sin, and peace stills the conscience."

This is important because there is great danger that we can lose sight of what all this is actually about, which is what was going on with the Galatians. They thought that grace and peace were just words. They had lost the meaning of the words; they were supplementing the gospel with various ceremonies. Of course, this was leading to friction. Some were on the inside track and others felt on the outside. There were divisions between Jews and Gentiles. They had begun to think that something other than grace and peace lay at the heart of their fellowship, because they had begun to think that something other than grace and peace lay at the heart of their salvation.

When we say "good-bye," we just say the word without thinking that we are actually saying, "God be with you." There's nothing wrong with just saying "good-bye," but there is something wrong with thinking that grace and peace are just religious words and not about the sacrificial death of Jesus Christ for our sins. If we don't keep that clear, we'll soon lose our way and have friction about other things, as well as an uneasy conscience. When Paul says, "Grace to you and peace," he is not just wishing them peaceful feelings. He is referencing the death of Jesus for our sins, which means we can have peace with God for all eternity.

Good novels and stories have diverse elements, but one thing they all have in common is a tight plotline. The Galatians had lost the plot. Paul's words were designed to serve as a compass, their guiding star, their GPS telling them the way to go. Those involved in political campaigns are always saying to each other, "You've got to stay on message." Paul does that with the Galatians, and he says the same to us. In our last chapter we looked at Paul's authority as an apostle and that we should believe his message because God had sent him. Now he is beginning to tell us what that message is. He is urging us to stay on message.

Stay on Grace

Paul writes, "Grace to you and peace from God our Father and the Lord Jesus Christ, who gave himself for our sins to deliver us from the present evil age, according to the will of our God and Father, to whom be the glory forever and ever. Amen" (Gal. 1:3–5). Every word of that is grace.

First, it is *grace from God our Father and the Lord Jesus Christ.* Our salvation does not start with us. We do not initiate the process. We did not come up with the plan. We did not start it. God did. This is the very central point and greatest truth that distinguishes Christianity from other religions. I have travelled around the world. I have worked with people of different religious faiths, and I can tell you that all the religions I have come across are human in their view of salvation.

C. S. Lewis was once walking past a room of academics arguing over what is unique about Christianity. He walked into the room and told them that the answer is grace. It is grace in that God is the initiator. Christianity is not a religion of pulling yourself up by your boot straps. It is a faith in God's grace. A. W. Tozer liked to say that "God is always previous." We are never the initiator. God is. He was before us—better, he *is* before us. Everything comes from him, and salvation is by his grace.

Second, it is *grace that Jesus gave himself for our sins.* The phrase "gave himself" means that he died on the cross. Jesus was not made to do it. One idea is that God the Son's death was forced upon him by the God the Father. But Jesus did it willingly. He gave himself. This is a wonderful grace. He did not have to. He chose to. And he chose to because he loves his people. He loves you. Soak in that truth of grace. Let nothing and no one take that away from you. Enjoy it. Celebrate it.

There is a debate over the Greek word "for" in verse 4. The word "for" might refer back to the sacrificial system in the Old Testament, thereby rendering the image of the sacrificial lamb slain for our sins. It could also simply mean "on account of" or "in the place of," an idea that is also conveyed via the theological truth of the sacrificial system that lies at the back of this in the Old Testament. Either way, it is for your sins. That is the very thunderclap against all guilt.

I know what it is to have a guilty conscience. Pastors are sinners too. I've screwed up in my life, and I will again. We come as broken people to a broken Savior who gave himself for our sins. Can't you see it? Can't you stay on message? I need no reminder of the standard that I am to reach, and every day I feel my failure to attain it. What I need is a Savior. There he is "for our sins." When the Devil asks, "You are a sinner and how can you be forgiven?" we are to say, "I am a sinner. That is why I need to be forgiven." This is a word of grace.

Third, it is *grace to deliver us from the present evil age.* The New Testament expresses consistently that we as Christians are people of a new age while still living in the midst of this age, which is going to pass away and is under the control of the Evil One. Paul is not telling us that we have been taken out of the world but that we have been taken out of the influence of evil.

So, the cross of Jesus Christ does not just forgive our sins; it also gives us the power to live in a holy way. Because of grace I can break that habit. I am free. Holiness does not come from law. It does not come from more rules. Holiness comes from the cross of Christ, the Spirit of Christ, the fruit of the Spirit. Jesus did this for us in principle at the cross, and as we walk in the Spirit, we increasingly realize that potential within us, all by grace.

Fourth, it is *grace by the will of God our Father and to his glory forever and ever.* Because this is all from God, it is therefore something from which God alone gets the glory. People have often wondered why there is no thanksgiving at the beginning of Galatians, as was typical in Paul's letters. I do not think it is because Paul was mad, or did not care. He calls them his children later in the letter, so he obviously cared. I think he was worried for them, much like a dad over a child who hasn't come home by 3 A.M. Paul is concerned about where they are and what they are doing. He is praising God because he knows it is by grace, and he has to trust, and in all things he will give praise to God. That too is grace. "I long for your salvation, prodigal son, in a distant land, checking out Christianity by chance, apparently. I long for it. I've been up late for you, longing for you, and I'm praising God that he is able."

People ask me, "If you think salvation is all by God, why do you bother to preach?" I tell them that if I didn't think salvation was all by God, I'd never dare get in the pulpit. This isn't me. It isn't my message or power. It is his, and I know that he is able to deliver you from the trap, from the bondage, from the pain, from the bitter root that no amount of skilled pastoral care can dig out. Christ, who gave himself for your sins to rescue you from the present evil age, Christ by God's will—to him be glory. He has the power.

It is all grace. Paul didn't begin his letters saying, "Hard work, discipline, moral improvement, church structure, certain kinds of music, law, and ceremony." It is all grace. Stay on message, which means stay on grace.

Stay on Peace

Stay on message also means stay on peace. There is a great confusion in some circles about what is objective and what is subjective. Some say this message is all objective. "Don't get all gushy with me. Don't get all touchy-feely. This is an objective declaration of fact. It's not about what I feel; it's about what God has done." Others say it's about a changed life, a relationship; it's about a subjective experience. The great wonder and truth of Christianity, of course, is that it is about both. The objective reality of God's salvation through the death of Jesus Christ becomes grace and peace *to you* for *our* sins according to the will of *our* God and Father.

The grace of God means that we who believe have peace of conscience. I beg you not to move away from the message of grace. If you do, you will move away from the experience of peace. I see a man who is always torturing himself over some sin he committed ten years ago. It was a very terrible thing. He has been to counselors. He has prayed. And, as people say, he cannot forgive himself. My friend, you are proud. Who are you to think you need to forgive yourself? What matters is that God has forgiven you. Don't be so arrogant. You are playing at God with your conscience. You are not the judge; God is. It is for *our* sins. It is peace to *you*. It is the will of *our* God and Father. If Paul can say, *you, our, our* to these Galatian Christians who were an inch away from getting circumcised and going back to the basic principles of this world, don't you think he can say the same to you?

I see a woman who was greatly sinned against. It was many years ago. She carries the wound like a badge. You can't see it, but she thinks you can. It is always with her. She won't let it go. She thinks she cannot let it go. She holds on to what he did, and now the sin is multiplied by years of spoiled years after the original great sin against her. Sister, you who were so greatly sinned against, be free. Stand firm on peace. It is for freedom that Christ has set you free; don't let yourself be burdened anymore. It is for *our* sins, and *our* God and Father, and it is peace to *you*. There is no shame. There is no dirt.

I once knew someone who had been a terrorist before his conversion. He was late on in life and he felt terribly depressed that so many years had been wasted. Then he read, "I will restore to you the years that the swarming locust has eaten" (Joel 2:25), and he knew that the Lord would give him back the wasted years.

At the cross of Jesus Christ we can not only be forgiven but also learn to forgive. The great truth is that every sin will find its judgment either at the cross or in hell, and the great truth of life is that if we let the sins that people have done against us build in bitterness, we are only hurting ourselves. We are letting a seed of hell—sin dealt with but not at the cross—grow in us. Take that sin that was done against you to the cross. Look at the blood and gore. There is violence there, yes, but it is the outpouring of God's love, the breaking of his heart that you, dear sister, might not carry that burden any more. Be free. Stay on peace.

Within a Christian movement of students a theological controversy arose. In the end, the leaders from the two groups got together to hash it out. I don't know all the details of the conversation, and I suppose they were not recorded, but it is a matter of record that at one point the leader of one group asked the other this question: "Is the cross of Jesus Christ central to your message?" The leader of the other group replied, "It is very important but not central." Friends, there are many matters over which we may—and must—this side of heaven disagree, and others over which we give ground in gentleness and humility. Some of the current theological discussions in Western Christendom appear to the rest of the world not that dissimilar from the infamous medieval debate about how many angels you could fit onto the head of a pin. But we are not to go to the other extreme either. We must stay on message. The liberal group in that discussion was, at the time, much larger and more powerful, but it dwindled. The evangelical group stood firm. It looked marginalized, but then it grew in strength and numbers and influence.

We must preach grace and peace, not just as "Hi" or "Dear so-and-so." We must preach in reality and power with the cross at the heart of our message. That is the only hope for peace for sinners like us, for guilty consciences, for broken families, for sleepless nights, for the next generation, for life now and for eternity. By his grace may we be given peace now and forever.

As we get a sense of this gospel of grace and peace, in many ways a summary of the whole of Paul's letter to the Galatians, we are prepared for his next foray as he outlines the one true gospel. He has greeted them, but he invested in that greeting a summary of the true gospel. Next he comes to show them that this gospel is the only gospel, and there is no other.

3

A Different Gospel

I am astonished that you are so quickly deserting him who called you
in the grace of Christ and are turning to a different gospel—not that
there is another one, but there are some who trouble you and want to
distort the gospel of Christ.

GALATIANS 1:6–7

The verses before us, Galatians 1:6–7, are worth spending time looking
at because we have a tendency to lose track of the path we're meant to
walk when there are so many other seemingly appealing paths offered
to us. None of us finds it easy to stick to the straight and narrow. As the
poet puts it, "The best laid schemes of mice and men go often astray."
This is a general rule in life, where entropy tends to bring disorder,
requiring our constant energy to maintain, let alone move forward. But
this tendency is especially the case in spiritual matters, for not only is
there a natural leaning toward the chaotic, but there is a gravitational
pull toward the rebellious. Of course, we are not in the situation of
the Galatian churches exactly, where there was one distinct group of
agitators that had come to offer a different gospel. Today, the situation
is more like a supermarket of religious options. The result is that the
Christian church is getting confused.

If you are new to Christian things, you will have noticed it. Which
church do you go to? There seem to be more brands of Christianity than
there are fast-food chains. After a while we tend to think that it's all just
food, and we can choose whichever brand we happen to like. But part
of what the apostle Paul says is that it really does matter. "There is no
other gospel."

That's at least as difficult for us to believe as it was for the Galatians.
There is this great cacophony of voices. I've got a couple of images in
my mind of what this is like. You're listening to some piece of music

on your iPod when you happen to walk through an industrial building site. The loud noises, the drilling, and the pure volume of other sounds make it hard to keep track of the tune. There are so many alternatives today—different takes, slightly different emphases—that in the midst of the din of human gospel production (the "industrial building site") we can lose track of the biblical gospel that comes from God.

In *The Hobbit* there is a scene in which the dwarves and Bilbo are meant to stay on the path through a dark wood. Eventually they get hungry and go off into the trees, and then they can't find their way back to the path again. It's a bit like that. There is a lot of pressure to leave the straight and narrow, the sole path that exists through the dark leaves of Mirkwood.

The Galatian churches had the gospel, the *evangel*; they were evangelical. But these agitators, "some who trouble you and want to distort the gospel of Christ" (v. 7), had come and were saying, "Unless you are circumcised according to the custom of Moses, you cannot be saved" (see Acts 15:1). This other message was confusing them; it had troubled and confounded them. They were losing track of the tune of the real gospel. They were being led off the path.

In my view, it makes best sense to see what was happening here historically as referring to the churches in South Galatia, which we know from Acts that Paul had planted, and that this controversy arose immediately before the Jerusalem Council, which comes later in Acts 15. It seems to fit best there. However you put it together, they had come down "from James" (Gal. 2:12), claiming implicitly the authority of the Jerusalem church, adding to the potential for confusion. Many from prestigious schools seem to like finding a way to put that affiliation on their latest book; similarly here, in terms of the kudos it gave the false teachers, they said they were "from James." They were proposing that law was necessary for salvation on top of the free grace that produces the peace that Paul has just summarized as the entire gospel (1:3–5).

This was obviously a powerful confusion. The Gentile Christians were presumably told that Jesus was the Jewish Messiah and that therefore they needed to become fully Jewish to be saved. Those who did not get circumcised and adopt the whole Mosaic Law were barred from table fellowship with Jewish Christians. These non-Judaized Gentile

Christians were, then, practically speaking, excommunicated, not part of the fellowship, and therefore symbolically declared in a public fashion as not part of the saved community.

This was the siren voice pulling them away from the pure gospel. So, Paul said to them, "Don't get muddled." There is troubling confusion. Yes, but don't get confounded by it. Paul makes an essentially negative point in these verses. He has summarized the gospel as centering on the death of Jesus Christ, which is purely by grace and therefore provides peace, without mention of the law. Now he says, "Don't go off the path; don't lose track of the tune."

Don't Get Muddled by a Different Gospel

First, don't get muddled by a different gospel. He says right away that he is astonished that they are turning to a "different gospel" (v. 6). He is quick to clarify that he doesn't mean that there is a different gospel: "Not that there is another one" (v. 7). So why does he talk about a "different" gospel if there is no other? He might be picking up on language that was being used in the debate, a practice typical of Paul. Perhaps the Galatian Christians were being presented with a "different gospel," something new and different.

This is always the way it works. For a false teaching to be effective, it must be presented as just a bit different, as something that fulfills or completes what you already accept. "I'm not asking you to reject Paul's message. I'm not asking you to reject grace. You just need the law of Moses and to be circumcised as well." We could list any number of ways this has happened historically. The Mormon religion presents itself as the church of Jesus Christ of Latter Day Saints. The appeal is that it's a little bit more, on top of what we already accept, and Jesus and the church are still included. It's Jehovah's Witnesses, emerging again from the Christian heritage, they say. The appeal is to something we already accept with a bit more added on. Someone once said to me that a cult always has another book, something that goes along with the Bible. That other book gradually takes over and becomes authoritative. False teaching is always parasitic upon true teaching.

The same historically has been true of liberalism in the Christian church. Great liberal professors and teachers were largely converted in

evangelical homes. There is no power in the liberal religion to build a
church, for the foundation of the church is the gospel of Jesus Christ.
There is only power to distort, alter, confuse, and offer something a bit
different.

It seems to me, as someone not from the Christendom of the evangelical Bible Belt, that the evangelical movement is particularly in danger
these days in this regard. There are many different ideas and teachings
out there, some good, some mediocre, some just plain odd. But I see a
subtext to a lot of the poor teaching, which is this drive to find something new and different. It seems that people are tired of hearing the
same old thing. They want something new, or, because the world thinks
that evangelicals are stupid, evangelicals think they need to come up
with a fancy new way of expressing an old doctrine. As someone with
three degrees from Cambridge and a fellowship at one of Yale's colleges,
I can tell you that, in my experience, the biblical gospel of Jesus Christ
can stand up tall against any academic intellectualization. We certainly
need to think, but we don't need to think up something different or new.

So the Galatians were doing, and we are often tempted to do likewise. Paul writes, "I am astonished that you are so quickly deserting him
who called you" (v. 6). Paul is astonished, this loving father with his eyes
bulging out of his head, at his children doing something he can't fathom.
The word *deserting* was used of someone betraying one philosophical
school for another. They are not just betraying a philosophy; they are
betraying the one who had called them—Jesus himself. It is a remarkable turnaround, and Paul is trying to get them not to leave the path but
to keep singing the tune. They are in the process of turning, and he is
trying to get to them before it's too late. "Don't get muddled," he says,
and the first way not to do so is to realize that this new message is really
just a parasite living on the true message. It is being presented as something different, new, and exciting, when really it's as old as the hills, the
same tactic the Devil employed with Jesus by quoting Scripture, for, as
Shakespeare put it, "The Devil can cite Scripture for his own purpose."

Don't Get Muddled by Personalities

Second, don't get muddled by personalities. Paul says in the middle of
verse 7, "There are some who trouble you and want to distort the gos-

pel of Christ." It is always that way. It is always a person or a group. In this particular case in Galatia, it appears to have been a group of people. Galatians 5:10 mentions "the one who is troubling you." So, most likely, and typically, the agitators had a leader. A sort of minor personality cult was developing.

You may think we do not need to spend as much time considering this as the more doctrinal aspect of the issue at Galatia, the teaching that led them and can lead us astray. Certainly the doctrinal aspect is crucial, and Paul will be talking about that repeatedly in various ways and at deeper levels throughout this letter, but my guess is that the personalities involved are almost as important at least for the more easily led.

We don't know much about the people who were leading the Galatians down the wrong path. This group and their leader were probably the same people whom Paul describes as those who "spy out our freedom" (Gal. 2:4). They were likely the same ones claiming to be "from James" (2:12). They could be lumped together as the "circumcision group." They were very zealous for their agenda, the kind of group that sought to gather adherents to their cause by sheer passion. The leader apparently had an aggressive demeanor. But behind all this apparently strong activity, Paul discerns a cowardly motivation to avoid the persecution that would come from being exorcised from the synagogue if they no longer kept the ceremonial law of Moses (6:12).

All this is Paul's description of his theological opponents, but even if we take the most cynical view of Paul's tactics in this debate—that he was caricaturing his opponents—there must have been some element of truth to his description of them as basically personality driven. Otherwise, the rhetoric would have fallen flat. I think that we are to accept the apostle's trustworthiness in this as in other matters.

The reality is that people rarely leave the straight and narrow path simply through force of an idea. It is normally through the force of a *new* idea as presented by a forceful personality. Humans are tribal. They like to gather around a chief. It makes them feel safe. If someone swings through town and presents himself as having all the right connections with all the powerful people, if he has an entourage of impressive supporters with him, if he is passionate and zealous for his message, and if the idea he presents is tantalizingly new and just a little different from the gospel, the combination is a cocktail that can go right to the head of even the most normally steady follower of Jesus.

It is important to realize that this is what we are like as people. We are sheep. We need to focus not on the personality of the shepherd but on the message he delivers and the fruit of the Spirit that is created. Even Paul was apparently personally unimpressive, or at least that's what his opponents in Corinth said. As sheep, we are to follow someone, even if unimpressive or "weak," who teaches the Bible and preaches the biblical gospel. We are not to follow someone, however impressive or "strong," who does not teach the biblical gospel. We are sheep, and our aim is to follow Jesus as our Shepherd through the means of his various under-shepherds. Just as false doctrine is usually presented as something new or different, a parasite on the gospel, so false teachers tend to present themselves as new and exciting, in the hope that we won't look too closely at the snake oil they are selling.

Don't Get Muddled by a Changed Gospel

Third, Paul wants them to realize, as it were, what's really at stake here, and what the agitators, with their little tribal chief, are trying to achieve. They are trying, Paul says, "to distort the gospel of Christ" (Gal. 1:7). At stake is an attempt to change the gospel for something altogether different. Paul says that the Galatians need to realize this so that they don't get muddled by the wolves in sheep's clothing and think it is only a minor matter. We need to realize the same when presented with forceful personalities presenting a new or different so-called gospel as an addition to the biblical one.

First, *we need to realize that behind false teaching is false desire*. Out of our hearts, our mouths speak, and the perverting of the gospel is, Paul says, what false teachers actually desire to achieve. Those of us who teach, then, need to be especially careful of our hearts. We come to the Bible on our knees. We pull the plank out of our own eye before we pluck the speck of incorrect doctrine out of someone else's. We are wary of selfish ambition. It is fine to be zealous, as Paul says, provided the purpose is good, and we should be zealous always. But it is impor-tant that our zeal is genuinely and truly for God and his church—not *apparently* for those good purposes, when in actuality we are trying to put ourselves forward by means of our latest idea to carve a niche for ourselves.

My guess is that much wrong teaching is rooted in a desire to set oneself apart as more important or better, or just different, from one's peers. We need to realize that behind false teaching is a false desire. Conversely, those of us who listen to the true teaching of the Bible are to realize that behind that is normally a deep, true desire to serve God's people for their good and God's glory.

Second, *we need to recognize that false teachers have a desire to distort the gospel itself*. This is a heavy truth but an important one. The real motivation of false teachers is not to help us but to change the very message. The gospel of Jesus Christ is humbling because it tells us that we are broken and need fixing. All false gospels appeal to our human vanity because they tell us that we are less broken and can at least participate in fixing ourselves. Behind false gospels is a great desire to actually change the gospel so that we don't need to be so humble, or meek, or poor in spirit in order to be blessed. The word *distort* can suggest broader gross perversion in other contexts in English, but the heart of the meaning here is simply changing the gospel for something else. That, of course, *is* to pervert the gospel, but the act that causes this perversion is that of replacing the gospel with something else. The word for *distort* in the original Greek was often used for replacing something with its exact opposite. The sun is replaced with darkness (Acts 2:20), laughter is replaced with grief (James 4:9) and the gospel of grace and peace is replaced with a so-called gospel of law and bondage.

Don't get muddled by a different gospel. Don't get muddled by personalities, however attractive they may be. Don't get muddled by a changed gospel. Realize that this is an attempt to change the good news of the gospel for the bad news of religious moralism.

Once that change takes place, the church begins to look more and more like the world. We start to divide up into different racial groups. We start to orient our fellowship along class lines. We start to organize ourselves around political or social agendas. In short, we start to look a lot like the evangelical church in the West today. The answer to that is not more law or a new and different gospel. The answer to our immorality, our tribalism, our ageism (one generation doesn't worship with another), our structural racial division, and the world's charge that historic Christianity is no longer intellectually or morally credible in a pluralistic world, is not a new or different message. The answer is a rediscovery of the message from which the church is in danger of drifting away. The siren voices are calling, but the path is straight through the wood. We need to stay on that gospel path and thereby find that in Christ there is neither Jew nor Gentile, slave nor free, male nor female, and that in the power of the Spirit through the proclamation of the gospel we may increasingly become more like Christ himself.

4

The Gospel Antithesis

But even if we or an angel from heaven should preach to you a gospel contrary to the one we preached to you, let him be accursed. As we have said before, so now I say again: If anyone is preaching to you a gospel contrary to the one you received, let him be accursed.

GALATIANS 1:8–9

I would not be surprised to find someone angered by the words of Galatians 1:8–9. In religious circles of days gone by, concepts such as hell and eternal condemnation and God's judgment—even his curse—were common. People today find such ideas beyond the pale. Those ideas are vicious, violent, and judgmental. Even among Christians, the idea of God's judgment, or hell, is seldom if ever mentioned nowadays. We want people to come to church, so we try to stay upbeat, and talking about hell doesn't seem, well, very upbeat. When people today say, "Go to hell," they don't mean it literally; they simply mean "Go away" or "I don't like you." But the apostle Paul seems to be saying it literally here: "Let him be accursed," *Go to hell.*

In culture more generally, we might be able to accept that some go to hell. Hitler, for instance, is the usual example. We do not find it impossible to believe that certain actions are worthy of eternal condemnation, if they are sufficiently extreme and rare. Nonetheless, we expect, typically, that just about everyone will go to heaven (if we believe in its existence at all), and the few poor souls we think might miss out are the serial child rapist or genocidal maniac. But, of course, in this passage Paul does not say that certain actions are worthy of God's curse; he says that if we teach certain things, we are worthy of that. If I believe something wrong and teach others to believe something wrong, it puts me under God's judgment. That is a thought so strange to modern ears that it feels like, with this passage, we are entering an alien world. In a religiously relativistic world, the idea that Paul teaches here is very difficult to swallow. I want to show that what Paul says not only makes sense but also is very important for our lives, our homes, our sense of hope, and the future of our church and our world today.

Paul has in mind here an *either-or*. There are certainly things that are *both-and*. You can have *both* cookie dough ice cream *and* strawberry shortcake. There are certain things that are *either-or*. You can be *either* at church *or* at home but not at both at the same time. With religion these days, we tend to think in terms of both-and. We think you can have both Islam and Christianity, both vague religious moralism and the pure gospel, both—for many of us today and for the Galatians—law and grace.

But Paul says it's either-or. So much of life is. As Jesus taught, you can't serve both God and money. We like syntheses, following the dialectic of Hegel. Hegel presented a view of logic, world history, and all human development whereby the standard process began with a thesis, turned to its antithesis, and finally culminated in synthesis. In so doing, he crafted a philosophy that balked at opposition and embraced cooperation. Yet, worthy as that may or may not be at one level, when implicitly applied to Christianity it misses the boat. The gospel is antithesis. Most startlingly, Paul says here that the antithesis is *gospel* or *curse*. This is the very nature of reality and life.

Curse

Paul says it twice: "Let him be accursed" (vv. 8–9). The word *anathema*, translated "accursed," is the Greek translation of a Hebrew word used to indicate that which is devoted to God, in either a blessed or (as here) condemned sense. Perhaps the best way of looking at it is with the contemporary phrase "It's in God's hands." That can be either positive: "It's in God's hands; we can trust him with that," or negative: "It's in God's hands; he's the judge." Paul is saying, "God's going to deal with this; we can leave it in God's hands. He is the judge."

Paul assumes that there are two groups. He shows us that the Galatian false teachers were living and encouraging others to live in the group that lives under the judgment or curse of God. That is the Bible's worldview. There are only two groups of people, spiritually speaking.

We are not divided into races, genders, or classes. We are divided into those living under the judgment of God and those living under the grace of God. Spiritually speaking, the division is not between the clean-living nice people and everyone else. It is between those who have received the free grace of God as a gift, with all simple humility, and those who attempt to stand before God in the power of their own righteousness.

Ever since man and woman left the garden of Eden, it has been like that. After Adam and Eve had been unable to believe that God was good and that God wanted what was good for them, God pronounced a curse. Cursed is the ground. Cursed is childbirth. Cursed is work. So Paul says here that these Galatian false teachers, with their desire to encourage the Gentile Christians to become fully Jewish by being circumcised, were actually moving the Galatian Christians back toward the land of the curse and away from the land of grace.

The law was added to show us what the perfect moral life is like and therefore how much we need God's grace. It was a standard, and its message was that we do not meet that standard. "You need the law as well as grace" is a synthesis, not an antithesis. For the Galatian false teachers to claim so was actually to take away grace. Paul says, again and again in different ways, that a Jesus-plus gospel is really no gospel at all. In fact, he says, it is back to the curse.

Perhaps you are wondering why your life does not seem to amount to much. Perhaps you try hard. Perhaps you live cleanly. Perhaps you still sense that your best efforts are futile. We live in a world with thorns. What we need is to be taken out of this world by the miracle of grace so that we are no longer under the curse.

There is this contrast, an either-or. Paul even includes himself in it. He is not angry. He is not declaring some magical curse on his opponents. Twice over, calmly, he simply describes the spiritual reality. It is gospel or curse. If we are not under the gospel, not under grace, then we are still under curse.

Be very careful, then, not to add things to Jesus. We are not to trust in our works. We are not to trust in our financial nest egg. We are not to trust in our friends, home, business, or reputation. All these things can be added to grace in much the same way that the law can. We want to mix our human effort with free grace. We long for a synthesis, but it is an antithesis, an either-or. It is gospel or curse, which means it is not only a warning not to stay in, or be taken back to, curse, but also a clear message of hope and joy.

Gospel

The answer to this curse is found in Galatians 3:10: "All who rely on works of the law are under a curse; for it is written, 'Cursed be everyone who does not abide by all things written in the Book of the Law, and do them.'" Paul has declared the reality. There is this curse. It would be true for him or for an angel. There is the reality that we cannot get ourselves back to paradise. Yet there is hope, once we face up to the true state of things and receive the gospel. The curse is taken so that we can have grace in the gospel. The law is the standard, but we do not keep it. Paul continues, "It is evident that no one is justified before God by the law, for 'The righteous shall live by faith.' But the law is not of faith, rather 'The one who does them shall live by them'" (3:11–12). There is the contrast, the antithesis—the law is not of faith. It is a standard we do not meet.

And here comes the gospel: "Christ redeemed us from the curse of the law by becoming a curse for us—for it is written, 'Cursed is everyone who is hanged on a tree'" (3:13). The curse has gone. Christ was cursed for you and me. He became the curse for us. He took the *anathema* on our behalf "so that in Christ Jesus the blessing of Abraham might come to the Gentiles, so that we might receive the promised Spirit through faith" (3:14). Receive the promise of the Spirit. It is grace, by faith, that we might receive the promise of the Spirit. The curse has been taken by Christ himself.

I first heard the gospel through the ministry of a man who, in his spare time, did magic tricks. He used to explain it this way: "All we like sheep have gone astray, we have turned everyone to his own way, and the Lord has laid on him the iniquity of us all." He'd take his Bible and say, "We are here, and God is up there, and we have all gone astray. There is a big barrier between us and God. But Christ has taken our iniquity upon himself. We now have access to God. Christ became a curse for us to redeem us from the curse of the law." There is no more curse for those who believe.

> Joy to the World, the Lord is come!
>   Let earth receive her King. . . .
> No more let sins and sorrows grow,
>   Nor thorns infest the ground;
> He comes to make His blessings flow
>   Far as the curse is found,
>   Far as the curse is found,
> Far as, far as the curse is found.

Wherever it is found, there Christ became a curse for us. Cursed is the ground. Cursed are you. Pain. Sorrow. Sadness. The curse taker has come. Christ has come. The gospel has come. Curse is no more. So, in these two verses (Gal. 1:8–9) Paul is simply declaring the antithesis. He is saying, "Don't be taken away from the gospel, for the alternative is the curse. Only in Christ, the curse taker, is the curse no more."

Avoiding the Curse, Receiving the Gospel

I want to conclude with a word to teachers, a word to those new to the things of God, and then with a word for all of us.

To teachers I want to underline what is surely obvious from this passage, which is that what we teach is of great importance for our own souls. Paul says to Timothy, "Keep a close watch on yourself and on the teaching. Persist in this, for by so doing you will save both yourself and your hearers" (1 Tim. 4:16). There is a temptation, sometimes, to try to come up with something new, to set ourselves apart as different, and to treat teaching as a matter of play. But whether we teach at a university or a Christian institution, through writing, through Sunday school or children's ministries, or through discipleship of other Christians, it is of eternal significance, not only for those we teach but also for ourselves, that we stick to the biblical Christian gospel.

At the beginning of his letter to the Galatians, Paul has outlined two ways to know we are sticking to the biblical Christian gospel. First, we are if we teach what the apostles taught in the New Testament. If we are, our authority is from the Bible, not from human tradition or contemporary culture. Second, we are if we teach the gospel of grace through faith alone in Jesus alone, which is what the apostles taught in the New

Testament. We teachers must stick to the Bible as our authority and to grace through faith alone as our message in order that we do not slip back to the land of curse.

To those new to the faith, I want to assure you that the message here in this passage isn't aggressive. The Bible isn't saying, "Curse you!" The message is more like a doctor who goes into an African village where a plague has broken out and he has the medication to cure it. He needs people to understand that the situation is serious, even if the symptoms might seem relatively minor at first. He wants people to understand that the strange vial in his bag is really going to take away the curse.

There are lots of signs of curse in our world today. Religious violence is one. Injustice is another. Climate change is a third. The economy might be first on people's minds. We live in a world where there is both structured oppression and great psychological pain. The gospel is the solution to both the physical and the emotional violence of men's and women's souls. When people argue, there is one who took the guilt. When people are oppressed, there is one who has the power to free. When someone comes to church looking for God to show up, he is here, not as the oppressor but as our redeemer from slavery. So if you are new to these things, we have a curse bearer to take away the curse of this world.

For all of us, the Word is gospel, not curse, and for that it needs to be grace, not law. Let us be unabashedly clear about that, as well as overwhelmingly joyful because of it.

5

The God-Pleasing Gospel

For am I now seeking the approval of man, or of God?
Or am I trying to please man? If I were still trying to please man,
I would not be a servant of Christ.

GALATIANS 1:10

Personal memoirs have become an art form in which the bare truth is sometimes peppered with liberal inventions to make the memoirs more interesting. They can be the facts of someone's life presented to gain approval—and good economic return—from the readers. Paul is beginning the process of, as it were, introducing his memoirs, but he is doing the very opposite of crafting them for approval. In fact, he is telling us that the record of his life, which he will unabashedly display, shows that his ultimate objective has been solely to please God. By this means (his memoirs, if you like) the Bible tells us that the true gospel is presented to show that is more concerned with pleasing God than with pleasing us.

Seemingly, by contrast, Paul was well known for his willingness to jettison his Jewishness when speaking to Gentiles and his Gentile ways when going to the temple with Jews. When he preached to the Galatians, he did not insist that they get circumcised. But when he and Timothy began to work together, he had circumcised Timothy for the sake of the Jews. Paul, it seems, in the situation in the churches in Galatia, was being accused of being a people pleaser. He was the kind of leader, it was said, who would do anything to get a following. "Seeking the approval of man" (v. 10) translates a technical term for the art of rhetoric in the ancient world. Paul was being accused of being a spin doctor, a demagogue, someone who cut the suit of his message to fit the tastes of his hearers.

In this letter so far, Paul has declared eternally condemned those who do not preach the one true gospel. How then, he says, can he be fairly accused of being a people pleaser? Then he goes on to describe his personal biography to show that behind his missionary flexibility there was great consistency. Verse 10, therefore, is not a random, disconnected, intemperate rant on but a concentrated restatement of the basic message of Galatians. Paul is going to show how, in his own personal memoirs, he has presented the true gospel, which is more concerned with pleasing God than with pleasing us.

The interesting thing about the classic self-help book *How to Win Friends and Influence People* is that when you read it, it almost feels like a manual for the contemporary church. The Christian church has become a technique for how to win friends and influence people. We don't criticize. We seek to arouse in others an eager want. We are, in other words, people-pleasers.

What is most relevant about this passage is that Paul himself was accused of being a people-pleaser. His flexibility made him look like some form of sophist, an ancient kind of travelling speaker who earned his wages from his speaking, someone who would say anything to get a following. The Judaizing agitators, who insisted on getting the Galatians circumcised, claimed the higher moral ground by saying that they were doing it because God's Word told them to, whether or not people liked it. They were saying that Paul was the people pleaser and they were the high-octane theologians who took the Old Testament law seriously. They had the temerity to insist on their disciples' getting circumcised— an unpleasant procedure at the best of times—because they were the God-pleasers, whereas Paul was the people pleaser. Really the reverse was true. The Galatian false teachers appealed to the basic human desire for self-righteousness and to seem morally better than others, whereas Paul presented a way to get right with God based on God's action in Christ, a way to be pleasing to God, not doing impressive moral actions to look good to other people. This was neither seeker sensitive nor aggressively frozen chosen. It was the God-centered gospel.

My guess is that many of us spend our days living to please others. We are nice and kind. There is nothing in the Bible to encourage rudeness but everything to discourage arrogance. But when we are presented with a wrong gospel, are we going to be God-centered enough to oppose it or nice and pleasing to people so that we run with the hares as well as hunt with the hounds?

This is of deep relevance to our personal lives, the life of the church, and the future of Christianity in an age where there are many subtle false gospels that proclaim various forms of self-righteousness. We need to ask ourselves, then, the question that Paul asked of himself: Are we trying to impress men or God? That question is the main theme of this chapter.

Are We Trying to Impress Men or God?

First, it cannot be both. Paul asks, "For am I now seeking the approval of man, or of God?" (v. 10). He assumes that it cannot be both. This assumption—that we cannot please both men and God at the same time in some cosmic sense—is totally foreign to our normal way of thinking. We tend to feel that God is there to help us win friends and influence people, or at least that approval with God and with man frequently, or at least sometimes, overlaps. Paul says that, at a fundamental heart level, it cannot be both.

In the original writing, Paul used the word meaning "persuade," literally, "Am I now persuading men or God?" Some people think he used the word *persuade* about the art of rhetoric, when actually the word *persuade* in this verse is used with relation to God, his point being that he is not like a magician trying to persuade God inappropriately or improperly. Most likely, though, he is using a form of grammar called a *zeugma* or *syllepsis* in which the same word is used one way in part of the sentence and then in a slightly different way in another part of the sentence. This technique tends to emphasize the incongruity or strangeness of the opposite way of thinking. Groucho Marx said, "You can leave in a taxi. If you can't get a taxi, you can *leave* in a huff." Scar in *The Lion King* said, "My teeth *and* ambitions are bared; be prepared!" Charles Dickens wrote, "[She] went straight home in a flood of tears, *and* a sedan chair."[1] So Paul asked, "Am I persuading people or God?" meaning, "I've been accused of doing anything to persuade people, but now do you think I'm doing that or trying to persuade God?" He used "persuade" in the second sense, meaning "entrust to," "rely upon,"

---

[1] Emphasis added.

"appeal to" or even "reconcile you to God rather than reconcile God to you." A God-centered gospel is what he's talking about.

The phrase "persuade people" was sometimes used negatively in the ancient Greek-speaking world of snake oil salesman who were just trying to pull one over on others to get what they wanted. The word *persuade* as related to God in the Old Testament Hebrew was used for trusting and relying upon God. So Paul is saying, "No, I'm not the traveling salesman who goes around Galatia selling stuff you don't need for prices you can't afford. I'm the prophet of the biblical kind who has come to you and said 'be reconciled to God!' I'm on bended knee, and I'll have nothing stand in the way of that gospel, but it's a God-centered gospel, not a people-pleasing gospel."

What is the point of this analysis for us now? There are many man-centered gospels today. Some are obvious and some are more subtle. We need to resist them. The religious salesman who gives us god on our own terms, the perfect addition to a perfect life, is to be resisted, as is the religious salesman who comes and tells us that we don't need to be justified by faith alone but can follow the law and so justify ourselves before God. The God-centered gospel is justification by faith alone in Christ alone; it is about reconciling us to God, not God to us, and anything else cannot be accepted. Trying to do so is not like mixing a few extra flavors into your ice cream at Cold Stone Creamery; it is like trying to mix oil and water. *It cannot be both*. Persuading man and God at once is like trying to be in two places at the same time. It is simply impossible.

Are we trying to impress men or God? It is either one or the other but not both at the same time. As Christian people, we are going to have to learn to be more attuned to the different theological notes within evangelicalism, because in some places it is a movement of people pleasers rather than one seeking to reconcile people to God.

The Goal Cannot Be to Please People

Second, the goal cannot be to please people. This sounds similar to what we just examined, but it's really more practical. Paul asks, "Or am I trying to please man?" (v. 10). This is a question about the goal of his life, and we need to ask that question about the goals and priorities of our lives too. "Do I seek to please men?" That word "seek" in the original resonates with the force of Jesus' word to "seek first the kingdom of God" (Matt. 6:33). So what does a God-centered gospel mean in practice? It means that those who put their faith in Christ become those who seek not to please people but to please God.

Every society in our fallen world is full of people caught in the bondage of what the Bible calls "the fear of man" (Prov. 29:25). We are naturally people-pleasers, but the fear of man is a trap. Perhaps you don't think you are a people pleaser. People-pleasers are not only those who are quiet or mousy, but also those who erupt in anger because they are unable to express what is really going on inside them. They fear no longer being impressive to people. Some of our internal thought language gives us away: "If I say this, what will she think?" "If I do that, will he still love me?" "If I make that decision, will this powerful person in my life be pleased?" Extreme people-pleasers sometimes find it hard to know their own opinions because they have buried them for years beneath a concern to adapt to the opinions of those around them. Being a polite or gentle speaker does not make you likely to be a people-pleaser, for you can with gentleness and kindness bring challenge. Likewise, just because you are more rambunctious does not mean you are not a people-pleaser, for that can be a way to impress those around you.

If you don't think you are a people-pleaser, ask yourself whether, as a Christian, you have considered not telling non-Christians about Jesus because you are concerned that they will think less of you. If you don't really think being captive to the fear of man matters, just replace that phrase, "fear of man," with more contemporary terms for broadly the same issue, such as "peer pressure" or "co-dependency." *I must have that item in the store because then people will be impressed by me. I must stay in that relationship because then people will be impressed by me. I must adapt my morality to this group because otherwise they will reject me.* The list could go on.

Again, Paul is not asking us to stop pleasing people in the sense of being deliberately rude or insensitive to those around us; he is asking whether our *goal*, whether what we *seek*, is to please people. The solution to this fear of man, of course, is the fear of God. That's why, when people say they want more practical sermons—i.e., more sermons that tell how to have the perfect marriage in three easy steps beginning with the same letter—they are really missing the most practical matter of all: the fear of the Lord. "Fear the Lord, you his saints, for those who fear him have no lack!" (Ps. 34:9). "He will be the stability of your times, abundance of salvation, wisdom, and knowledge; the fear of the Lord is Zion's treasure" (Isa. 33:6).

The God-centered gospel is the key to this treasure. The gospel is not made by man. Paul did not invent it, he will go on to say. The gospel is not from man; Paul has already said that he'd been called by God. The gospel is not a legalistic understanding of the law but the proclamation that Jesus alone saves, which means that we are justified—made right—before God by faith in him alone. This gospel is a fearsome thing. It is the means for a Copernican revolution in our hearts, whereby we are no longer centered upon people but upon God, and we revolve in his orbit happily.

For years I never quite understood Psalm 130, but now I think I do. "With you there is forgiveness, that you may be feared" (v. 4). It doesn't say, "With you there is forgiveness, *therefore you are loved, admired, cherished, cuddled up to, and appreciated.*" No, there is forgiveness, and therefore *God is feared.* The one thing we need above all rests completely in the gift of God. It is not by our effort or keeping the law. It is purely a justification by faith alone in Christ alone. Therefore, this Copernican revolution takes place, and we are fearers of the living God.

Become that. Be set free from the trap of the fear of man. Be nice. Be pleasant. Be kind. Don't become a snake-handling religious extremist who gives the Bible and bile too. Become like Paul, who could answer the question, "Am I trying to please man?" with a clear no by means of his personal life story and his preaching of the God-centered gospel. That is the freedom of the gospel of grace and peace—a Jesus-only gospel, not a Jesus-plus-law gospel, which is so rife today and will only keep us more trapped in our people pleasing co-dependency, the slavery of which Christ has come to set us free.

Are we trying to impress men or God? First, *it cannot be both.* They are mutually exclusive in the foundation of our heart. We cannot worship God and money. We cannot do spiritual prayers or religious deeds to impress people and expect that to impress God. Second, *the goal cannot be to please people.* At the most practical level—our daily lives—this

God-centered gospel sets us free from being people pleasers to become God-fearers. This is the freedom in which Paul is urging the Galatians to stand firm and not get circumcised or adopt a legalistic understanding of the law in order to look impressive to the very religious false teachers who were in the near vicinity of the congregations in Galatia. They had a different perspective on the gospel. They claimed it was the old and original one, but it really did nothing but set up a religion that was human orientated and designed to look impressive to other people.

In the last part of this exploration of what the true gospel does to the human heart, Paul shows us how we can be sure that we are pleasing to God. In our world's times of turbulence, there is great opportunity to realize that nothing is more important than knowing that we stand right before God for all eternity. We are perhaps convicted by Paul's questioning: are we trying to impress men or God? It leaves us wondering where we really stand. Paul now shows us, at the end of this concentrated summary of the gospel, how we can know for sure.

I Must Be Pleasing to God

Third, *if I am a servant of Christ, I must be pleasing to God*. Ah, what a relief! Who can always be focused on pleasing God? Who does not sometimes mix a little oil with a little water in this regard? Who has a perfect theology or a perfect life all the time? No one! As Paul concludes, we find how deeply these accusations had searched him. "Paul, you're just a people pleaser! You are just a religious spin doctor, doing anything to get people on to your team!" It must have shaken him. We know how he loved the people of the churches he founded.

When you read Paul, you realize how emotional he was. He cared deeply, and for these, his children, to come back and repeat to him the accusations of the false teachers, well, it must have hurt deeply. Perhaps he engaged in some soul searching: "*Am I* trying to impress men or God?" At any rate, the answer he gave was a resounding no. He was sure that at the basic level he was securely in Christ, for he was serving Christ. He writes, "If I were still trying to please man, I would not be a servant of Christ," or literally, "If still men pleaser Christ's slave I wouldn't be." Paul is applying gospel logic. He is saying to himself, "Christ alone lived the perfect life, and only in him can I be pleasing to

God; am I in him? Yes, for the fruit of my life shows that I live to serve Jesus."

It is the message of the whole letter in summary applied at the most personal of levels. No, we do not need the law. The law is good, but we do not need the law to be saved; in fact, if we take the law in this way, we make it to be what it was never meant to be. We have a legalistic understanding of the law and treat it as something that was intended to be saving, when really it was intended to be convicting and to expose our need and so lead us to Christ as our savior. No, we do not need the law to save; we need the gospel of grace. Christ has come, he has died, he has risen again, and he offers his perfect life and death in our place that we might be justified before God solely through faith in him.

Does that mean, then, that we can do whatever we like? It means that what we like has changed. If we are in Christ, the fruit of our lives is different. We are regenerate, we have the fruit of the Spirit, and we begin to live a life of love, joy, peace, gentleness, kindness, patience, faithfulness, goodness, and self-control. We start to live like Jesus because we are in Jesus, and we have Jesus' Spirit in us. We are free from the law and free from the sin of which the law convicts us. Don't get burdened again by that legalistic understanding of the law that every culture all around the world has, those basic principles of human religion that enslave. Don't get burdened by them. Instead be free, trust in Christ and his death, and therefore walk in the Spirit—"against such things there is no law" (Gal. 5:23).

So What Does This Mean?

So, what does this mean? First, if you have put your faith in Christ and are therefore showing the fruit of the Spirit in service of Christ, then be assured that you are pleasing to God. "I have been crucified with Christ. It is no longer I who live, but Christ who lives in me" (Gal. 2:20). Rejoice and be free in that.

Second, if you want to be pleasing to God, you need to put your faith in Christ and become *in* Christ and therefore a servant *of* Christ by the fruit of his Spirit. "Know that a person is not justified by works of the law but through faith in Jesus Christ" (Gal. 2:16). It is not works. It is not circumcision. It is not Buddhism, atheism, Christendom, moralism, Islam, Judaism, or Mormonism. It is not the law or any attempt to reintroduce a legalistic perspective on the law. It is Christ, and only by him and only by faith in him.

I write that to you unapologetically. I will stand up against human-centered gospels, for they are no gospel at all. I will appeal with every bone in my body and remove all unbiblical stumbling blocks so that the gospel can be heard. But I will not—I cannot—just say to you what you want to hear or give a message designed to please you. I do not have that luxury. I am not here as an author with a little book designed to be pleasurable. I am here as a messenger of heaven with a message from God's Word, which is defined by him, is about him, and is intended to glorify and please him.

I want you to be reconciled to God; I make no attempt to try to get God to be reconciled to you, that is, be defined by your desires, for God is God, and you are not. This God-pleasing gospel (the only gospel) is the hope of all people. It is God-centered, but it is blessing, freedom, and life—it is the fear of the Lord, and in that fear is freedom from peer pressure, co-dependency, and all the traps of the fear of man. We speak with wisdom and gentleness, but the message we speak is from God, the message of the gospel of grace and peace. We stand up against the prevailing perspectives that seek to redefine the message for a new age. In our hearts, as we all do so, we are assured that we are at peace and rest and that we are serving Christ, and therefore we are pleasing to God.

We have freedom, therefore, and joy, peace, and the boundless fruit of the Spirit. Today put aside your goal to impress people with your clothes, money, accent, or talents. Today put aside the people-pleasing poison in the water that ruins it all, and in your heart set aside Jesus as Lord. Be a servant of Christ and find in Jesus that in his service is perfect freedom.

6

The Relevance of the Gospel

For I would have you know, brothers, that the gospel that was preached by me is not man's gospel. For I did not receive it from any man, nor was I taught it, but I received it through a revelation of Jesus Christ.

GALATIANS 1:11–12

This passage is a great summary of the distinction between the Christian gospel and any other message that claims our allegiance. It says that other messages are essentially the gospel of man. They are made up by men, they are taught by men, and they are received from men. Paul says that the Christian gospel is totally different from this. Instead, the Christian gospel is by revelation from Jesus Christ.

This matters because *all other gospels don't work*. We see this everywhere today in the failure of Western society as it tries to enter a new age built upon a gospel of man—the gospel of wealth creation, the gospel of the United Nations. The United Nations is a great gospel of man. There's nothing wrong and much right with it, of course, but it's essentially a gospel of man. It's not based upon revelation from God but upon tradition of humans. The same could be said for Communism or secular capitalism. There is the gospel of education: as soon as we educate everyone properly, they will become better rather than simply better able to do what they are inclined to do. If you want a sense of how much we are surrounded by various gospels of man, note the items marketed as you go through the checkout line at a grocery store. You too can have the perfect abs. You too can be wealthy. Yoga to a peaceful life.

These things are not working. What is the real message of an economic crisis? Surely it is that money is not the answer to everything. We cannot negotiate, buy, or fight our way to peace. The only way to peace is through the Prince of Peace, Christ himself.

Even more important is that these gospels *do not honor God*. That is why, in the end, God chose to save us in the way he did. God chose the weak things of this world to shame the wise so that no one can boast before him (1 Cor. 1:27–29). The gospel of God, revealed by Jesus Christ, honors God as no other gospel does. If you want a litmus test for the true gospel, that would be it. Does it honor God because it is all from God, or is some other institution, person, or technique getting the glory?

This is why Martin Luther, in his teaching on the book of Galatians, noted how different the true gospel is from the gospel of the Roman Catholic Church. The gospel is not passed along from man to man. The papal succession that claims to go all the way back to Peter is a great historical myth. At one point in the Middle Ages there were two popes at the same time. Which was the true one? Some of the Medieval popes did not show a great holiness. So, the idea of a tradition being passed along from man to man is just not historically accurate. We do not need to know that to realize the problem. It's not just that it doesn't work, though that is true; it's that it doesn't honor God. It puts the authority in the hands of a man. But it is all from Jesus.

People have argued about why Paul can say he received the gospel by revelation from Jesus Christ. Do we really think he received everything in that Damascus road experience? Was he taught it all then? You have to remember that Paul, when he was Saul, was a great scholar and religious leader already, and his scholarship was in the Bible, the Old Testament Scriptures. Paul did not start from scratch. He had all the infrastructure in his mind; he had all the logs ready for the fire carefully laid, and when he met Christ on the Damascus road, the bonfire was kindled and all the pieces put together, and light was shone in his mind's eye. He'd studied the Christ. He knew the message of the Old Testament law; he was a Pharisee. But he needed, like the disciples on the Emmaus road, to have his eyes opened to realize that all this was about Jesus.

The Gospels of Man

This is of great importance to us because all gospels of men do not work, and because only the gospel of God as revealed in Jesus Christ gives sole honor to God. But there's another reason why we need to think about this: it tells us *how we need to make sure that we are believing in the true gospel.*

Human gospels do not work. In fact, I think you could say quite simply that the Western world looks like it is crumbling at present because it has moved away from its moorings to the Christian gospel. If you read even nonreligious documents from years ago, you'll find them honoring God and getting their sense of right and wrong from God and Jesus. The trade guilds in London did that. Businessmen did it. Why have people cheated on the Stock Exchange? Why have they swindled investors out of billions of dollars? It's not because they don't have "values" and statements of the right way to act. It's that they don't have the power to act that way. Humans, naturally, have a conscience, and they know, roughly speaking, right and wrong. But human gospels can't make us do what's right. We need the gospel of Jesus Christ for that.

Human gospels are not working. It is very important that the Bible Belt hear that. It is easy for Christians to think that a more humanistic approach to life is better, because that's what the advertising at the checkout line at Cosco tells us. But that's not the case. These so-called gospels don't immediately and dramatically fail, but, like a frog in water, the temperature gradually rises and before too long the moral behavior has changed. The gospel of sexual liberation is a gospel of man that hasn't worked. Why are our inner cities facing great difficulties? Why do our men cave in to the addiction of lust? Why is there rising risk of abuse? The gospel of sexual liberation is running its course. We are told that the Victorians were too strict and prim with their sexual repression, but now we have the fire of sexuality let out of the fireplace and running rampant through the house and setting ablaze and burning out and destroying people in our society. These things are not working, and we need to face up to it. We must not be conned by the marketing of secular society that such so-called gospels are the great future. There is nothing new to them. They are just the gospel of man, a new paganism.

Religious activities that puff up religious teachers end up detracting from the glory of God. There should be no papal succession, but then neither are we to have our evangelical gurus who gather their adherents on a pedestal and repeat their sayings. That's a kind of gospel of man too. It doesn't work and it dishonors God.

The True Gospel

What are we to do instead? We are *to give ourselves to God's Word*. We are to study it. We are to preach it. We are to let it come inside us and shape us. We are to be changed by it. Paul urges the Galatians to see that. This gospel, the true gospel of God, is by revelation of Jesus Christ.

That means it is a revelation *of* Jesus Christ and a revelation *by* Jesus Christ. Both were true for Paul on the Damascus road. It was not just a blinding light outside but a change inside. Jesus, the risen Jesus, revealed himself to Paul. Paul was commissioned to be an apostle of Christ, given the special and unique task of founding the doctrinal framework for the church and having that recorded for us by the work of the Spirit in our New Testament. Paul, as Peter said, wrote things hard to understand (2 Pet. 3:16), as we find in the other Scriptures. This is not always simple stuff, but it is now in this revelation of Jesus Christ part of the Scriptures.

It is also *of* Jesus Christ. The whole Old Testament points to Christ. That is its purpose. "The Scriptures bear witness about me," Jesus said (John 5:39; cf. Luke 24:27). This New Testament is God's last word. It is the record of the revelation of Jesus Christ. When we read the Bible, we are reading a word from heaven about Jesus. That is its point, purpose, and message. Instead of a gospel of man, we are to have the gospel of Jesus Christ, which means that the Word is at the heart of our lives and our churches. Christ is at the heart of that, for he is the one of whom the Word speaks.

This means the same thing for us that it did for the Galatians. Like them, we need to get rid of any Jesus-plus gospels. They were on the verge of succumbing to the law as a means of salvation, as something necessary for the Christian life. What things are we on the verge of believing are necessary for our church life other than faith in Jesus through the centrality of his Word? Could it be a certain music style? If your faith is centered upon a certain music style, are you on the verge of a Jesus-plus gospel? Could it be a certain way of dressing? If your faith is centered upon wearing certain kinds of clothes to church, are you on the verge of a Jesus-plus gospel?

It comes down, therefore, to our practical attitude to the Bible. I heard someone say once that it was terrible, all these fast-growing churches in the developing world with no books but the Bible. If you came to visit me, you would see that I have many books. I love second-hand bookstores; before I had a family, my budget priorities were books, food, and clothes in that order. But the more we learn, the easier it is to have a Jesus-plus gospel or a Bible-plus gospel. Perhaps churches in the developing world are growing so fast because they contain a Bible-only people, as we must be too. John Wesley liked to call himself a man of one book, and he was an Oxford professor.

Perhaps the greatest gospel of man that threatens our grasp of the real gospel is the gospel of constant busyness. Perhaps our Jesus-plus gospel is Jesus plus the perfect suburban life. We are often very busy as Christian people these days. When was the last time we had space simply to say that it is God and his Word and faith in Christ, and rest in that?

Out of that place, as we reorient ourselves to a Jesus-only and Bible-only faith and lifestyle, will come freedom from anger, lust, worry, the idol of success, loneliness, and the constant burden of being busy. It's that which will help us live life as a Christian on Monday, not just on Sunday. It's that which will help us find Christ in a community of mutual lovers of Jesus, in the warmth of connectedness and caring.

7

Gospel, Not Religion

For you have heard of my former life in Judaism, how I persecuted the
church of God violently and tried to destroy it. And I was advancing in
Judaism beyond many of my own age among my people, so extremely
zealous was I for the traditions of my fathers. But when he who had
set me apart before I was born, and who called me by his grace,
was pleased to reveal his Son to me, in order that I might preach him
among the Gentiles, I did not immediately consult with anyone;
nor did I go up to Jerusalem to those who were apostles before me,
but I went away into Arabia, and returned again to Damascus.

GALATIANS 1:13–17

Being in church often makes us feel that we have come to a place of
spiritual safety, a sanctuary where there are very few if any spiritual dan-
gers. But, actually, according to the passage in front of us, and the whole
remarkable story of Paul's Damascus road experience, there is a great
spiritual trap in religion. Paul was not converted from a background of
sex, drugs, and rock 'n' roll. He was very moral. He was a student of
the Bible. He was a religious leader of growing reputation and influence.
But Paul found that there is a certain "religious" interpretation of the
Bible that is at least as great a trap spiritually as flagrant immorality,
and often more difficult because it is more subtle.

Perhaps you like to drive, and perhaps you like to drive fast. It is
sometimes joked that the last part of Christians' anatomy to get converted is their right foot (perhaps after their pocket). I once managed to
make it from a radio interview in the middle of London to speak in a
church on the south coast in under an hour, which, if you know London
geography, is an achievement only possible through a divine reworking
of the laws of physics or a vigorous application of the right foot. I'll
leave up to your imagination which. I am aware that there are speed

traps around for the unwary. Perhaps you are good at maneuvering that sort of thing and keeping yourself clean through the challenges of the day, but when you get home and the kids are thrown at you, as it were, you are immediately grumpy. Life can feel like little more than a series of challenges, and then you get blindsided by something out of left field. I like the story of the woman who once listened to a man preach on sin. After the service she said to the pastor, "I haven't sinned for ten years." The pastor looked at her slowly, smiled, and then said, "You must be awfully proud of that," and she said, "Yes, I am actually."

Here in Galatians we are dealing with an unexpected trap that hooked Paul and how God got Paul out of it. In the movie *Jurassic Park* there is a scene in which a hunter goes after the velociraptors. He has one in his sights that isn't moving, and then suddenly he realizes that another is to his left. He'd thought he was trapping them, but really it was the other way around. It's a bit like that. We can be focused on trapping immorality and wrongdoing and suddenly find we've been caught by this religious trap.

Paul continues to urge the Galatians to have a Jesus-only gospel, and he builds on the idea that the gospel is from God. He shows them the truth from his own biography—the story of his conversion on the Damascus road—that we are to *reject the "religion of I" and receive the faith of God*. In Galatians 1:13–14 the word "I" is very prominent. Here Paul was recounting his life in the "religion of I." John Stott noticed that it switches in verse 15 to where God becomes prominent.[1] We are to reject the religion of I and receive the faith of God.

Reject the "Religion of I"

Paul recounts that he had been persecuting the church. He adds, "I was advancing in Judaism beyond many of my own age among my people" (v. 14). At that stage in Paul's life, he was captivated by the religion of I.

1) *The religion of I is a way of life* (v. 13). It is a code, a series of rules. It is easily defined and quantified. It is something that I can feel good about having achieved. It is a series of boxes on my to-do list that I can check off. Particularly, the "former life" is likely to refer to the *halakhah* of rabbinic Judaism, the oral tradition of rules used to

---

[1]John R. W. Stott, *The Message of Galatians* (Downers Grove, IL: InterVarsity, 1984).

interpret the Bible; the word here is also used to translate the Hebrew *halakh* as "walk" or "conduct." When Jesus said, "You have heard that it was said . . . but I say to you . . . ," he was referring to the rabbinic interpretation of the Old Testament, through which they brought the rules down to an achievable standard in their human flesh. Actually, the law was intended to point to Christ, who alone could achieve the standard for us. The religion of I is a way of life, a conduct, a behavior. It is concerned with the external, not the internal, with good doing, not good being. There is a constant temptation to interpret the Bible that way. People view Bible-believing Christians as those who are for certain moral positions and against certain behavior, not as a people who proclaim a message of good news to all nations.

2) *The religion of I has a nationalistic interpretation of the Bible.* It was Paul's way of life in Judaism (v. 13), and he was advancing in Judaism (v. 14). This is the only time "Judaism" is used by Paul to describe his former lifestyle, and here it is used twice. *Judaism* as a term was developed by the Maccabees in response to Jews who were beginning to live more like Greeks. Judaism then became a nationally defined movement with certain particular criteria (circumcision, sacrifice, the Sabbath) that defined a proper Jew living like a Jew.

The religion of I typically becomes nationalistic, for, in the corporate entity of the nation, we find a larger than life *I*. We become proud of our nation in a religious sense. Most vicious totalitarian regimes cultivate a religious feeling toward the nation. We tend to feel that God is on our side and that God speaks our language. I suppose Mormonism is the ultimate extension of this, where, despite all the archaeological evidence, Jesus is viewed as having walked the sacred turf of America.

When I did mission work in the Republic of Georgia, I noticed that the pictures of Jesus contained a good, handsome Georgian man, whereas, of course, the Western Jesus tends to look Western, when surely, if anything, he looked Jewish. The British Israelites movement believed that the British nation was one of the lost tribes of Israel. Every nation has this temptation. It is a religion of I, where we see projected onto the big screen our national characteristics and claim God as an Englishman, an American, or whatever nation it is from which we come.

3) *The religion of I is opposed to the church of God* (v. 13). Paul vio-

lently and vigorously persecuted the church like a good zealous fanatic who had been commissioned to seek the punishment of those thought to have blasphemed by calling Jesus "God." Looking back, he realized that those he had persecuted were actually the church of God, not a blasphemous sect. Today, the religion of I tends to persecute the church too, for in the gathered community of God's people there is a deep and prevailing threat to the religion of I. Church is not individualistic. It is a community, and a community requires commitment. To find community in a church, you need to make a commitment, get involved, take the initiative, and have time together. The religion of I tends to sit back and let it all flow by. "What's in it for me?" is the great question, not "What I can give?" and, of course, this is opposed to the community of the church of God, even if only passively.

4) *The religion of I is competitive*. Paul was "advancing in Judaism beyond many of my own age among my people" (v. 14). That is the classic feeling of the religion of I. Who is the best theologian? Whose Greek is the best? Whose is the best and biggest church? Whose prayer is the best? All this is vanity, for what is best with regard to God is defined only by God. When we are captivated with the religion of I, what matters is what other *I's* think, not what the Great I Am thinks. We strive for heaven in order to impress earth, and heaven is not impressed.

5) *The religion of I is zeal without knowledge* (v. 14). It is fine to be zealous, Paul will say again (Gal. 4:17–18), provided the purpose is good, but the agitators were trying to make the Galatians zealous for them. He knew all about that. *Zeal* was almost a technical word at the time, and later the zealots became a defined movement. Paul was not a zealot, we think, but a Pharisee of Pharisees, yet *zeal* was a technical defined word for being zealous for traditions, for codes of behavior. The Judaizing false teachers were trying to turn the Christians back to what they had interpreted the Scriptures as being about—zeal for the human traditions of their fathers—rather than zeal for Christ and his gospel, as the Scriptures purely and simply spoke.

Classically, the religion of I is this zeal without knowledge. It is passionate, but it is the kind of zeal that blows up buildings and causes wars and fights. The solution is not relativistic tolerance or a vague "anything goes" attitude. The solution is zeal for what is good and godly. No one can be too zealous for love or too zealous for the gospel, but the religion of I is zeal without knowledge; it is barking up the wrong tree.

6) *The religion of I is tradition overwriting the Word* (v. 14). One caught up in this religion is zealous for the traditions of his fathers, this oral law and way of life. He is not zealous for the Bible or the gospel. This is typically what happens. A movement gets more concerned with "how we have always done it" or "what we did before" and not with the truly radical thought of what the Bible actually teaches us to do.

So reject the religion of I, which means religion as a way of life, a nationalistic interpretation of the Bible, individualism opposing church commitment, fractious competition, zeal without knowledge, and tradition overwriting the Word. Paul, by means of his autobiography, is telling us that we need to reject the religion of I and receive the faith of God.

Receive the Faith of God

Through Paul's personal story, we are to learn that we need to receive the faith of God (vv. 15–17). God intervened in Paul's life, and he wants us also to have the kind of faith that comes from God and his initiative.

This means that God initiates. Immediately, God is brought into the picture. "But when he . . . " (v. 15). The faith of God is that faith which begins with God and that God begins. God comes first. There are many people who do not believe in the Christian God because they feel we make him too small. Einstein may have been one of those. Even someone like Richard Dawkins, when backed in a corner, recognizes there may be some great original higher power, but not one like the small tribal deities that he thinks Christianity represents. We need to repent of any attempt to bring God down to our level. Certainly God is intimate with us as his children, but the transcendent, magnificent, above all and over all is God. God begins. God initiates. Receive the faith of God, which means that God initiates.

We receive the faith of God, which means that God sets us apart. The Greek word for *set apart* may be referring to the Pharisees, whose name perhaps came from the idea of being set apart. Paul then could be saying that the true faith is not that by which we set ourselves apart (the religion of I), but that which is set apart by God. God sets us apart. He calls us. He makes us his own. It is not something we work up or project. It is something that God does, pure and simple, in his sovereign power and on his decision.

We receive the faith of God, which means it's all grace. ". . . called me by his grace" (v. 15). Because God initiates and sets apart, this means it is grace, a gift. This is the heart of it. The religion of I is scared to emphasize it. What will happen if we really let people know that it is all a gift? What will happen if they truly understand that it is not by works? What will happen if they get that all they have to do is receive the faith of God? I tell you what will happen: revival will break out, the church will be reformed, missions will go to the farthest corners of the earth, and it will stop being always winter but never Christmas in the Western world. We will understand the message of Christmas, the gift that simply needs unwrapping.

We receive the faith of God, which means not only that God initiates and sets us apart by grace, but also that the pleasure of God is in the personal dynamic of the sight of his Son. He was pleased to reveal "his Son to me" (v. 16). This is what Jonathan Edwards called "the sense of the heart." Yes, there was a great, flashing, blinding light on the Damascus road. Yes, Paul saw Christ not mystically but truly as the risen Jesus. But he also saw him in a different way from those others on the road with him. The son was revealed *to him*. What does it mean for the Son, for Jesus, to be "to us"? It means this sense of the heart. The heart in the Bible is not merely the feelings. For Christ to be *to* us does not just mean that we have warm emotions about him, but neither does it mean only that we think well of him. For Christ to be to us means "in our heart," in a biblical sense, which means the thinking-willing-feeling unit of who we are. We sense him. He is who we are about in our minds, feelings, and wills, and there is a connection with Christ today in our sense of him. We see him, as it were; we touch him and hear him. His Word is not a dead letter but a living voice of his Spirit. We receive the faith of God, which means that the personal dynamic of the sight of his Son pleases God.

When this is real, what benefit! What change! What a difference it makes to the whole world. Receive the faith of God, which means not just that God initiates, and that it's by grace, and that there's a personal change of the sight of the Son, but that this leads to worldwide benefit. There is always this purpose: "In order that I might preach him among the Gentiles," that is, the nations (v. 16). Those who get Jesus move from being nationalistic and trying competitively to advance in a way of moral superiority to being those who give worldwide benefit to all the nations.

We're not sure exactly what Paul did when he was in Arabia (v. 17), but most likely he did exactly what he had just been told to do, which was to go to all the nations and preach the gospel. Arabia is likely Nabean Arabia, nearby or including Damascus at times, with populous cities in it, and where Paul most likely began his immediate vision for worldwide benefit.

We receive the faith of God, which means good news to others. It is "in order that I might preach him" (v. 16). The message of the gospel is the message of Christ. If we are not preaching him, we are not preaching the gospel. A Christian preacher must always preach Christ or he is not a Christian preacher. The word Paul uses here for "preach" means "evangelize this good news," this announcement of the Christ, who came to rescue people from the religious trap as much as from the immoral trap. This is good news to us and others. It spreads. When we really get the Son in us, it is not like a campaign that has to be marketed, though I'm sure there are organizational practicalities to evangelism; it is more like a virus that is caught. Christ to us, then, is Christ that is "gospeled" to others as good news.

All of this means *that it does not require professional authentication.* Paul says that he did not consult any man or go up to Jerusalem (vv. 16–17). Paul has been building to this point. This is not the gospel of man; it is the gospel of God, for he got it directly from Christ. Now he says that he did not even "consult" (a special word used for those consulting with professional interpreters of mystical experiences) with any of the experts, those other apostles. He is not denigrating them but just clarifying. For him, uniquely, he just got on with what God had told him to do—evangelizing the nations in Arabia and Damascus.

For us too, although the faith of God is in God's Word and in the apostolic Word in the New Testament—so different from Paul in that respect. Nonetheless, there is a direct communion with Christ through the Word and by the Spirit that does not require professional validation; it is its own witness, Christ in us, and the fruit of the changed life that all can see which verifies this in our own autobiography, as in

Paul's. Rather provocatively, the Danish theologian philosopher Søren Kierkegaard once said that he who studies the Bible with ten open commentaries is probably writing the eleventh. We need to go beyond that and actually come face-to-face with God himself in his Word.

Reject the religion of I and receive the faith of God. Reject the religion of I, which means religion as a way of life, a nationalistic interpretation of the Bible, individualism opposing church commitment, fractious competition, zeal without knowledge, and tradition overwriting the Word. Then receive the faith of God that God initiates. He sets us apart, all by grace, and gives this internal dynamic sight of the Son. This leads to worldwide benefit, which is good news to others and does not require professional authentication. We find a connection at a personal level in our hearts between us and God. Reject the religion of I and receive the faith of God.

That is Paul's autobiography and the purpose for which he retells it, to urge the Galatians and us to follow him away from the religion of I to receive the faith of God. What does (or would) our personal autobiography say about where we are with regard to those two options? Perhaps you are reading this expecting to be given religion. I don't want to give you religion; I want to give you God, and those are two very different things. Don't be confused by the infrastructure of a traditional church. Church is about being a vehicle for the faith of God. Receive not just that but him.

Perhaps you're from a religious background, not Judaism but Christian-ism. I want to set you free from that. I want you to feel the pleasure of God as the Son is revealed in you. Paul didn't stop having a basic commitment to standard morality. What he stopped was being *I* focused, and he became Christ focused. He understood what the Bible was really about—good news to the whole word—and he let that message shape everything about him. I want you to have the pleasure of God in you, and as you do, you will find the "so that" and take the gospel to the nations.

I want us, Christian people, by the power of the Spirit to live on the side of the faith of God, not on the side of the religion of I, to have Christ, by his Word, revealed in our hearts (our minds and feelings) so that our wills are set upon God. I want us to have his pleasure, and for that we need to pray.

8

The Authority of the Gospel

Then after three years I went up to Jerusalem to visit Cephas and remained with him fifteen days. But I saw none of the other apostles except James the Lord's brother. (In what I am writing to you, before God, I do not lie!) Then I went into the regions of Syria and Cilicia. And I was still unknown in person to the churches of Judea that are in Christ. They only were hearing it said, "He who used to persecute us is now preaching the faith he once tried to destroy." And they glorified God because of me.

GALATIANS 1:18–24

It was early Sunday morning, cold and damp. A grim day, it might even have been snowing. The mother of the house was trying to get everyone ready for church. She looked at the clock: they had to leave in ten minutes! She called upstairs to her son, who had not yet emerged from his bedroom. "We've got to get ready for church!" There was no reply. She tried again. This time wafting down from above came the complaint, "I'm not going." The mother heaved a sigh and dragged herself up the stairs outside her son's bedroom door. "It's time to go to church," she said again. "I'm not going," the son replied. She decided to try a different tactic. "You know lots of people at church, and lots of people know you." The son said firmly, "I don't have any friends, and no one likes me, and I'm not going to go to church." The mother said to her son, "You've got to go to church because you're the minister and you're preaching!"

One of the themes in the letter of Galatians is this conflict between church authority and the authority of the gospel. The Galatians were being presented with the trump card of the authority of Jerusalem. They were being told that this gospel of Paul's was inadequate and that the true gospel was different, and that they could know this because the people telling them this were "from James," and from Jerusalem. Paul, they were saying, had his authority from Jerusalem too, but he'd gotten some of it wrong; he was a man-pleaser who had made the gospel fit the shape of his hearers.

This whole theme of the conflict between church authority, or that of "Jerusalem," and the authority of the gospel is coming to a head in this passage and in the subsequent verses of Galatians 2. Paul is going to make two points. He is going to argue that actually his gospel is not in conflict with that of the Jerusalem apostles, but he is also arguing that the gospel has the authority, not the church, and even if he (1:8) or Peter (2:11) were to go off track, they must not be followed, because the gospel of Jesus Christ itself has the authority.

This is of great importance today, for those both inside and outside the church. For those inside the church, there are various strong movements urging us to go back to the true "ancient" church. Some people say that the ancient church is Orthodoxy, whether Greek or Russian. Other people say that the ancient church is Roman Catholic. Some say that the ancient church is the Celtic church. But according to the Bible, the ancient church is that which sticks to the ancient message of the gospel. That's where the authority lies, for it is authored by God himself.

For those outside the church, Paul is still often thought to have distorted the message of Jesus. It's popular to write books about the "secret message of Jesus" or the "really truly lost message of Jesus that I just discovered." There's a sort of Indiana-Jones fashion among religious publishing at the moment. What we're going to discover is that Paul truly represents the ancient Jesus—the Jesus of history, if you like.

So Paul is arguing that our gospel is true; i.e., what Paul says, God says. He very firmly wants to make that point: "(In what I am writing to you, before God, I do not lie!)" (v. 20). So, in this travelogue between him and the ancient Jerusalem church, that means a couple of things.

Our Gospel Is True

First, our gospel is true, which means that the church cannot change it and therefore must not try to. Church, don't try to change the gospel, for the church cannot change it. The church is not the author; God is.

"Then after three years I went up to Jerusalem to visit Cephas and remained with him fifteen days. But I saw none of the other apostles except James the Lord's brother. (In what I am writing to you, before God, I do not lie!)" (vv. 18–20). This is really important for our current discussions about the ancient church but also for all that stuff about whether we can really trust Paul's record of what Jesus was like. Paul says that his message was not authored by the Jerusalem church apostles because (1) he didn't go there for information but for a personal visit; (2) he was in Jerusalem only a very short time; and (3) he saw only Peter and James.

1) *He didn't go there for information but just for a personal visit.* The word Paul uses for "to visit Cephas" could be used of sightseeing an ancient monument. Paul, having been converted by Jesus on the Damascus road and commissioned by him personally, went off to Jerusalem to see the apostles, not to learn but to visit.

2) *He was in Jerusalem only a very short time.* Paul tells us that he was there fifteen days, which was certainly long enough to get to know people but not to construct a sophisticated theology. These fifteen days were after the three years that he'd already spent preaching this gospel, so the couple of weeks in Jerusalem were very much by contrast a brief visit.

3) *He saw only Peter and James.* He saw only Peter, as his house guest, and James the brother of the Lord, which probably means (Acts 9 describes Paul's visit to the apostles) that James was included among the apostles, though not among the original Twelve.

So if Roman Catholicism is true, then surely we should find Paul learning from Peter. But we don't. In fact, we find that Paul confronts Peter because Peter is in the wrong (Gal. 2:11). That doesn't mean that Paul is better than Peter; it means that the authority is in the gospel, not in man, whether Paul or Peter. It's important that we see the contemporary relevance of this discussion about Paul's itinerary. He is being detailed. The Holy Spirit recorded this detailed travelogue for us because it shows us where the authority is. If Orthodoxy is true, then surely we would expect to find the authority for the origin of the gospel in a communal council discussion among the apostles, but again we don't. The authority is from God, and it is his gospel; and no one, whatever his religious title, gets to change it. It's very important for the so-called emergent church, of which there are many different types and kinds these days. If we want to emerge from the corruption of the contemporary church (and we can be sure that the contemporary church has its corruption), what we will need to do is get back to the Bible and to the gospel and find there this ancient message that cannot and does not change—and that we must not therefore attempt to change.

But, of course, this is hard for people. Very often this is because we think, *How do I interpret the gospel?* Paul also answers that, at least by implication in verse 20: "In what I am writing to you, before God, I do not lie." Before God, or in the face of God, or in the presence of God, he is writing. We may know that this gospel is true, in the face of God, in the presence of God. Yes, it's good to have teachers and to learn from history. Human writings can help. But the Protestant Reformation has always taught, and, much more importantly, the Bible itself teaches, that there is a self-authentication. The Bible interprets the Bible. It is the work of the Holy Spirit, of God himself, in these writings preserved for us. As Paul says to Timothy, "Think over what I say, for the Lord will give you understanding in everything" (2 Tim. 2:7). There is always the process of thinking and discussing, but our interpretation and the authority of that also belong in the presence of God and in the work of the Holy Spirit.

This means that our faith is not built upon the sand of men. Isn't that comforting? You can be sure that you have the rock of God himself under the gospel that Paul is preaching here in Galatians, that gospel of justification by faith alone. It's not a tradition or a fad. It's not an innovative idea. It is eternally rooted in God himself. It means that what Paul says is what God says, and that to disobey Paul's writings in the New Testament is to disobey God. It means that we should be committed to the local church—find a church, join it, stick with it, and love it through its mistakes, as long as that church is committed to the one true gospel of Jesus Christ. It means that we don't have to be blown around by any pretended new, secret message of Jesus from the Jerusalem apostles because the point is the gospel, and where that is, there is the ancient church. That is Paul's first point. Our gospel is true; therefore, he shows through his travelogue, the church cannot change it.

Praise God Because of It

Second, our gospel is true; therefore it's not just that the church cannot change it but also that the church is to praise God because of it. "Then I went into the regions of Syria and Cilicia" (v. 21), Paul writes, continuing his alibi describing in detail his movements so they know he got the gospel from God, not from Jerusalem. "And I was still unknown in person to the churches of Judea that are in Christ. They only were hearing it said, 'He who used to persecute us is now preaching the faith he once tried to destroy.' And they glorified God because of me" (vv. 22–24).

Why is this good news? Why does this mean that people get all excited and praise God? It's because this gospel of God actually changes people. There is the bitter old woman who lives in anger at her husband. They live in the same house, but they ignore each other apart from disagreeing about when something happened or who said what. There is the rebellious teenager who is like the ugly duckling, almost beautiful and yet gangly and awkward, and his parents are going mad. There is the guy who thinks he's really right on in every way and much better than all other people. Paul is the extreme example of what God does by his gospel all the time: he changes people. You may say you haven't seen it, but maybe that's because you haven't seen the gospel in its purity for a while. How are we going to mend fragmented families, or build a strategy for world evangelization, or bring the Western world back to Christ? It is going to happen one Paul at a time through the power of the gospel.

Lots of things are remarkable about how Paul describes this praise to God and the change that brought it about. He was *personally* unknown to the churches of Judea. They'd heard of Paul. They'd heard of his conversion. But he wasn't known *by face*. He wasn't making the most of his change to get celebrity. One of the background colors in the painting of Galatians is this issue of face, flesh, and humanity. They were all very interested in what looked good to other humans. Paul, previously so concerned to look good, was quite happy to be unknown. He spent fourteen years just preaching without anyone getting all excited about who he was, and then they praised God because of Paul. Once God gets hold of a man or a woman, that can happen. He is exalted, but in exalting him, people do not praise the man; they praise God. Perhaps that's something you can be asking God for, that people would praise God in you. What is most remarkable is the turnabout. He who was persecuting is now preaching. This still happens through the power of the gospel. It does not happen through the power of the church.

A woman was a drug dealer in New York City, and then she came to New Haven, Connecticut, where she ended up on the streets and then in a homeless shelter. A couple of Yale University students went to the shelter, told her the gospel, and invited her to church. After hearing the Word of God, she was convicted it was true, and she began to believe. Sometime later she was baptized. She began to tell her friends and family about Christ. It was quite a change. She died a few years ago of complications from her past drug use. Before she died, still getting used to the new life she had been given, she said to me, "Pastor, if you ever need any help, just let me know. I know people, you know what I mean? And if you ever need me to take care of anyone, I can just make a phone call, and it's done."

I also know a young, bright Asian couple. They are coming to church and hearing the gospel. They were converted, and they are serving now, inviting friends and telling people about Christ. There are businessmen, homeless people, intelligentsia, simple men and women, those of high class, low class, and middle class; there are the intellectually convoluted and the drug addicts, and those from Western culture and Eastern culture. A man in Central Asia who was coming to our Bible study group broke his leg, and I went every week up a long winding road to see him. I found him in his apartment reading the Bible, underlining parts he didn't understand. By the time his leg was healed, he'd given his life to Christ. Then there was a Moslem man converted through a portion of the New Testament who had to flee for his life across the border.

Paul. Me. You.

I want you to understand that this is the gospel of Jesus Christ. It is not a proclamation of law. It is not vague notions of the kingdom. It is the cross of Jesus Christ. It is his death for our sins. It cannot be rewritten by the church; the church must not attempt to do so. Instead, the church has the wonderful, joyful duty of praising God because of what he is doing by means of the gospel in real people's lives.

What makes us do that is the realization that it is all from God and by God, and therefore to God goes the praise. It is not made up by humans, even human apostles. It is not changed by the church. It is not to be reinvented by the latest religious fad, marketed as "Ten Ways to the Perfect Church." It is not about human tradition. It is not by flesh and blood at all. This is God's doing. It wasn't the church or Jerusalem; it was God in Christ. He called Paul. He commissioned him. It is God's gospel. There is no other. It changes people. God by the gospel changes people. We don't give our praise to humans. We give our praise to God. And when the church is about that, it's worth getting out of bed for.

9

The Gospel of Freedom

Then after fourteen years I went up again to Jerusalem with Barnabas, taking Titus along with me. I went up because of a revelation and set before them (though privately before those who seemed influential) the gospel that I proclaim among the Gentiles, in order to make sure I was not running or had not run in vain. But even Titus, who was with me, was not forced to be circumcised, though he was a Greek. Yet because of false brothers secretly brought in—who slipped in to spy out our freedom that we have in Christ Jesus, so that they might bring us into slavery—to them we did not yield in submission even for a moment, so that the truth of the gospel might be preserved for you.

GALATIANS 2:1–5

Woke up, fell out of bed, dragged a comb across my head; found my way downstairs and drank a cup; and looking up I noticed I was late. Found my coat, and grabbed my hat, made the bus in seconds flat"—so the Beatles sang in "A Day in the Life" from their *Sergeant Pepper* album. If you want a more contemporary feeling of the slavery of modern *homo economicus*, you need look no further than the noisy if peaceful complaints mounted outside a meeting of the G-20 global leaders dealing with an economic crisis. Or if you prefer something slightly less cerebral, you could watch a YouTube video of GM dealership workers getting into a fight over their feelings of economic slavery.

For the first time in the letter, Paul says that if we get the gospel wrong, it's not just a mistake; it's a form of slavery. We tend to think of slavery in terms of the power dynamics of the workplace. There were slaves in America. There are still slaves around the world. In our lives we tend to think we are free if we are, as it were, the queen bee in the hive, and a slave if we are just one of the worker drones. We attempt to get our freedom economically. If we become the queen bee, then we are free, but the Bible tells us that true freedom is freedom from guilt. The ultimate slavery is not to the workplace, to the boss, or to the nine-to-five grind of life, but to the law.

Circumcision in Galatians is not just about the physical act of circumcision. In another place Paul will himself circumcise Timothy. He will say that circumcision is nothing. If we think it is something, then another factor is at work. In Galatians 4:8–10 Paul describes the underlying principles, those gods, those special seasons and days, to which the Galatians were turning back. Because we feel guilty, we are attracted to religious ceremonies that seem to make us feel less guilty, and circumcision, not inherently an attractive option for adults, was appealing in particular to these Galatians because, by getting circumcised, they were identifying themselves with the grandfathered religion of Judaism in the ancient world and so avoiding the persecution that would come the way of this newfangled faith called Christianity.

Jerome was wrong to say this letter is just about circumcision. It's not. It's not just about ceremonies and rituals but about the underlying motive that makes those rituals attractive. It's about guilt and freedom—slavery and freedom—and the means to avoid slavery, which Paul now is beginning to address in his letter. The image of the exodus is behind this. They had been slaves, but the gospel had set them free. By this legalistic interpretation of the law they were becoming slaves again to guilt. In these few verses here, we have Paul describing how he stopped being enslaved, and so for us this is about *how not to be a slave*.

Word and Spirit

First, *don't divide the Word from the Spirit*. "I went up because of a revelation and set before them (though privately before those who seemed influential) the gospel that I proclaim among the Gentiles" (v. 2). When I am being legalistic—thinking of myself as better than others, finding my confidence in how good I think I am at keeping the rules, adopting as necessary certain behaviors that are only a matter of conscience—it is normally because I am getting less into the Bible. People think that if you study the Bible too much, you will get enslaved. The reverse is true. There is no danger in too much Bible, only in too little. You can't have too much of the Bible any more than you can have too much of sunlight in midwinter, or rain in the desert, or love letters from your beloved, for that is what the Bible is. The Bible is the voice of the Spirit, and we are not to divide the two from each other.

Paul goes in response to a revelation. He has used the word *revelation* twice already (1:12, 16), and both times have been about the revelation of Jesus Christ. So I think Paul is saying here that this gospel, which Jesus himself had revealed to him, was what motivated him to resist being enslaved. Jesus Christ, the gospel of Jesus Christ, as revealed in the Bible is what empowers us by his Spirit not to be slaves.

If you're an expert car mechanic, you haven't just been listening to *Car Talk* on PBS Radio in Boston each Saturday morning. You really know your stuff. You take your car in for an oil change, and the guy at the garage tells you that you don't just need an oil change but thousands of dollars' worth of repairs. Well, you know cars—you know *this* car—and you can resist that kind of daylight robbery. Just so, if someone comes up to you and says, "I've got this new way of looking at the Bible, and it's rather different from that preached by some well-known forebear, and it means that you've got to do this, that, and the other, and then you'll be right with God"—well, however spiritual that person may be or however clever, if you don't divide the Word from the Spirit, and you are confident in the biblical revelation of Jesus Christ, you can resist that form of new legalism.

It doesn't mean that we don't change at all in terms of how we do things; it means we know Jesus and can spot a fake. Christ is revealed by the Spirit through the Word. If we know that, if we know him, we won't get enslaved by any new form of legalism. But Paul didn't just resist it himself; he went up to Jerusalem to deal with it alongside some others. Not being a slave means not only having the right theological principle ("don't divide the word from the Spirit") but also dealing with it actively in the right way.

The Fifth Column

Second, *resist the "fifth column."* I call it the "fifth column" because Paul is using a lot of military metaphor in verse 4: "Yet because of false brothers secretly brought in—who slipped in to spy out our freedom that we have in Christ Jesus, so that they might bring us into slavery . . ." It was war. Paul and Barnabas were pioneering a Christian mission to Gentiles in the cosmopolitan city of Antioch. Some within the fellowship were saying the Gentiles needed to be circumcised to be a part of God's people. Paul, knowing Jesus as he did, realized that this was not a minor matter of ceremony but a matter of salvation. So, as we read in Acts 11 and 12, he and Barnabas went to Jerusalem for the public purpose of poverty relief (which he mentions again in Gal. 2:10), and privately discussed this matter with the Jerusalem leaders to find out if they agreed. If they had not, the conflict would have grown even worse, but they did. In the heat of battle, Paul employed four tactics that we are to emulate.

1) *He did it privately.* He did not do it by e-mail. He did not send a letter. He did not talk to others about it first to get support. He went privately, face-to-face, and sorted it out in closed personal discussion. There is no more important principle for maintaining the sweetness of Christian fellowship. Never send anything negative by e-mail. Don't do your rebuking by letter. You must have the courage to say personally to someone, "I'd love to get a coffee with you and chat about that sometime; when could we do that?"

2) *He did it deliberately.* He was not overly hasty in anger, nor did he procrastinate, giving in to his fears. Many of us try to be nice and avoid any offense, but the only way to avoid harboring hurt feelings is to have the guts to say what you are feeling. The Bible calls it "truthing in love" (see Eph. 4:15). Truthing in love is not hitting someone over the head with the truth, saying, "Hey, don't complain; the truth hurts." Nor is it hoping that others are mind readers and know what you are thinking without your having to say so. Nor is it assuming that you are right. If you are to truth in love, you have to have the humility to have your mind changed by the other people's truth in love to you, as well. It is simply saying, "Brother, I'm not sure your gift is singing in the choir" as well as "Sister, that ministry you lead is excellent; just keep on going."

3) *He didn't do it perfectly.* I don't mean that Paul was a sinner, though he was; he didn't do everything perfectly in that sense. I mean that his approach here was not grammatically perfect. The commenta-

tor J. B. Lightfoot calls verse 4 "that shipwreck of grammar."[2] Paul was a passionate man, and though the grammar in this sentence is not correct, his heart was. Rhetoric is the art of learning to speak as if you really mean it. This is why Paul eschewed the formal ancient tactics of rhetoric. His approach was plain speaking, meaning *not boring* but *straightforward*. He didn't need to learn to speak as if he meant it; he really meant it.

Some of our speaking should not be grammatically perfect. I have never heard anything more rhetorically compelling than two people arguing, or two lovers wooing, and those who speak only as if they are in a school declamation are not speaking as Paul sometimes spoke and God's Holy Writ inspired. It may not be perfect to boldly split infinitives like no man has split them before, but when someone is weeping for my soul, I expect a slip or two, just like I would at the bedside of a woman mourning for her husband, or a young man telling me that "she finally said yes," or the apostle Paul standing up for the gospel through which we can be saved.

4) *He didn't always do it.* The trouble with Protestants, some people understandably criticize, is that they are always protesting. Paul understood this was a central matter. It took significant discernment. (Circumcision itself was nothing, but the way it was being used meant that they were trusting circumcision and the law, not Christ—a terrible tragedy, for the law is all about Christ.) Don't get your nose put out of joint by the color of the carpet, or the style of the music, or the clothes people wear. These are external things. One of the Devil's great tactics is to get God's holy people arguing about things that don't really matter. First, it causes tension; second, there is probably another far more important matter (the fifth column) in our hearts—pride, or envy, or what have you—that God really wants us to be focusing on.

How Not to Be a Slave

Third, *make pure gospel doctrine your purpose.* "To them we did not yield in submission even for a moment, so that the truth of the gospel might be preserved for you" (v. 5). I know doctrine sounds doctrinaire and the gospel sounds like it's the basics. Neither is true. The gospel is

---

[2]J. B. Lightfoot, *The Epistle of St. Paul to the Galatians* (Grand Rapids, MI: Zondervan, 1974), 104.

not the ABCs of the Christian faith; it is the A to Z, for Christ is the Alpha and Omega. Doctrine is not only for professors and pastors; it is the truth of the gospel for which every Christian must be concerned. Paul says that the whole purpose of this is so that the truth of the gospel might remain with us, and we are to have that purpose for ourselves, our church, our neighborhoods, and the world. Our purpose is not to have a happy life; our purpose is the furthering of the gospel. Our purpose is not "Now that I've become a Christian, I can slip into cruise control"; our purpose is to go deeper with God in doctrine.

Be set free from the slavery of a wasted life. If my life is about getting a paycheck, and cleaning the car, and tidying up the yard, and going to family weddings, then just put me out of my misery. You've got to have a bigger vision for your life than that. To live, you have to have something worth dying for. The great question is not "What do I want people to say about me at my funeral?" The great question is "What is there to do that I'm willing to give my life's blood for so that the truth of the gospel might be preserved?" Get up early. Stay up late. Pray like heaven and hell depend on it. If Christianity is just about singing nice, perfect hymns and preaching pretty sermons, then just put me out of my misery. I don't do ministry so that I can sit in leather armchairs in a boardroom. I'm in ministry to maintain the truth of the gospel. Don't make a career of ministry. You seminarians, you full-time Christian workers, don't waste your life with career moves. Don't give your life to ministry; give your life to Christ and the truth of his gospel.

Be set free from the slavery of the lie that there is no truth. I was amused when I was told that when Bill Clinton spoke at Yale, he said that anyone who believes in absolute truth is just plain wrong. What an extraordinary statement! Yet that is what many people believe. "There is no absolute truth so just go with the flow; anyone who believes in absolute truth is just plain wrong." Well, if it's just plain wrong, that's an absolute truth.

Be set free from the slavery of lies about your committed personal relationships—the lie that says your marriage is a dead-end. Be free from the lie that you can trade up to a better wife, like you trade in a car. Marriage is a relationship. You can no more trade in your wife for a newer model than you can cut your arm off and then find a dead body with a more deeply tanned arm to stick on yourself. In marriage, you are one; that's the truth. Be free from the slavery of the lie that says a little bit of adultery on the side is okay as long as no one finds out. God sees. He knows. Be free from the slavery of the lie that your value is determined by your job. No, you can be unemployed and of great value to Christ because he values *you*, not what you do for him. Be set free from the slavery of the lie that your value is determined by your looks. Christ looks on the heart, and if someone else doesn't, that's their fault, not yours.

Be set free from the slavery of money. It looks like Wall Street is learning this lesson. God does not care how much I give; he cares how much I have left. Money is a great tool but a very bad master. When money is your master, you cannot sleep at night for worry about your investments. When money is your master, the one who inherits wealth is ruined by it, for he finds no motivation to succeed. When money is your master, the Bible would say, Christ is not. When money is a tool, you invest it in heaven. God does not need your money. He is looking for your heart. To wean us off money, he asks us to give it away. The rich man who gave $2.5 million anonymously to a project did so out of his riches; the shaky handwritten note sent with a dollar bill came out of a woman's poverty. I remember both, and Christ looks on the heart.

Be set free from the slavery of the law. Our gospel is not about not drinking, or not smoking, or not playing cards as long as they have no pictures on them but only numbers. I was told of someone applying for a certain mission organization that forbade alcohol who was refused sponsorship because he had cooked with wine in the last year. The poor man was a chef. A gospel church is of great morality—the fruit of the Spirit (Gal. 5:22–23)—and little Pharisaism.

How to be set free?

Inside the doors are sealed to love
Inside my heart is sleeping. . . .
Inside it's colder than the stars
Inside the dogs are weeping
Inside the circus of the wind
Inside the clocks are filled with sand

Inside she'll never hurt me
Inside the winter's creeping
Inside the compass of the night. . . .

Outside the stars are turning
Outside the world's still burning

Love is the child of an endless war
Love is an open wound still raw
Love is a shameless banner unfurled
Love's an explosion,
Love is the fire of the world
Love is a violent star
A tide of destruction
Love is an angry scar
A violation, a mutilation, capitulation, love is annihilation.

So Sting sings. Inside we're broken; outside there is the facade. Love breaks down the barrier. If he'd said the cross (not circumcision) I would have agreed.

10

The Unity of the Gospel

And from those who seemed to be influential (what they were makes no difference to me; God shows no partiality)—those, I say, who seemed influential added nothing to me. On the contrary, when they saw that I had been entrusted with the gospel to the uncircumcised, just as Peter had been entrusted with the gospel to the circumcised (for he who worked through Peter for his apostolic ministry to the circumcised worked also through me for mine to the Gentiles), and when James and Cephas and John, who seemed to be pillars, perceived the grace that was given to me, they gave the right hand of fellowship to Barnabas and me, that we should go to the Gentiles and they to the circumcised. Only, they asked us to remember the poor, the very thing I was eager to do.

GALATIANS 2:6–10

There is a lack of structural unity in the church today. There are many different denominations, different types of Catholics, different brands of Orthodox, different sorts of Protestants. There are Presbyterians, Baptists, Episcopalians, and various subsets of each. You are no longer just an evangelical but a conservative evangelical, or a charismatic evangelical, or a Reformed evangelical. There is certainly lots of energy—as one Texas senator said, "There are more Baptists in Texas than people"—but it is diffuse.

The other thing to observe about the church today is a lack of patience with doctrine. This is ironic, because those who trumpet doctrinal vagueness, or liberty, often do so because doctrine, we are told, divides. Yet today while, on the one hand, we have great structural disunity, on the other hand, we have a great impatience with doctrine. But that is what we would expect, for, according to the passage in front of us, what really divides is not doctrine but personality, and what truly unites is strong, firm, biblical doctrine that helps us move beyond human personalities.

Paul continues to explain to the Galatians how justification by faith alone is the true gospel of God proclaimed by him as well as the leaders in Jerusalem, and he does so in these verses by saying, *one gospel, two apostles*.

One Gospel Ministry

First, there is one gospel ministry. There are four parts of this unity in gospel ministry: (1) *one message*; (2) *one preaching*; (3) *one equipping*; and, as a result of this gospel being powerfully proclaimed, (4) *one love* that is transformative.

1) *One message*. "From those who seemed to be influential (what they were makes no difference to me; God shows no partiality)—those, I say, who seemed influential added nothing to me" (v. 6). Paul is not being rude about the Jerusalem leaders by calling them "those who seemed to be influential"; he is refusing to join in the divisive game of personalities that the Galatian false teachers were playing. So J. B. Lightfoot thought that the references to "those who *seemed* to be influential" should really be "those who *seem* to be influential" (the present tense), making it clear that the target of Paul's criticism was the Galatian agitators and what they were saying in Galatia about what they thought was the superior personality of the Jerusalem leaders.[1]

The Galatian false teachers were emphasizing the direct connection that Peter, James, and John had with Jesus by virtue of their knowledge of him before he died and rose again. They referred to them as "pillars" of the new Christian temple, or as those who have "reputation," and so downplayed Paul's authority and divided Paul from Peter.

In response, Paul does not disparage the Jerusalem leaders; he has already respectfully called them "those who were apostles before me" (1:17), and will shake hands with them in the "right hand of fellowship" (2:9). But while he recognizes they were apostles before him, he is clear they are not thereby more apostles than he, for he, like them, had been commissioned by the risen Christ, and he, like them, has the same message: "those who seemed to be influential . . . added nothing

---

[1] J. B. Lightfoot, *The Epistle of St. Paul to the Galatians* (Grand Rapids, MI: Zondervan, 1974), 104.

to me" (v. 6), meaning the message that he represented in himself to the Galatians.

2) *One preaching.* "On the contrary, when they saw that I had been entrusted with the gospel to the uncircumcised, just as Peter had been entrusted with the gospel to the circumcised . . . " (v. 7). This phrase in the long sentence of these verses is contrasting "the gospel to the uncircumcised" of Paul with "the gospel for the circumcised" of Peter, so some have mistakenly wondered whether this means different gospels were now accepted—a Pauline gospel and a Petrine gospel. But in context it cannot mean they had different gospels. The whole point of this discussion is to prove their unity in the gospel. So Paul says that this gospel agreement was that "we should go to the Gentiles and they to the circumcised" (v. 9); that is, each going to preach the same gospel with different areas of responsibility.

This does not mean that Paul and Peter had hermetically sealed boundaries of missionary work (one labeled "Jew" and the other "Gentile"), whether that airtight boundary is defined territorially or ethnically. Paul, we know from Acts, would habitually, as his missionary strategy, go to the synagogue and preach first to the Jews and the Gentile God-fearers he found there. Paul and Peter recognized in each other not only the same message but also the same entrusting from God to preach that message in primarily, but not exclusively, different spheres. The phrase is rightly interpreted as the "preaching of the gospel" or the "gospeling of the gospel," as some might put it, for the gospel word is itself a proclamation word and can be used verbally as preaching. The *evangel* is to be evangelized in different but overlapping spheres. They are united, then, in one preaching.

3) *One equipping.* "He who worked through Peter for his apostolic ministry to the circumcised worked also through me for mine to the Gentiles" (v. 8). They see that God is working through both of them effectively. They recognize a similar empowering, or equipping, from God, which is bringing blessing from God.

Faithful preaching of the gospel does not always produce large numbers of converts, for, as Paul said elsewhere, the preaching of the gospel means we are the aroma of life to some and the aroma of death to others (2 Cor. 2:15–16). But the Word of God preached always has some impact, some effect, and some attendant working of God, honoring God and producing the results he desires. The prophet Isaiah was told that his ministry would not be believed, yet he was mightily equipped and empowered by God, and God's word through him still speaks today. They are united in the same God working through both of them, to different degrees and in different ways, as they discover *one equipping*.

4) *One love*. They embrace each other in mutual recognition of their ministries (v. 9) and then commit together to express this one gospel in a loving care for the poor (v. 10). Because they recognize that they have one message and that God is at work in both, they offer each other loving fellowship, and the gospel overflows in love to others through their ministries. Care for the poor is not their gospel, but it is an implication of their gospel. Martin Luther said, "A true bishop must be concerned also about the poor, and Paul here admits that he was."

Keith Green was a passionate Christian rocker from the 1970s, whose flared pants were wider than your average highway. In one pamphlet he produced a cartoon caricaturing the wrong approach to Christian unity. There was an old-fashioned telephone kiosk and into it were being squeezed a lot of people. Outside the kiosk was a trash can labeled "truth." As each person attempted to cram into the kiosk labeled "unity," they discarded truth into the trash can. Unity is never achieved that way. Humans always need a point of unity in order to unite, and if it is not doctrine, then likely as not it will be personality, and personalities end up dividing. If the unity is not around the truth of the biblical gospel, it is not unity worth having, and that so-called Christian unity will rapidly disintegrate and be revealed as the ephemeral creation of man. It won't be the unity of the Spirit in the gospel of Jesus Christ.

I want you to be passionate about the message of the gospel. I believe that if you are, you will be increasingly one, as we are one in Christ. I don't want you to be passionate about Christian personalities, or the latest fads, or the oldest traditions; I want you to be passionate about the gospel. I want you to focus on that and have your heart placed there.

I want you to be passionate about biblical preaching. A church or Christian institution that has the gospel written in its books but not preached from its lips is one step away from not being Christian, for it is not just the gospel that is the foundation of the church but the preaching of the gospel. The Bible needs to be not just in the pew racks but open on the pulpit stand. Don't go to a church that has a correct doctrinal statement but does not preach the Bible.

From this comes the equipping of God, who honors his gospel, and the love he gives us for each other, even the disadvantaged among us. It is a series of cascading priorities: the gospel at the heart, the preaching of the gospel necessarily following, which leads to God's honoring of his message, which leads to the fellowship of love for each other, whether rich or poor. It is like a seed that must be sown, and when received into the ground grows to be the largest of all the trees, bearing much fruit for God's honor and glory. Focus on this. Honor this. Love this. Be passionate about this: God's gospel, Bible preaching, and all the fruit from that. Don't focus on personalities and styles and "flesh," for God does not judge by external appearance.

Two Apostles Ministering

The conclusion of their conversation, that they are two apostles ministering the one gospel, is a remarkable victory of the gospel over a potential war of personalities. They recognized that God was using both in different ways: "He who worked through Peter for his apostolic ministry . . . worked also through me for mine" (v. 8). As God used their ministries, Peter therefore recognized Paul, and Paul and Peter shook on it, recognizing each other: "When James and Cephas and John . . . perceived the grace that was given to me, they gave the right hand of fellowship to Barnabas and me" (v. 9).

It is all too easy to let personal differences spoil spiritual relationships. We all tend to think we know the kind of people that God uses, but time and time again God surprises us with whom he picks, and sometimes he picks people we find hard to get along with or just find difficult to believe that God would choose. Samuel had to go down the whole list of siblings before he finally got to David. If we think this discussion was hard for Paul because of being undermined by the Galatian agitators boosting Peter's credentials (and no doubt it *was* hard for Paul) it must also have been hard for Peter, recognizing this man called Paul who so recently had been Saul, the arch Christian persecutor. How did they do it? How is this victory for the gospel won? They did it by seeing beyond appearances, fighting for the truth, and fighting for fellowship around that truth.

They see beyond appearances. Paul tells us that the reputation of the Jerusalem leaders was not important to him, even though they are called "pillars." We can only guess, but I think it is a fair assumption that Peter had to work hard to get beyond Paul's reputation. In any ministry situation, it is important get beyond appearances. Once while I was preaching on pastoral staff at a church in England, I looked out at the large congregation, and a sudden thought entered my head: "Every person here has some hurt." Our world tells us to view people by their position. In fact, some of us spend a good deal of energy gaining a reputation. When we meet someone we have heard about, we can carry those former perceptions into the meeting. If we are to gain a real sense of collaboration, it is important that we see beyond appearances. God does not judge by external appearances, nor are we to do so.

Corrie Ten Boom was deeply wounded personally by the Nazi regime, yet she was given the message of the gospel to preach afterward. One time after having shared at a meeting, a man approached her to shake her hand. She immediately recognized him as a concentration camp guard. What a test! She had been witnessing to the gospel of forgiveness of grace, and before her was this former guard extending his hand. I'm not sure that Peter and Paul shaking on it was as tough as that, but if it is hard to get over people saying nasty things about us, it can be even more difficult to say nice things about our competitors, especially as here in Galatia, when such competitors were apparently seeking to diminish if not destroy the ministry of Paul.

Seeing beyond appearances means to see others as God sees us all. God does not judge by external appearances; he sees the reality behind the persona. We are all made in the image of God. We are all, if Christians, in Christ. We are all sinners. As we focus on the gospel ministry and then celebrate the two apostles ministering, seeing beyond appearances is the initial step.

We have to fight for the truth. I don't mean a physical fight. I mean the kind of spiritual fight that Paul was engaged in here. The truth of this gospel ministry was essential, so he went up to Jerusalem to straighten out the truth of the matter between him and Peter and the rest of the leaders. We also must be willing to straighten out the essential truth at times. That means we will have to make the effort by spending some of our personal precious energy. We may have to sacrifice some of our treasure to proclaim the truth widely. We may have to risk much-loved relationships by confronting a doctrinal issue. Fighting for the truth does not mean fighting for every kind of thing that may or may not be true. We are not to be people who fight over whether Bach was the greatest composer, or whether our favorite sports team will defeat its opponents, or whether certain minor doctrinal things are true or not. We are to be people who fight for the truth of the biblical gospel.

It is vitally important to have a right sense of perspective to orient our passion to the right degree. We can become passionate about minor matters, but the reverse is to be true. When the authority of the Bible, the exclusivity of Christ, the atonement, justification by faith alone, the cross and the resurrection—all those central matters that Galatians is really about—are up for grabs, we make sure that we stand up and grab them for Christ and his kingdom. But I don't find here Peter and Paul discussing with great intensity those things over which Christians can disagree and still make their way fruitfully to heaven. I may get to heaven and find out that it's infralapsarianism after all (but I doubt it). I may get to heaven and find that football is a better game than rugby (but I doubt it). I will not get to heaven at all if I do not believe the biblical gospel. The authority of Scripture, the exclusivity of Christ, and justification by faith are of such central importance that we will need to go to the mat for them. Let them have our jobs, our lives, our talents, and our time, but they will not have our souls.

I want you to realize that the fact that we are Christians does not protect us from having to be willing to stand up for the Christian gospel. In fact, there are so many winds of doctrine in Christendom that it is especially important that we learn to see beyond personalities and accept each as made in the image of God and, if Christians, remade in the image of Christ. At the same time, we must discern what is essential and what is not and let go of what is not and stand unwaveringly firm on what is.

They see beyond appearances, they fight for the truth, but then also we come to a most remarkable conclusion. Despite all the tension that surrounded this meeting beforehand, they leave joined in one gospel ministry as two apostles ministering, because they also *fight for fellowship around that truth.*

When I was a younger man, I used to think that fellowship was a slightly wimpy word, connected with coffee and donuts and Christian cheesy smiles. I do so no longer. Fellowship is the communion connection we have with God the Father through faith in Christ and therefore with each other also. Fellowship is something won for us by Christ's work on the cross, but nonetheless the Bible consistently teaches we still need to work at it ourselves in order to maintain and develop it. As Paul says in Ephesians, "*Eager to maintain* the unity of the Spirit in the bond of peace" (4:3). We see that applied here in Galatians. Do whatever it takes, if you're talking about fellowship with a Christian brother or sister, to live at peace, so far as it lies in your power to do so, and if that fellowship is around the truth of the gospel. Fight for that fellowship. Often it means great humility. Often it costs a lot to keep fellowship.

People have said that Paul is being rather arrogant here, with his characterization of those who "seemed" to be influential (Gal. 2:6), though, as we have discovered, that is really a criticism of the way the Galatian false teachers were talking. But there is great humility, even in Paul making this journey to Jerusalem at all. He leaves his current ministry, he travels, he goes and sees them face-to-face. He gets beyond appearances, he fights for the truth of the gospel, and he fights for fellowship, and they end up offering each other the holy hug of fellowship in Christ. They shake on it formally as an expression of their deep personal commitment to each other and to each other's ministries in Christ. Go on one knee if you have to. Say you're sorry without fear of being corrected, for, as Charles Simeon said about his critics, "If they only knew how bad I really was, they'd have a lot worse things to say." Do what it takes. This brother or sister is someone whom Christ gave his life for, and so we are to make every effort to keep that bond of fellowship.

I hope you can see how relevant this passage is. This gospel unity has been won for us by Christ, but we can't take it for granted. We have to fight for the truth and fellowship and see beyond appearances, and when we do and see the gospel, we have one gospel ministry—one message, one preaching, one equipping, one love—even with two apostles ministering. When there is no gospel unity, as Paul is declaring that there is not between him and the Galatian false teachers, we have to be willing to declare that too. If we discard the truth of the gospel into the trash can in order to squeeze into the kiosk labeled "unity," we will continue to find fragmentation, and, ironically, disunity, for then our unity is around the powerful personalities that we follow.

Flesh is as the grass and will fade away. Only if we refuse to be sidetracked by what is not true and stand up loud and clear for the essential truth of the gospel, only then will we find the kind of truth in love that marked the conclusion of Peter's dialogue with Paul. Then our unity will be in God and in Christ Jesus. May it be so, may we be faithful to the gospel, and may we find the joy of fellowship together.

11

The Gospel of Second Chances

*But when Cephas came to Antioch, I opposed him to his face,
because he stood condemned. For before certain men came from
James, he was eating with the Gentiles; but when they came he drew
back and separated himself, fearing the circumcision party. And the
rest of the Jews acted hypocritically along with him, so that even
Barnabas was led astray by their hypocrisy. But when I saw that their
conduct was not in step with the truth of the gospel, I said to Cephas
before them all, "If you, though a Jew, live like a Gentile and not like a
Jew, how can you force the Gentiles to live like Jews?"*

GALATIANS 2:11–14

This story is usually told from the standpoint of Paul, who was the hero
confronting this issue, and that's fine. But Paul is not boosting his ego
to the Galatians about how great a guy he is to stand up for truth; the
point of this story is to showcase what can go wrong. Paul recounts this
story to show the Galatians why Peter messed up, how not to mess up,
and what to do if they do mess up.

Why Peter Messed Up

Peter and the rest of the Jews were not "in step with the truth of the
gospel" (v. 14), and that's why they messed up. It really matters to figure
out why you mess up. If you don't, you'll just keep on doing the same
thing over again. You've got to get to the root of it and figure out what's
really going on. They messed up because they didn't get four things.

1) *They didn't get that what you do as a Christian needs to come
out of what you believe.* So many people don't get that. They get all
the theological degrees you can imagine. They study hard. And then
somehow or other they act in ways that are contrary to what they've

learned. Part of the reason is a failure to understand that there needs to be a connection between what you believe (the truth of the gospel) and how you act. I see this all the time.

People can believe that Jesus is the only way to God and that everyone who doesn't believe in Jesus is going to spend eternity in hell, yet they spend forty years living next door to someone who doesn't believe in Jesus and never tell him about Jesus. You ask them if they love their neighbor, and they'll say yes. You ask if they believe in heaven and hell, and they'll say yes. You ask them if they tell their neighbor about Jesus, and they'll say no.

We can believe that God is no man's debtor and that we are to invest our treasure in heaven, where moth and rust don't destroy, and that God promises to take care of us, and that if we seek first the kingdom, all the other things will be given to us as well—yet we hoard money like a miser. People can believe that sex is for marriage and marriage is for life, and that they are to love their wife as Christ loves the church—yet they have pornography all over the computer screen. What's going on is that we're not acting in step with the truth of the gospel, and part of that is just that we don't get that we need to.

2) *They didn't get that what you do actually shows what you really believe*. A lot of people don't get that. If you want to find out what you really believe, just look at your calendar, because your time is the one commodity you can never get back after it's spent. If you spend three hours every evening playing *Halo 3* on your Xbox, then what does it say about what you really think is important in life? Your schedule tells you more about what you believe than your tax return; your tax return tells you a lot about what the government believes. It's who you spend your time with. If you spend time with only a certain portion of the Christian fellowship yet refuse all the others because they eat pork, then what does it say about what you really believe? It says that you really believe there is a super-elite Christian group.

It's really pretty amazing that Peter messed up. He'd already gotten that Jews and Gentiles were part of the same family, but then he wouldn't eat with them. He wasn't acting in step with the truth of the gospel. He didn't realize that what he did—refuse to eat with people who ate pork—was saying something about what he believed. If you believe in justification by faith alone, that means you have fellowship with other people who believe in justification by faith alone, because if you don't, you're saying that whatever the difference is between you and the other is what really justifies you.

3) *They didn't get that what you do will change what other people believe.* Even Barnabas was led astray by what Peter and the Jews did. What we do tends to be what people follow, and if what we do doesn't go in step with what we believe, likely as not people will follow what we do rather than what we say we believe. That's why you get so many Christians who look like their pastors and sound like their pastors; they are little clones of the leader. From their mannerisms, you can spot who their leader is if you are familiar with the leader. So, if you are a leader, you need to watch out for this. You can say what you like till you're blue in the face, but basically, in the end, people who follow you are going to do what you do, and if what you do doesn't come out of what you believe, it will undermine everything you stand for.

4) *They didn't get that what you do changes what you believe.* You believe one thing, but you start to do something else. Likely as not, soon enough, you'll begin to change what you believe to fit what you're doing. What you do has an impact on your own belief systems. That's what was going on here; Peter believed in justification by faith alone but because he began not to eat with others who believed the same thing he began to believe something different. It was undermining the gospel not just in its influence on others but in his own heart too. This happens all the time; it usually starts with small things, like a little bit of not doing your devotions here, an occasional let's not bother to go to church this week there—a little thing—and bit by bit it not only influences others but starts to influence your own faith as well.

So why did Peter and the rest of the Jews mess up? They messed up because Peter wasn't acting in step with the truth of the gospel. They didn't get four things: what you do as a Christian needs to come out of what you believe; what you do actually shows what you really believe; what you do will change what other people believe; and what you do changes what you believe.

How Not to Mess Up

This is a little more encouraging I suppose. Yes, let's dig out the root (the *why*), but let's also get a strategy to make sure that we don't mess up. Paul tells us what Peter did. To not mess up we need to do the opposite of what Peter did. He was afraid, which is why he messed up. He was also hypocritical. So to not mess up, instead of being afraid of men we need to have a primary and overruling fear of God, and instead of putting on a good, pretentious, hypocritical show we need to take off the mask. You may know that the word *hypocritical* comes from the Greek word for "actor." Actors in the ancient world used to wear masks while performing, which is why the word came to mean "hypocritical" in the sense of wearing a mask. He was afraid; we're to fear God. He was hypocritical; we're to take off the mask.

How are we going to do that? We get big into who God is. There will come a moment when there will be intimidation from some powerful group to do something that deep down we know is not right. It might not be quite like when Romanian minister Richard Wurmbrand went to jail, but there will be some intimidation. Maybe it will be some guys at school who want to go out and get drunk. Maybe it will be some deal at work that you know is not really quite kosher. Maybe it will be some trendy theological idea that you know is not in line with the truth of the gospel. Whatever it is, at some point there will come something where you just have to know that God is big.

When I went to boarding school as a scared little thirteen-year-old, I was already a Christian, but there I was, surrounded by people before whom reading the Bible and praying was not going to be cool. I couldn't really kneel by my bed at night in front of them, with a dormitory of other teenagers cat-calling as I prayed. But I found a way. I let them know I was a Christian, and I read the Bible in the only place in the building where one could get some alone time—the john. Jesus said that when you pray, go into a quiet place and shut the door (Matt. 6:6), and I took him at his word. While at Cambridge I wanted to play rugby for the college team, but I found out that in order to do so, I'd have to join the 21 Club, and obtaining membership meant that I'd have to drink twenty-one pints of beer in one evening. I couldn't do that, but I wanted to play rugby. So I went to the team captain and said, "I'm a Christian, so I can't do this twenty-one pints thing." He looked at me like I was an alien, he blinked, and he then said, "All right," and it was done.

You have to stand up for what you believe, and the way to do that is to get a really big view of who God is. I came with my family to America with a laptop, a printer, three suitcases, and nowhere to stay. We changed homes ten times in one year, and people said, "Oh, how brave." I don't think we were brave at all. If God is in it—and he is always in the gospel—then what's the problem? Do you really think the one who flung the stars into outer space can't get you the few dollars you need to survive this month? The way not to fear man is to get a really big view of God, which is what it means biblically to fear God.

While I was a missionary in Republic of Georgia, I was taking a day off, exhausted from God's work. I walked up a little hill with an ancient church on it near where we were staying, and suddenly a man approached me to rob me. I was a Westerner, so he thought I had money. He said to me, "My friend has a gun, so if you don't give me money— bang, bang—do you understand?" I thought, *I'm so fed up. This is my day off, and I can't get any peace and quiet*, and I just walked off.

I'm not telling you these things to make me look big but to make God look big. You just need to realize that the very breath you are breathing, the beating of your heart, the words that another is forming, are all part of the sovereign power of God. God is for the gospel, and God loves you, and that's what it means not to get freaked out by "some men from James." A big view of God—that's how to do it.

But then how are we not to pretend? How are we to take the mask off and stop acting? That's very important too. We get the sense that Peter didn't quite mean it when he separated himself. He was just going along with it for an easy life; he was scared. Peter here is putting on the mask and acting or pretending.

The only way you're going to stop putting on the mask is to realize that you are okay as you are. Remember that the picture behind the word *hypocrisy* is acting, going on the stage and pretending to be something or someone that you're not. It is to wear the style of others because you think they are okay and you are not. It is speaking with the accent and intonation of others because you think they are okay and you are not. It is walking like others because you think they are okay and you are not. The only way to realize that you're okay is to realize that God loves you and that Christ died for you as you are, warts and all. This isn't mere future justification, because that just means that maybe one day you will be okay. All that means is that you're going to have to keep on pretending and hoping that one day you're going to get to be okay. This is present justification. This means that you are okay because you have Christ's blood shed for you, and you are righteous in God's eyes through the righteousness of Christ. Right now, today, you're okay.

Whenever there is significant mask wearing in Christian circles or in church, it's because justification has been forgotten somehow. Present justification is the only cure for mask wearing. Any other message tells you that you're not okay, and that you've got to work at it, but that you need to pretend you're doing much better than you are, because you mess up. Only when you realize that even though you do mess up, you're okay because you're righteous with God's righteousness. Only then can you be real and take the mask off. There's no other way, so the cure for mask wearing is always justification, right now, by faith alone.

How can someone approach a pastor and say, "Pastor, I'm sleeping with my girlfriend. I know it's wrong, but I am. Help me." How do you get that kind of frankness? You get it only if the pastor is operating out of justification by faith alone and is able not to judge but to accept that person and offer help. The person receiving the help will know he won't be forever in the doghouse but will get a chance to start again.

So the way not to mess up is not to do what Peter did, and what Peter did was fear man and put on a mask. The way not to fear man is to fear God, and the way to take off the mask is to get a firm understanding that we are okay because Christ's blood was shed for us as we are, right now, pure and perfect in God's eyes, covered by Christ's righteousness. Without those two things, we will mess up again and again. I don't mean that we believe them in theory but that we actually believe, and then we practice so that we are acting in step with the truth of the gospel. If you can't take your mask off, then the sin that you struggle with (and we're all sinners) will just keep on growing. If you can take your mask off and get someone to pray with you about your sin, the sin will be dealt with. When people mess up their life after years of what seems to have been stellar service, it's almost always because they've been wearing a mask.

The sin has been building and building, but they never talked about it and found someone to keep them accountable.

Homosexuality is difficult to talk about in church, so when people struggle with that temptation, what do they do? Do they keep it a secret and never tell anyone? Romans 1 makes it clear that homosexuality is wrong, but then it also makes clear that disobeying one's parents is wrong. Some sins have bigger consequences than others, so we can joke about teenage rebellion but not teenage sexual role confusion. Whatever the issue, it is better to find someone who can help and pray with the tempted about it, and the way to do that is to have a strong church culture whereby people are accepted as they are for Christ's sake.

The issue in the background in the Galatians passage is race. Certainly it's about religious food rituals, whether you can eat kosher meat or not, but there is a strong racial undertone to it. I've never personally come across any Christian white supremacists in any church, but I've come across many folk who wear a mask before others. They are afraid of each other in one way or another, that if they say something wrong, it will be misinterpreted. Wouldn't it be great if we weren't afraid of others, and if we didn't wear a mask, sort of acting out subliminal role definitions unconsciously? If instead (because of justification by faith right now) we could take off the mask and, because God is incredibly big, act in love toward each other?

Peter messed up because he didn't act in line with the truth of the gospel. He didn't understand that what you do as a Christian needs to come out of what you believe, and that what you do actually shows what you really believe, and that what you do will change what other people believe, and that what you do changes what you believe. We won't mess up if we do the opposite of what Peter did. He acted in fear of man, but we are to act out of the fear of God; Peter put on a mask, but we are to take masks off because we know we're all right since Christ died for us.

What to Do If You Do Mess Up

And then there's what Peter did do, which is really pretty amazing. This incident probably took place before the Jerusalem Council (see Acts 15). Paul had confronted Peter here, so when it comes to the council, you might expect that Peter would stick to his guns. His pride had been hurt, and he was even more entrenched now, or perhaps he was just stubborn and didn't want to be shown as having been wrong. But at the Jerusalem Council he stood up and added his enormous influence to Paul's by actually being the first person to speak against the Judaizers. When Paul came to speak, he needed only to tell the story of what God has being doing because Peter had cleared the way for him. That is amazing.

The other amazing thing about this, from Peter's point of view, is that Peter never mentions this instance again, certainly not publicly in any of the records we have. He could have spent time subtly spinning the event to make himself look a little better—"Oh, yeah, Paul did talk to me about that, but he wasn't saying anything I didn't know already."

What this means is that when you mess up, you need to repent. There's no other solution. It can be painful and difficult, and it can take longer for humans to accept your repentance than it takes God. One man I worked with had messed up big-time. When I first talked with him, I was convinced he was sincere and that he was done with the sin, but it took those closest to him almost a year to get over it. David messed up near the end of his life by counting all God's people. God had promised that his people would be like the sand on the sea shore and the stars in the sky, so to count them was a form of doubting God's word. As punishment, God gave David a choice between famine, pestilence, or invasion, and David replied, "Let us fall into the hand of the LORD, for his mercy is great; but let me not fall into the hand of man" (2 Sam. 24:14). It can be hard to repent, and people can be less forgiving than God because they have messed up as well, or because they're not operating through justification by faith alone but through some other form of basic works-righteousness, or because maybe they're just really hurt by what you did.

So, when I simply say, "Repent," I don't mean it's easy; it's simple, but it's not easy. Yet it is the only solution. Repentance means change. It doesn't mean feeling sorry or even saying you are sorry, though those things are normally present. It means acting or believing differently.

That is why Peter's response to this is so astonishing. A little while later he was advocating for the position his action had denied, and then he never brought up the matter again. He never tried to justify himself; he knew he was justified before God by faith alone, so he was silent about it.

I find this convicting. I have made mistakes in my life. I've been a hypocrite. I've feared man. I've acted in ways contrary to the gospel. I've found it hard to repent cleanly and be different as a result. To me, and I hope to you, it's important we get to the root of it. We need to figure out why and realize the connection between what we believe and how that needs to lead to the fruit of how we behave. We need to avoid those mistakes by getting a big picture of God, thereby not fearing people's intimidating us to do what's wrong.

We have been like Paul at times, in this sort of situation, but we have also been like Peter. It may be easier to think about how we've been like Paul, but the point of this is that the Galatians are in a Peter-like situation. Paul is telling them this story so that they won't mess up, and so if they have, they'll stop it and get it back together again. My prayer for all of us is that when we have the opportunity to be like Paul was here, we'll have his loving boldness, and when—not if—we're in a situation like Peter was, we'll get back into acting in step with the truth of the gospel.

12

The Gospel and Justification

We ourselves are Jews by birth and not Gentile sinners; yet we know
that a person is not justified by works of the law but through faith in
Jesus Christ, so we also have believed in Christ Jesus, in order to
be justified by faith in Christ and not by works of the law, because by
works of the law no one will be justified.

GALATIANS 2:15–16

The first time these words were read in the native Sio language they caused an immediate reaction. As they were read out for the very first time the Sio tribesman who heard them slammed down his fist and said, "No! It is by the law!"

You need no exposure to the technicalities of Second Temple Judaism to understand the issues that are addressed in these two most compact verses. There is a universal tendency of humanity to go back to self-justification by works of the law. Our default mode as people is to try and prove ourselves to God by our works, though to be sure this tendency is manifested in different ways in different cultures at different times. Here, Paul says, actually it is by Christ and our faith in him that we are justified.

Paul is perhaps continuing his conversation with Peter and allowing us to overhear this extraordinary debate between the two apostles. He is telling Peter (and thereby instructing us) three things: (1) *works of the law do not justify*; (2) *faith in Jesus does justify*; (3) *this is what the Bible consistently teaches.*

Works of the Law Do Not Justify

There are five ways that Galatians 2:15–16 underlines the point that the works of the law do not justify, each of them striking. First, it is apparent from the context, and from the culture at the time, that there is a sense in which, at its worst, it is even possible for a wrong approach to the works of the law to enshrine sinful attitudes to other races. The statement in verse 15 puts Jews against Gentile sinners, but that is not how the Bible intended God's people to look at the Gentiles. Going back to Abraham, God's promise to his people is that they would be a blessing to all nations, not a means of excluding them from his covenant. It is possible that when I take the law and I make it a work ("works of the law"), I can be not that far away from feeling morally superior to other races.

People look at the context of this passage and say that it's "just" about food fellowship between Gentile and Jew and nothing else, but they don't realize that Paul is saying that the attitude of separation between Jew and Gentile is really about something much deeper. It's really about who we believe we are by birth, what we believe we have achieved by keeping to our "works of the law" (whatever they are in our culture), and who we think the other people are—in this case "sinners," which was a sort of technical term that excluded people from God's people.

It happens in very different ways even today sometimes. Perhaps the caste system is at root a form of the works of the law, which leads to a form of one group feeling morally superior to another. Perhaps the real issue in some forms of slavery was not only an infringement on the universal rights of man but a wrong understanding of how we get right with God. It may be that, in God's providence, it is no accident of history that an evangelical Christian was at the forefront of abolishing slavery around the globe. That might be an application of a theological truth, that all peoples are to be made right before God, not by works of the law but by faith in Christ. It may not, then, be surprising as we sometimes find it to be when we discover than on occasions human-made religious systems have capitulated to the evils of slavery. A wrong approach to the works of the law can foster a feeling of moral superiority from one group over another.

Second, Paul might also have been hinting that a wrong approach to the works of the law could foster a form of chauvinism. When he says, "We know that a person [literally "man"] is not justified by works of the law" (v. 16), his use of "man" there might be just the universal term for "mankind" with the grammatical male head, but perhaps he is also referring to the works-of-the-law tendency to view the actual male in a chauvinistic way. Perhaps Paul is referring to the tendency of the works of the law to create situations like the well-known rabbinic prayer of thanks for not being born a woman!

Using the law as a work that will get us right with God tends to elevate our sense of self; it can lead to a tendency to elevate the man over the woman, or vice versa. Human religion can create this sort of gender friction. Paul may also be alluding to that in this concentrated form in these verses, a theological concentration typical for Paul when he was packing in a lot of theological dynamite to create the maximum possible explosion.

Third, "works of the law" is not always hard legalism, or what's sometimes called "Pelagianism," from the later heretical teacher Pelagius, but can be (as it probably was here) more subtle forms of the "works of the law," a semi-Pelagianism.

It was "just" about table fellowship in Antioch, but behind that thin end of the wedge was a whole host of "works of the law" attitude. It was the tip of the iceberg. Some people say that the table rituals and other markers were just covenant markers of what it was like to be in the community at that stage in Israel, and were therefore not really legalistic. Let us say, for the sake of argument, that it is just this table fellowship matter, leaving aside the thin-end-of-the-wedge argument that Paul clearly teaches was going on here. He wrote, "I testify again to every man who accepts circumcision that he is obligated to keep the whole law" (Gal. 5:3). The thin-end-of-the-wedge idea is very important (all the works of the law that you have to work to get right with God come along with it), but let's leave that aside for the moment and, for the sake of argument, say that it is just about markers of being in the community of the covenant. Even then, so-called soft legalism, or nomism, is the same thing at heart. That's what Jesus taught.

In Mark 7 Jesus is criticized because the disciples do not wash before eating (which wasn't a way to deal with Swine Flu but was for religious reasons of purity, and for the same reason that Peter wouldn't eat with Gentiles). He was criticized for that and said, "Well did Isaiah prophesy of you hypocrites, as it is written, 'This people honors me with their lips, but their heart is far from me; in vain do they worship me, teaching as doctrines the commandments of men.' You leave the commandment of God and hold to the tradition of men" (Mark 7:6–8). That wasn't because they couldn't point to texts in the Old Testament that would have supported (or so they thought) their washing and separating from "Gentile sinners." If you go through Leviticus, you could cherry pick things that would support that; the point is they'd forgotten what the law was really about and were making it (in Paul's phrase) "works of the law." So it is just soft legalism, just nomism, but in "only" doing that, as Jesus said, they were "straining out a gnat and swallowing a camel" (Matt. 23:24).

Fourth, the "works of the law" here was something that the Jews knew did *not* justify them. Whatever it was, they knew it didn't work. It never did, from birth. It was not their experience that it justified them; it was their experience that it did not justify them. They knew they were not justified by works of the law. You might not think that's important, but it really means that this "works of the law" is a wrong use of the Bible, even for those living in Old Testament times. They never thought that circumcision and food ritual and Sabbath keeping and all that would justify them; they knew, according to Paul, that it did not.

To tell the Galatian Christians that they needed the works of the law was to tell them they needed something that even Old Testament Jews knew did not justify them. It was a wrong use of the Old Testament. Of course, the Old Testament is not legalistic—there are many records in the Bible of faithful believers in God knowing they were saved by grace—but this "works of the law," so predominant at that time, did not and could not justify, and had never done so. The law was not meant to justify.

Fifth is Paul's slam dunk argument, which he'll explain more at the end of Galatians 2: if the works of the law could justify, what's the point of Jesus? "If righteousness were through the law, then Christ died for no purpose" (Gal. 2:21). If you could get justified by circumcision and eating only with other Jews who had kept the hand-washing and food preparation rules, then why would God in Christ have to become a man, get beaten and crucified, and rise again? If the rituals worked, why did

Jesus need to get crucified? It's absurd and gross because it suggests that Christ's death was not necessary.

Paul is making a similar point here in verse 16 where he says that faith in Jesus Christ does justify, in contrast to the works of the law, which don't. "Faith in Jesus Christ" could also be translated *"faithfulness of Jesus Christ,"* and I think it probably does mean that here; otherwise he's just repeating himself in the next verse. He says that works don't justify; the faithful living and dying of Christ in our place is what justifies.

So for all these reasons Paul says that the works of the law don't justify, which is the first thing he tells Peter. It can create a toxic environment of racism and chauvinism, even the more subtle "works of the law." We know it never worked from the Old Testament; otherwise, what would be the point of the sacrificial faithfulness of Christ Jesus?

Faith in Jesus Justifies

We know that faith in Jesus does justify. First, however, not all who seem to believe in Jesus actually believe in Jesus. Paul puts it in an interesting way: "We also have believed in Christ Jesus" (Gal. 2:16). It is not just about Jesus but being entrusted into Jesus. This means that those who really believe in Jesus are those who have committed themselves to him actively and purposefully. This is very important because of all the surveys we read about what born-again Christians do, or what the Crusaders did, or what fundamentalist fascists do. *Not all who believe in Jesus actually believe in Jesus.* Not everyone who calls himself "Christian" is Christian. Faith in Jesus is not like being or not being an American. You know whether you're an American by getting out your birth certificate, or you look at your citizenship card. How do you know whether you actually believe in Jesus? You were baptized? No, Paul doesn't say that here. You're on a church roll? Paul doesn't say that here. This is kind of an old-fashioned point in some ways, but if we're not clear on it, we'll end up having to defend things that are done by so-called Christians without being able to say that not everyone who believes that Jesus exists, or grew up in a Christian country, actually believes in Jesus. In the Crusades, was Europe ever really converted? I don't think so; not when you read how the tribes were converted: at sword point. That's not entrusting yourself to Jesus.

Second, our experience is that trusting Jesus does justify. We too have put our faith in Jesus, and look what Jesus has done for us. It is the experience of Christians, of Peter and Paul, that this total trust in Jesus is what works. Experience isn't everything, but it is something. They (Paul and Peter) had tried the works of the law, Paul says to Peter, with one eye over to the Galatians; that didn't work. Then they tried faith in Jesus; that did work. This actually makes a difference; it changes, it justifies.

Third, faith in Jesus Christ justifies because it is *into* Christ Jesus. He is the righteous one. Those who put their faith in Jesus Christ become joined to and connected to Christ in such a way that his righteousness is theirs, and their sin is his. They are in him.

Fourth, faith in Jesus Christ justifies because it is in the *faithfulness* of Jesus Christ. I think that's a better translation here, not that it matters much for the general sense of the passage, but if it's "faith in Jesus," that means Paul is bringing out the same thing twice in this one sentence. I think Paul is saying, "Those who really entrust themselves *into* Jesus are righteous because of the faithfulness of Christ Jesus' righteous life and death in their place."

Fifth, this faith in Jesus Christ is mutually exclusive to the works of the law. The law does not work. Faith does. They have put their faith in Jesus Christ, not in the works of the law. It is not a bit of one and a bit of the other. It is only faith in Jesus Christ, or faith alone in Jesus alone.

What the Bible Teaches

Works of the law don't justify and faith in Jesus does justify, and we know this *because this is what the Bible teaches*. Of course, we've been studying the Bible all along, but crucially Paul actually quotes from the Old Testament to back up his point here. He says we know this "because by works of the law no one will be justified" (v. 16). This is a quotation from Psalm 143:2: "For no one living is righteous before you." This is crucial for five reasons.

1) The context of Psalm 143:2 is judgment. People look at the context of the word *justification* in Galatians 2, table fellowship, and say that justification is about covenant markers for membership of the community. This is wrong; it is not what the word *justification* means, and the point that Paul is making to Peter and to the Galatians who are

listening in (as it were) to their conversation is that behind these apparently small things, such as food rituals, is the much bigger issue of how we're accepted before God, and, therefore, who we accept into God's family.

Justification is a word that has a breadth of meaning, but it comes out of the sense of the law court; it is about how someone gets acquitted before the judge. But don't take my word for it—it's a quotation from Psalm 143:2. Most of the technical commentaries on this Galatians passage recognize it. If you reference a Greek New Testament, you'll see it as a quotation from that psalm.

What is Psalm 143 about? It is about judgment. It is a prayer of David, who is saying, "God, don't bring me into judgment; instead justify me." He wrote, "Enter not into judgment with your servant, for no one living is righteous [justified] before you" (v. 2). How will his life be preserved? "In your righteousness bring my soul out of trouble!" (v. 11); in other words, "justify me."

You need to realize how massive this is. Paul is saying, "When you refuse to eat with brothers and sisters, you are saying that you get acquitted from God's judgment by what you eat; but you don't!" How do you get justified? You get justified by faith into the faithfulness of Jesus Christ (his death and resurrection, which Paul is about to explicitly mention). So Paul points to what the Old Testament teaches: "No one living is righteous before you." David said it. He was kosher. He was not justified by Sabbath, circumcision, or food ritual. He knew it. We know it. God's Word says it.

God's Word says it everywhere else, particularly in the Old Testament, because the point is that the law is leading to Christ (as Paul will say in Galatians 3). But this "works of the law" is the Pharisaic interpretation, which tells us we're justified by external things, not the change of life that comes through faith in Jesus Christ.

2) Genesis 15:6 is the test case that Paul uses in Romans 4 to make the same point that he is making here in a different context. I studied this passage carefully with a Yale rabbi. It reads: "[Abraham] believed the LORD, and he counted it to him as righteousness." Paul's point in Romans 4 is that this happened before Abraham was circumcised, so the Old Testament law is not to be interpreted as the works of the law, but

the law leading to Christ. The word for "justification" or "righteous-ness" in the New Testament is translated in the Old Testament mainly by this word in Genesis 15:6, which has a similar range of meaning in terms of judgment and being acquitted from judgment. The word can be used to translate "covenant love," but most times it is used to translate a word that has this range of meaning in terms of the law court and judgment and being declared right by the judge and not in the wrong.

3) From 2 Samuel 15:4 we can begin to see that this idea of justifica-tion is more than simply being forgiven. In 2 Samuel, Absalom is going to use those who have complaints against David (if you are a king, there are always lots of people who have complaints against you) to curry favor. And Absalom is going to do so by seeing that they get justice. In the Greek Old Testament, it says that they get justified; the Hebrew word used there has a similar meaning. So the point is not just that they "receive justice," because if Absalom could do that, a lot of them would get in serious trouble, which wouldn't get him in their good books. The point is that he's going to "justify" them, that is, present them as in the right. In the Hebrew world, when someone was acquitted, they weren't just let off as not guilty; they were declared innocent, which is not the same thing. That means that here in Galatians, this faithfulness of Christ's is what we are justified with. We are declared righteous with his faithfulness; we are acquitted not just as forgiven but as just, right, innocent, pure, and holy.

4) There are places in the New Testament where this is clear in context: "For I am not aware of anything against myself, but I am not thereby acquitted [justified]. It is the Lord who judges me" (1 Cor. 4:4). That's not a context of "covenant faithfulness" but clearly of judging, acquitting, and being declared righteous, pure, and justified.

5) "Just as David also speaks of the blessing of the one to whom God counts righteousness apart from works . . . " (Rom. 4:6), which means that David, circumcised, kosher, and a Sabbath keeper, was righ-teous "without works," and that his righteousness came from faith also.

Technical, but Important

This has been a technical study but an important one. I want you to see that the works of the law don't justify, that faith in Jesus does justify, and that this justification by faith alone in Jesus is what the Bible teaches. Psalm 143:2, which Paul quotes here, teaches that. Genesis 15:6 teaches that, and 2 Samuel 15:4 shows the Old Testament context for the meaning of the word *justify*. First Corinthians 4:4 shows the meaning of the word *justify* in the New Testament context, and Romans 4:6 shows that the works of the law did not justify David but rather his faith, this faith that is now fulfilled in Jesus Christ. Jesus Christ is the one to whom the law points and of whom the law speaks, and before whom we worship and give praise that in him, because of his faithfulness, we can stand justified before the holy God, if we put our faith into him.

13

Answering the Common Objection to the Gospel

But if, in our endeavor to be justified in Christ, we too were found
to be sinners, is Christ then a servant of sin? Certainly not!
For if I rebuild what I tore down, I prove myself to be a transgressor.

GALATIANS 2:17–18

The sheer length of commentaries written about the bare few words of this passage reminds me of a story I once heard about a country farm laborer. This farmer was asked by his new pastor to read a large, technical commentary on a particular text of the Bible. The minister gave the man the book, and the farmer dutifully took it, promising to read it carefully. Sometime later, the minister saw the farmer again and asked him how the book was going. "Ah, it's a hard book, it's a very hard book" the farm laborer said, "but I do find the Bible sheds some light upon it."

Let's find out how the Bible sheds some light on Galatians 2:17–18. These verses are how the Bible responds to one very common objection to the gospel. The gospel—the central message of Christianity—is that Jesus was born, and he died and rose again, and that his death was for our sins that we might receive forgiveness and new life in relationship to God now and forever through faith alone. People have objections to that message, and Paul here is going to deal with one of the most common. That's what these two verses are about: how the Bible responds to one very common objection to the gospel.

I'm going to show three things with regard to this common objection and the way these verses deal with it. First, I'm going to show that if we don't or have never had this common objection, it probably indicates that we've never really understood the gospel. Second, I'm going to briefly survey the four answers that Paul gives to the objection, only one of which is present in this passage (v. 18); the others are in the rest of Galatians 2 as his argument moves forward. Third, I'm going to show that Paul's answer to this common objection really proves the necessity of the gospel message to begin with.

Doesn't Faith Alone Promote Sin?

If you have never had this objection, it probably shows that you've never really understood the gospel in the first place. The objection is this: if you get saved simply by trusting in Jesus, doesn't that mean (as Paul puts it) that Christ is a "servant of sin"? It is an obvious objection. You don't have to do anything to get saved. It's all done by Jesus. You're a sinner, you've messed up—we all have—and to be justified, to get right with God, here's what you have to do: nothing. Absolutely nothing. God has done it all.

One time after I'd preached someone said to me, "I've discovered what's different about this church. Every other church I go to tells me what I've got to do, but you're telling me what God has done." That's exactly right. That's the gospel, what God has done in Christ. It isn't the gospel you always hear in churches. The gospel you hear sometimes is that to get justified, you've got to do a whole host of things, but that's not the gospel. The gospel is what Jesus has done. So there is the message, and the obvious objection to that message is, doesn't that mean you can do whatever you like?

We find the same objection in Romans. Paul presented the gospel at much greater length there, and in his argument he dealt with the same objection: "What shall we say then? Are we to continue in sin that grace may abound?" (6:1). In other words, if Jesus saves you while you're still a complete sinner, doesn't that mean Jesus promotes sin? It is basically the same objection.

I want you to see, from the way in which Paul deals with this objection both here and in Romans, that there is a very important point: if you have never asked this question, it is at least probable that you have never understood the gospel. The gospel always raises this question. If it is raising that question in your mind now, that is a good thing, because it is a sign that the gospel is getting through.

The Objection Answered

I want to show you the four answers Paul gives to that objection. We're not going to go through them all in detail, but it's important to give you the lay of the land so that you can get a sense of the entire shape of Paul's thought regarding this objection. His first answer is found in Galatians 2:18; the second is found in verse 19 and the third answer is found in verse 20, both of which are flip sides of the same coin.

We will come to back to his first answer in a moment. In his second and third answers, he says that if you get saved while you're still a sinner, that cannot mean that Christ promotes sin, because to be justified (declared right by God) while still a sinner is connected to us being united with Christ both in his death (v. 19) and in his life (v. 20). These are extremely profound verses. They are based upon the idea that we are "in Christ" when we are justified by him. This is a strange idea to us but an important one.

When God declares us right in the judgment court of his holiness and gives us Christ's righteousness, it is not like saying that some inexplicable gas passes across the room from him to us. You have to understand ancient ways of thinking. Christ is our head, if we believe in him, so there is no legal fiction in us receiving his righteousness. It's much like how a wealthy man can adopt a child, and that child can be called rich, even though he will not formally own a penny until he comes of age (which is an image Paul will use to explain this in Galatians 3 and 4). So in Christ we have all the wealth of his righteousness right now.

The fourth answer to the objection is found in 2:21 "I do not nullify the grace of God, for if righteousness were through the law, then Christ died for no purpose." If we think that the law could have ever made us right with God, Paul says, then we are saying that Christ's death was pointless. Here he is going more on the offensive. What's the alternative, if it's not Jesus alone who declares us right? The only alternative is the law. However, if it is or ever was the law, that means you are really saying that Jesus' humbling himself and becoming a man, dying a gruesome death on the cross, receiving the just punishment for our sins, was actually unnecessary. No one wants to say Jesus' death was unnecessary, so Paul answers this objection in this fourth answer by pointing out that to hold to the alternative idea (that we can be justified by something that we do) actually means that Christ's death was pointless.

We've looked at three of his four arguments against the objection. The first is found in verse 18, and I've saved it for last because I want to take more time with it. His answer in verse 18 to the objection that is commonly raised against the gospel—that it means you can do whatever you like—is that while if you have never asked that question or a question like it, you have probably never understood the gospel. If you are still asking that question, it shows that you have never really deeply understood the gospel. Certainly, if you are living in a way that makes it look like Christ promotes sin, all that really does is prove the necessity of justification by faith alone, this message of the gospel, in the first place.

First, then, is the common objection that if you have never asked the question, you probably haven't understood the gospel, but then if you cannot get over it at some point, you still have not understood the gospel. That's why Paul so quickly says "Certainly not!" (v. 17). Paul always used this phrase to respond to an objection raised by those who have understood what he's saying, but at the same time, when they think about it, say it just can't be the case. You see this several times in Romans, once in 1 Corinthians, and then another time here in Galatians (chapter 3). "No way!" "Absolutely not." Well, why absolutely not? Absolutely not because you cannot possibly think that Christ promotes sin. We all know that Jesus is not like that, so, while the objection is a good sign at first, with a moment's thought we will realize it just can't be.

Second, Regarding this common objection, it is certainly true that if we are living in a way that seems to suggest that Christ promotes sin, this also means that we have never really understood the gospel. Ever since Jerome and discussions between the Alexandrian and Antioch centers of Bible study, people have discussed whether this is about ceremonial sin or moral sin, which is what Chrysostom said. But why can't it be both? There is a moral indignation in Paul's "certainly not!"

So the whole point of Galatians is that circumcision, in this context here, is really about a much bigger issue—justification and salvation. As Paul says in Galatians 5:3, anyone who gets circumcised is going to have to obey the whole law. Or as he says in Galatians 6:15, circumcision and uncircumcision are nothing. This issue of circumcision is really about how sinners (morally speaking) can get right with God. Do they do it by obeying the whole law? No, they can never do that, because no one keeps the whole law, as Peter and Paul both realized. How do you do it? You do it by trusting what God has done in Jesus' dying for us on the cross.

If we live as if Christ promotes sin, we show that we have never really understood the gospel at all.

The whole point of going to Jesus to deal with our sin is *going to him to deal with our sin*. If we just keep on sinning, it shows we've never understood the sinfulness of sin—Jonathan Edwards used that phrase to explain that Jesus is savior *from* our sins not *of* our sins. Say you've got cancer, and you find a doctor who has a miracle cure. So you go to him, but you never get the surgery, you never get the cure, and you hold on to your cancer. What does that show? It shows either that you never believed that the doctor could do anything about it, or that you never really decided to get rid of the cancer. You didn't understand the cancer-ness of cancer. You didn't ever, as the Bible would put it, repent and believe.

If, after coming to Jesus, I just go along and rebuild what I've destroyed—sin—then all it proves is that I never really went to Jesus to get my sin dealt with in the first place; it proves that I am a lawbreaker still. I'm not in Jesus. That doesn't mean that Christians don't sin, but it does mean that Christians don't love their sin.

If you are saved solely by grace right now, does not that mean you can do whatever you want? The Christian answer is, "I will tell you what I want—I want to be done with my sin and to please Jesus. That is why I became a Christian in the first place." If you go to the miracle doctor who can deal with cancer, does not that mean that you can keep the cancer if you want to? Are you out of your mind? Of course I don't want to keep the cancer! Why do you think I'm going to the miracle doctor in the first place?

So, the last thing this proves is that when the gospel begins to be understood, it actually proves the necessity of the gospel all along. All of us who are Christians sometimes do a bit of rebuilding what we destroyed. We all can be a bit like the dog that returns to its vomit; we know it was vomit, we know it was sin, which is why we went to

Jesus in the first place. But then, well, we are still in this world; we are not in heaven yet. We still struggle with temptation at times, but that proves that we are lawbreakers, which proves that we need Jesus. So the objection proves the necessity of the thing to which it is objecting. Augustine used a phrase that helps with this: "They wouldn't be seeking justification if they weren't sinners." The whole point is that it isn't just the Gentiles but all of us who need Jesus. This is another big theme in Galatians.

The circumcision aspect here actually meant something much bigger. Paul goes to the basic principle of the gospel, justification by faith alone, to show that circumcision is not necessary, and if you treat it as what would justify, then you are trying to impress God with your works, which is never going to happen. That is the big theme. But then there is also the theme of how we get holy as Christians, how we grow. A book by Jerry Bridges calls this the two bookends of the Christian life.[1] To live successfully as Christians, we need to have the bookend of justification. We constantly need to go back to the cross and realize that Jesus died for our sins, and that when the voice comes in and says we are rebuilding what we destroyed, we can say that is why we went to Jesus. In saying that we are sinners, that voice is just proving the necessity of the gospel that it's objecting to. That's the bookend of justification that we need, not just at the start of becoming a Christian but throughout our life.

In the other big theme in Galatians, there is the bookend of sanctification, or, as Paul calls it, the fruit of the Spirit. In relying upon Jesus' death, in being united with him by the Holy Spirit, we have power to bear the fruit of God's character, the fruit of the Spirit, and, as Paul will say, against such things there is no law (Gal. 5:23). In other words, it's the Spirit that does this, not the law. The law convicts; it shows that we are lawbreakers, which shows that we need Christ. From him we receive his Holy Spirit, and therefore we bear the fruit of the Spirit in our lives.

---

[1]Jerry Bridges and Bob Bevington, *The Bookends of the Christian Life* (Wheaton, IL: Crossway, 2009).

14

The Gospel and the Cross

For through the law I died to the law, so that I might live to God. I have
been crucified with Christ. It is no longer I who live, but Christ who
lives in me. And the life I now live in the flesh I live by faith in the Son
of God, who loved me and gave himself for me. I do not nullify the
grace of God, for if righteousness were through the law, then Christ
died for no purpose.

GALATIANS 2:19–21

These verses, particularly "I have been crucified with Christ. It is no longer I who live but Christ who lives in me," are well known in Christian
circles. You might find such words in a greeting card, or stuck on
someone's wall in a Christian college. But though they are well known,
I'm not sure how well comprehended they are. Typically, commentaries
on these verses talk about the "mystical union" between the Christian
and Christ, and there is that. The fact that we are "in Christ" is part of
Paul's answer to the question, Doesn't getting justified simply by faith
alone mean that Christ promotes sin? His answer is no; because we're
in Christ, we died, and we have risen again to a new life. That's a very
important and central aspect of what these verses are teaching.

But that absolutely accurate approach can still, if it is not taken
deeper, miss the main point. It can miss the exegetical wood for the
theological trees. The great big whacking, smack-you-over-the-head
point of these verses, in their context in the letter to the Galatians, is
that they are all about the cross. Paul is saying, "You Galatian agitators
and you Galatian Christians, the reason why you're not understanding
Christianity is that *you are losing sight of the cross.*"

I want to make the case that, given where this comes in Paul's argument, this is his *propositio*, as the literary theorists call it, referring to
the common ancient style of letter writing. Or, as we would say, this

is his thesis statement. I want to make the case that we may take it as axiomatic, that is, as a foundational principle, that whenever someone is misunderstanding Christianity, it is *because they are losing sight of the cross.*

Paul shows us this in three areas. This first is found in verse 19 and in the first phrase of verse 20, which go together. The best critical editions of the Greek New Testament seem to all agree that the first phrase of verse 20—"I have been crucified with Christ"—belongs to verse 19. It doesn't matter technically, because the verses and chapters were not in the original, but nonetheless, structurally, the first phrase of verse 20 really belongs to verse 19. It seems the first phrase of verse 20 is set in verse 20 because that's where the King James translators put it, and there it has remained ever since. Here Paul is really talking about conversion, how you become a Christian, and he's saying that we misunderstand conversion and evangelism (getting someone to the point where they get converted) when we lose sight of the cross.

The second area is found in the latter part of verse 20, which is about discipleship, or living as a Christian, in *view of this conversion reality,* all of which we misunderstand when we lose sight of the cross. The third area is found in verse 21, which I put under the heading of "salvation," which we also misunderstand when we lose sight of the cross. In verse 21 Paul is talking about righteousness or justification, but justification for Paul is the gospel. He defends the true gospel throughout Galatians, which began in 1:6–9 where he says there is no other gospel. When he comes to his *propositio,* his summary thesis statement, it's about justification. I'm going to call it "salvation," but you can call it "justification," if you like, because it's the same area.

So, we misunderstand Christianity when we lose sight of the cross. Paul addresses three areas where that typically happens: conversion and evangelism; discipleship and living as a Christian in view of this conversion reality; and justification and salvation.

Losing Sight of the Cross in Conversion and Evangelism

"For through the law I died to the law, so that I might live to God. I have been crucified with Christ" (vv. 19–20). Paul says that the law's function is to convict us of sin, and that when we understand the law aright, it does takes us to the cross of Jesus, where our sin is dealt with. John Stott puts it like this: "The law's demand of death was satisfied in the death of Christ."[1] What we're talking about here is how someone becomes a Christian, how they get converted.

People typically understand conversion and evangelism quite differently. Some years ago while I was participating in a university mission, someone wrote an anonymous letter to the student newspaper that said:

> Religion is dangerous, it tempts you when you are at your weakest, hooks you, and then slowly eats away at your identity and individuality. If you are in need of support or advice, go to a friend or a trained counselor. However bad it is, don't make it worse; if approached by the God squad, just say no.

That's a common attitude toward conversion, even though not as politely phrased as some would put it. Basically, conversion is seen as a process of manipulation, and evangelism therefore is seen as manipulative.

In a more intellectually sophisticated vein, Richard Dawkins has come up with a theory of how people become Christians. He says there are things called "memes" (taken as analogy to genes) that pass down from parent to child, or from influential individual to open-minded recipient. Memes are not rational but are instead inherited beliefs. In this attitude, conversion and evangelism are reinforcing outmoded ideas that, for the rational individual, have no place in modern life.

I remember at Yale having a discussion with some of the chaplains about whether it was legitimate to teach religious truth to impressionable young minds. The attitude there was that all should be allowed to choose when they are old enough to make an informed choice rather than to be influenced by powerful older mentor figures. We did point out that institutions like Yale have their whole *raison d'être* locked up in influencing impressionable young people by powerful mentor figures; they just call them professors, not evangelists.

There are various aspects to each of these attitudes. They have different philosophies of how to know reality, of the existence or nonex-

---

[1] John R. W. Stott, *The Message of Galatians* (Downers Grove, IL: InterVarsity, 1984), 65.

istence of God; they are variously more mature or less so. At the cross hairs of these is very often a loss of sight of the cross. This first became obvious to me when I was reading the French philosophers of the eighteenth-century Enlightenment who were, by and large, inventing various sophisticated ways to be anti-clerical and anti-religious. As I read them, I increasingly felt that I didn't recognize what they were arguing against. It wasn't that they were arguing against a straw man when it came to Christianity; it was that they had lost sight of the man upon the cross. Of course, if I'd read these verses more carefully back then, I would have gotten the point much earlier. The purpose of the law is that we might die to the law—it exposes our sinfulness, leading to death—that we might put our faith in Christ, who died for us.

Losing Sight of the Cross in Discipleship and Christian Living

The second area where we lose sight of the cross is in discipleship and Christian living *in view of this conversion reality*. "It is no longer I who live, but Christ who lives in me" (v. 20). These words can seem mystical to some, or, to people today, vague and ethereal. There is a union between us as Christians and Christ, which is mystical, but here, that mystical union is neither vague nor ethereal but explained clearly. On these verses John Stott is again helpful, and he explains verse 20 in these words: "Being united to Christ in his sin-bearing death, my sinful past has been blotted out."[2] There is a faith-union between us and Jesus *on the cross*.

This is very important because people misunderstand Christian living and discipleship when they lose sight of the cross. Oftentimes we are encouraged to go to Jesus to get something from him. We are reminded that salvation is a free gift, and we are encouraged to receive it. That is all well and good, but there something missing from that description as it relates to Christian living and discipleship: there is no teaching about repentance or about the cost of being a Christian. The gift of salvation is free, yes; that's a wonderful truth that Paul is emphasizing here. But to become a Christian means to turn away from the selfish "I" of our sinful self: "It is no longer I who live." Being a Christian is to live a life

---

[2]Ibid.

of death to the selfish self in order to live a new life in Christ. The cost of becoming a Christian is your sins, which cost is no cost at all, for all we lose are our sins; nonetheless, that cost of death to the selfish self is essential for the Christian life and discipleship to make any sense.

People today have misunderstandings of what it means to live as a Christian. We could mention perhaps some types of talk-show hosts whose descriptions of spirituality seem to revolve more around getting in touch with yourself than losing yourself. The same can be true at times for at least some of the various self-help books that speak about finding yourself, being kind to yourself, and unleashing yourself. This set of ideas is far removed from the "I no longer live" phrase of Paul's famous statement. Instead, we are told nowadays, that it is about believing in yourself and living your dream, and the emphasis is as far removed from dying to the selfish self as could possibly be.

Look at many of our popular Christian books. *The Life You've Always Wanted*—how does that compare to "I no longer live"? *Your Best Life Now*, which is very different from this verse.[3] In Galatians we have "Christ who lives in me." Perhaps we should say that as Christians our aspiration is therefore to be living "Jesus' best life now," for "I" no longer live and "Christ lives in me."

Still, people living in glass houses should not throw stones, and I wonder whether these same self-orientated attitudes (and lack of cross-orientated living) influence us more than we like to think. Take, for example, the typical well-meaning, church-going folk. We will call them Harry and Sally (that's a reference for the pop aficionados). Harry follows the rules. He's a stand-up guy. He knows what's right, and he's always going to stick to it. He works hard. He plays hard. He's on more committees than you could shake a leg at. Harry is doing all this because those are the rules. That's what his dad did; it's the right way to live. Then there's Sally. Sally is a free spirit. She also is an involved church-goer, but she floats on the breeze and goes with the flow and follows her instincts. If it feels good it probably is good, for Sally.

Neither Harry nor Sally have a firm grasp of the cross. Sally needs to reflect on the first part of verse 20, that she no longer lives, that becom-

[3] John Ortberg, *The Life You've Always Wanted: Spiritual Disciplines for Ordinary People* (Grand Rapids, MI: Zondervan, 2002); Joel Osteen, *Your Best Life Now: 7 Steps to Living at Your Full Potential* (New York: Faith Words, 2004).

ing a Christian means giving up the selfish self and having Christ and his mission and his agenda living in her. Harry needs to reflect on the second part of the verse, that he is to be motivated by the love of Christ, who gave himself for him on the cross. Harry may not be a legalist as such, but he is a *nomist*, someone who lives by the rules more than by faith. And Sally may not be licentious but she is loosy-goosy and lives more by gut than by faith. Both need not to lose sight of the cross.

My guess is that most of us have a little bit of both Harry and Sally in us. For verse 20 to become *more than a bumper sticker*, we need to see it as being about the cross—dying to our old way of life and rising to a new way, all because of the great love of Jesus on the cross. That's what Christian living and discipleship are about; that's when we won't have to persuade people to serve in children's ministries, or in disability ministries, or on various serving teams, or as missionaries, or to give up their careers to be pastors. They'll be lining up to do so because "he loved me and gave himself for me." They won't be looking for their best life now; they'll be looking to embody Christ's best life now. There would be gladsome, sacrificial self-giving on the basis of the love of the one who gave himself for us. That, amazingly, is actually what life itself is about. Paul is probably thinking here of Jesus' famous words on the subject: "For whoever would save his life will lose it, but whoever loses his life for my sake and the gospel's will save it" (Mark 8:35).

Losing Sight of the Cross in Justification and Salvation

We also misunderstand justification, which is the way we get saved, if we lose sight of the cross. "I do not nullify the grace of God, for if righteousness were through the law, then Christ died for no purpose" (Gal. 2:21). Paul has answered the question he posed in verse 17 in various ways, and this is his fourth answer—the slam-dunk answer: if you say that it's the law, or was ever the law, then you are saying that Jesus' death was pointless. No one wants to say that.

We've looked at that, but there's another aspect of it that I want to bring out, which is how someone could possibly get to the point in their Christian faith where they think "works of the law" is what justifies them. What would make that happen? Here we see that the only way we could go there is if we cease to really look at the cross. I'm going to show you five ways that can happen, each of which is intrinsic to the context here, and each of which I've noticed as tendencies either in my own life or in the life of those I've pastored.

1) *We lose sight of the cross when we listen to teaching that does not emphasize it.* That's what was going on here. Wherever the Galatian agitators got their initial entrance into the community, claiming authority "from James," they became teachers that the Galatians were listening to. It's okay to read heretical material occasionally; you've got to know what people are saying. But your diet needs to be mainly healthy. It is easier in some ways and more healthy to listen to the obvious wrong than the subtle wrong within the broadly Christian community. However, we must listen to teaching that emphasizes the cross.

2) *We lose sight of the cross when our teaching is theoretical, not practical.* Paul was the most doctrinally sophisticated teacher the church has known, other than Jesus, yet he addresses the Galatians directly. He calls on them to believe specific things and to avoid specific things. If our teaching is purely academic, then we are less likely to be impressed by the reality of the cross. We will know it in theory, but we need to have it as the controlling motivating force in our lives. That's why Paul will write in Galatians 3 about portraying Christ crucified before their eyes; it needs to be vivid, personal, real.

3) *We lose sight of the cross when our teaching is unemotional.* I don't mean we should all be weeping, crying, and laughing until we're in some sort of crazed frenzy. But he who can understand the cross and not be emotional about it is someone who has not understood it. You can hear of the Grand Canyon, but when you are there, you are moved. When we are "there" at the cross, we are moved. Paul here is very passionate. It does not mean he is *not* thoughtful; it means that his emotions are connected to the truth and the importance of the matter.

4) *We lose sight of the cross when our teaching is boring.* There's only one thing worse than boring teaching, and that is heretical teaching. Other than that, I'd rather have someone be interesting about God even if he doesn't parse his Greek correctly. This is God we're talking about. It's got to be fascinating, thrilling, appealing, exalting because God is. The most doctrinally exact presentation but one that has no

thrill is not actually by definition doctrinally exact, for God always interests, challenges, and encourages. Whatever you think of the book of Galatians, it is not boring.

5) *We lose sight of the cross when we don't ask ourselves the obvious question.* As we go on through the Christian life, it is easy to leave the cross in our rearview mirror, instead of looking to the present reality through which all our Christian evangelism, discipleship, and salvation is to be viewed. The way to keep that in the forefront of our minds and hearts is to ask the obvious question: who keeps the law? Who obeys the commandments? If righteousness could be gained through the law, Christ died for nothing.

15

The Gospel, Not Moralism

*O foolish Galatians! Who has bewitched you? It was before your eyes
that Jesus Christ was publicly portrayed as crucified. Let me ask you
only this: Did you receive the Spirit by works of the law or by hearing
with faith? Are you so foolish? Having begun by the Spirit, are you now
being perfected by the flesh? Did you suffer so many things in vain—if
indeed it was in vain? Does he who supplies the Spirit to you and
works miracles among you do so by works of the law, or by hearing
with faith . . . ?*

GALATIANS 3:1–5

If someone in our culture today were to speak like Paul does in this
passage, he would probably sound somewhat medieval, even aggressive
or presumptuous. You just can't go around calling people foolish; it's
not done other than perhaps in Prime Minister's Question Time in the
British Parliament, but even then there is a code of decorum. Here Paul
calls the Galatians "foolish." He does so twice. He says that they have
been "bewitched," meaning not that they've won a ticket to Hogwarts
but that they are loopy. He practically calls them numbskulls, dunder-
heads, or knuckleheads.

Whenever the Bible says things that do not seem to fit in with our
sensibilities, we need to ask ourselves a very important question: What
is it about the way we look at life, or religion, that makes this seem so
shocking? We need to resist the temptation to assume that the Bible is
wrong or that its language needs to be translated into a form that is
more acceptable to our culture. Of course, there was a particular context here in Galatians, which we have been considering all along, that
explains why Paul uses such strong language here when he doesn't use
it at other times. But I can't think of any situation today, even if that
situation were similar to the one in Galatians, where it would be viewed

as okay for some form of Christian leader to stand up and say, "Hey, brainless, what do you think you're doing?"

We are going to consider two general views of what this passage assumes and what our culture does not, which will help us see where Paul is coming from and where the Bible is coming from, and what this passage especially pulls out for us to see. Then, after looking at two general views of this passage, we're going to consider one particular aspect that this passage is focused on.

A Truth about God

The first general view that this passage assumes and our culture does not, which explains why we find this passage so strange, is that *there is an absolute truth about God*. Paul is assuming that there are some things that are true about God and some things that are not, and that we can identify what those things are. So, for Paul, God is like gravity in the sense that some things are true about gravity and some things are not. But God is not like a painting, in which it is much more a matter of personal opinion and perspective. This is so radically different from the attitude in our culture today toward God that we need to understand the Bible's attitude, especially here where that attitude goes a long way toward explaining why Paul uses such strong language.

If you were enjoying looking at a painting in an art gallery and someone came and stood next to you and said, "I can't stand that painting," you would not say, "Hey, you fool, what do you think you're doing?" You might disagree, but it's a matter of opinion. But if you went to the restaurant out on a balcony of the art gallery, and someone was to get up and stand on the railing as if he was about to jump to his death five storeys below, you might then say, "Hey, you fool, get down; what do you think you're doing?" For our culture God is more like the painting, but for the Bible God is more like the gravity.

Now I want to say that you, we, will never understand anything the Bible says about God until we get this through our thick skulls (I'm using apostolic language already!). Because our culture assumes that religion is a matter of private devotion and that God is a mysterious being about whom we can know precious little for sure, we all tend to default to the view that God is a matter of opinion. Because of that, we don't even think of feeling the kind of intense angst that Paul is feeling here toward these erring Galatians.

You know you've been drawn into the postmodern relativistic mindset when you walk along city streets and do not weep for the millions of lost people on the city streets. Do you weep? Do you say, "Lord, in your justice remember mercy"? I don't mean you have to weep all the time. E. J. H. Nash (Bash), the man who discipled John Stott, after one particularly intense talk when everyone had been sent to their rooms to meditate, was found instead flat on his back reading a comic book. Christian leaders know there can be a wrong kind of intensity, which is really a strange form of religious pride where we begin to think that it all depends on us. But do we have compassion on the needy crowds and say, "They are like sheep without a shepherd" (Mark 6:34)? Do we look at the harvest field around the world and say, "Send workers, Lord, send workers" (Matt. 9:37–38)?

Christianity versus Christian Moralism

The second general view here, which this passage assumes, and which explains why we tend to find the language of this passage remarkable, is really a subset of the first general view that there is a truth about God. The second general view is this: *there is a difference between Christianity and Christian moralism.* In fact, for Paul, not only is there a difference between them, but true Christianity really stands against fake Christian moralism.

This is very much a part of what's going on here. The Galatian agitators were acceptable within the broadly speaking Christian community. We mustn't think of them as people of a completely different religion, or people who were irreligious. They were moral; they had come "from James." Nonetheless, for Paul, and, very surprisingly, for us, there is a conflict between the true biblical Christianity and the claims to this sort of Christianity, which was actually non-Christianity. There is nothing of greater importance today than learning to distinguish between these two things, and also learning how to communicate to our society the difference between them.

When people today reject Christianity, they are very often rejecting Christian moralism. I'm not sure how much they have even begun to get to grips with Christ. All the trappings of Christendom—the externals, the institutions, the characterizations—can put off people needlessly from a true relationship with Jesus. It can be helpful to make a little graph with three columns. At the head of one column, list "What is the gospel." At the head of the next, list "What is not the gospel." At the head of the third, list "How do we promote the gospel." Under the heading "What is not the gospel," our staff team listed "religious" matters, such as legalism and formalism.

Paul here is making a distinction between the gospel of grace and this thing that the Galatians were getting into. We are distracted by different things, and our perceptions as to how non-Christians define Christianity will differ, but we need to understand that there is a distinction between biblical Christianity and a form of Christian non-Christianity, that is, what has the husk but has lost the kernel, the substance, the power, and the grace of Christ.

This is perhaps the most important challenge for the contemporary church today, because we live in a time when people have very confused understandings of what a biblical Christian is. They assume that we are aggressive because we are exclusive; they assume that we are judgmental because we hold to certain moral principles. We need to make a distinction and tell them that we believe in Christ, who was crucified for us as the ultimate love offering.

Those are the two general views, and now we come to the particular aspect of this passage.

The Way Forward

Our experience of conversion will show us the way forward as Christians. Paul is making an argument from experience, in particular the experience of becoming a Christian. In Galatians 3:6 onward he will make an argument drawn from the Old Testament Scriptures, but first he calls them back to what they know to be true: "Let me ask you only this." This passage is really about this one thing, this matter of our experience of conversion being what will show us the way forward as Christians. "Let me ask you only this: Did you receive the Spirit by works of the law or by hearing with faith?" (v. 2).

Paul says that this attempt to get holy by the works of the law, which the Galatian false teachers were offering to the Galatian Christians, is not just a *supplement* to grace, but it actually *supplants* grace. If those general views were extremely important, I can think of no more particular teaching that has greater significance for many Christians today. The gospel of Jesus Christ, Paul says, is not only for the start of the Christian life; it is for the whole of the Christian life. We are not to think of Christianity as step 1, becoming a Christian by grace through faith alone; and step 2, living as a Christian by the works of the law. Instead, we are to think of living as Christians also by grace through faith alone, what Paul will later call "walking in the Spirit." This attempt to *supplement* grace actually *supplants* grace.

He argues that this is the truth of the matter: "It was before your eyes that Jesus Christ was publicly portrayed as crucified" (v. 1); "Did you receive the Spirit by works of the law or by hearing with faith?" (v. 2), calling them back to their experience of being born again when they became Christians; "Having begun by the Spirit, are you now being perfected by the flesh?" (v. 3), showing them that *supplementing* grace is illogical because the Spirit comes through believing the Word; "Did you suffer so many things in vain—if indeed it was in vain?" (v. 4), appealing to what it cost them to accept that Jesus is the only way to be saved and how odd it would be if now, religious works could do it; "Does he who supplies the Spirit to you and works miracles among you do so by works of the law, or by hearing with faith . . . ?" (v. 5), recapitulating his point that it is through faith that the power of the Spirit enables us to grow and become more godly.

I will illustrate this by means of a section from John Bunyan's great old Christian classic, *Pilgrim's Progress*. In this allegory, Christianity is represented by the figure of Christian, who meets various figures along his pilgrimage, some helpful, some distracting, some troubling. Christian has a heavy burden on his back, the burden of guilt and sin. He meets Evangelist, who tells him the gospel and points to "yonder wicket gate" where Christian can enter into the life that is life and where eventually he will come to the cross where his burden will roll off his back. Christian has begun on his way, but then he meets Mr. Worldly Wiseman, who tells him that instead of going to yonder wicket gate, he needs to rest in the house of Mr. Legality.

So Christian turned out his way to go to Mr. Legality's house for help: but behold, when he was got now hard by the hill, it seemed so high . . . also his burden now seemed heavier to him than while he was in his way. There came also flashes of fire out of the hill, that made Christian afraid that he should be burned: and therefore he sweat, and did quake for fear. And now he began to be sorry that he had taken Mr. Worldly Wiseman's counsel; and with that he saw Evangelist coming to meet him, at the sight also of whom he began to blush for shame. So Evangelist drew nearer and nearer . . . [and said] "What doest thou here, Christian?"

Christian responds and explains how he came to Mr. Legality, and Evangelist says:

"This Legality, therefore, is not able to set thee free from thy burden. No man was as yet ever rid of his burden by him; no, nor is ever like to be: ye cannot be justified by the works of the law; for by deeds of the law no man liveth can be rid of his burden—Therefore Mr. Worldly Wiseman is an alien, and Mr. Legality a cheat; and as for his son Civility, notwithstanding his simpering looks, he is but a hypocrite, and cannot help thee. Believe me, there is nothing in all this noise that thou hast heard of these sottish men, but a design to beguile thee of thy salvation, by turning thee from the way in which I had set thee."

After this, Evangelist called aloud to the heavens for confirmation of what he had said; and with that there came words and fire out of the mountain under which poor Christian stood, that made the hair of his flesh stand up. The words were thus pronounced, "As many as are of the works of the law are under the curse, for it is written, Cursed is everyone that continueth not in all things which are written in the book of the law to do them" Galatians 3:10.

Christian is trying to make himself better by the law. He is supplementing his conversion by faith in God's Word, through which he received the Spirit, with works of the law, and in so supplementing he is really in danger of supplanting Christ. The Old Testament itself bears witness: cursed is everyone who doesn't continue to do all these things, as Paul quotes in Galatians. But "Christ redeemed us from the curse of the law by becoming a curse for us" (v. 13). The Galatians have listened to the counsel of Worldly Wiseman and gone to the house of Mr. Legality, and Paul (Evangelist) comes and points them back to the cross (v. 1), to their new birth (v. 2), and therefore to the craziness of attempting to get spiritual power by any other means (vv. 3–5).

That is what Galatians 3:1–5 is about and why it so startles us. It assumes that there is a truth about God, and it also assumes that there are religious messages that sound good but are actually opposed to real biblical Christianity. Then it points us to how the gospel is the means of our growth as Christians, as well as the method of our becoming Christians in the first place.

I suppose the questions for us to ask are these: Do we believe the truth about God? Do we distinguish between biblical Christianity and vague religious moralism? Are we in the house of Mr. Legality, or are we walking on the path of the Spirit?

16

The Gospel and Abraham

Just as Abraham "believed God, and it was counted to him as righteousness. . . ." Know then that it is those of faith who are the sons of Abraham. And the Scripture, foreseeing that God would justify the Gentiles by faith, preached the gospel beforehand to Abraham, saying, "In you shall all the nations be blessed." So then, those who are of faith are blessed along with Abraham, the man of faith.

GALATIANS 3 : 6 – 9

I don't know about you, but I don't spend a lot of time thinking specifically about Abraham. However, that is exactly what this passage is asking us to do. "Consider Abraham," Paul says. Church people probably recall a song, "Father Abraham, had many sons, many sons had father Abraham . . . " Generally speaking, apart from children's songs, if we're not doing a study in the book of Genesis, we don't usually "consider Abraham" at much length.

Yet what we think about Abraham makes a big difference. Christianity says Abraham is the father of Christianity; hence the song. Judaism claims Abraham as the father of the Jewish people for understandable genetic reasons. Moslems believe Abraham is the father of their religion. They call him "the first Moslem" because they view him as the one who originally reestablished monotheism; Ishmael, not Isaac, they say, was the child Abraham was instructed to sacrifice, and through Ishmael they trace their religious inheritance. So we have Christianity, Islam, and Judaism all claiming Abraham as their patriarch. If you want to get technical about it, there are also other religions that look to Abraham as their father: the Samaritans, the Rastafarians, and the Bahá'is. For most purposes though textbooks on world religion mainly list Christianity, Judaism, and Islam as the three Abrahamic, monotheistic religions.

As soon as we categorize these religions by the term "Abrahamic," we potentially introduce another way of looking at religion based on our view of Abraham, which is that all these monotheistic religions might *legitimately* trace their lineage to him; they are *all*, by this view, "Abrahamic" in origin. What we think about Abraham, therefore, has great implications. World evangelization, the uniqueness of Christianity, and even what some call "interreligious dialogue" are all impacted to some extent by what we think about Abraham. Whose father *is* Abraham?

A similar question was raised in Galatia. The false teachers had come to the Galatian churches planted by Paul and taught the recent Galatian Christian converts that to be saved, they had to be circumcised according to the Law of Moses. That's how Acts 15:1 helpfully summarizes their message; they were arguing from Moses. Paul now makes his case for justification by faith without the works of the law by appealing to father Abraham.

So the question is, who was Abraham's father? This is a question of great importance, because only the true children of Abraham will receive Abraham's inheritance. To answer the question Paul wants us to consider Abraham's righteousness, his children, his gospel, and his blessing.

Abraham's Righteousness

First, Paul shows us that Abraham's righteousness was credited to him by faith: "Abraham 'believed God, and it was counted to him as righteousness'" (v. 6). Paul wants us to consider Abraham because, by doing so, we will see that Abraham did *not* behave perfectly righteously; rather, God gave him righteousness as credit through faith. If that's how Abraham got righteous, Paul says, so will we.

It is true that in the Genesis account of Abraham we are told that he was a very godly man. But as the story of Abraham is told, we hear also time and again that Abraham did not always behave righteously. Abraham deceived Pharaoh by pretending that Sarah was merely Abraham's sister; he also deceived King Abimelech in similar fashion. Abraham even slept with Sarah's maidservant Hagar, who bore him Ishmael.

No, the story of Abraham is about trusting God. Abraham left his home country trusting God's promise; he let his nephew Lot choose what was apparently the best land, trusting God's promise; he went to sacrifice Isaac, trusting that God could raise the dead and therefore would keep his promise. I'm not sure we can even say his *faith* was perfect, for we also hear of Abraham laughing at God's promise of a son so late in his life (Gen. 17:17; Sarah also laughed later in the story, 18:12), but despite his imperfections, he still believed God.

Paul expounds this theme about Abraham's faith elsewhere in his writing, and in Romans 4 this quotation from Genesis 15 about Abraham's faith is especially important, because it was said about him before he was circumcised (Rom. 4:1–3). Abraham's righteousness was therefore not on the basis of his acts of moral obedience *or* through circumcision but a credit from God by faith.

Justification by faith often seems an abstract idea, but as you enter into the story of Abraham, there are readymade illustrations of righteousness being credited through faith. Abraham's promised child came when he was one hundred years old and his wife was ninety. That son, Isaac, was not achieved by their natural ability, any more than Abraham's righteousness was. Justification credited by faith is as much about the pure promise of God as a man siring a child at one hundred and a woman bearing a child at ninety.

This means that even we can be righteous. Perhaps you feel that your being righteous is about as likely as a man bearing a child at one hundred, but if you believe, God's righteousness will be given to you just as it was to Abraham. We tend to think we're as holy as, if not Abraham, at least any other person, but if Abraham needed righteousness as a gift, we need the humility to receive it that way too. Consider Abraham, Paul says, and learn about righteousness by faith.

Abraham's Children

Second, Abraham's children are those who believe: "Know then that it is those of faith who are the sons of Abraham" (v. 7). Because the Bible teaches that Abraham's righteousness was received as a credit through his faith, it means that Abraham's "sons" are therefore those who believe.

Then, as now, it was common to think of Abraham's children as those who were genetically descended from him, but Paul is arguing that Abraham's *true* sons are those who believe like Abraham believed. He explains this point further in Galatians 4:22–23. There, he reminds his readers that Abraham had two sons. Which of the two inherited from him? One was born in the ordinary way and did not inherit, while the other came by promise and did. So those who are Abraham's sons, in the sense of being inheritors of the promise of God's blessing, are those who believe as Abraham believed, for the child born in the ordinary way did not inherit, while the child of the promise, received by Abraham's faith, did.

This argument seems difficult to swallow at first gulp because it is not a common way of thinking. If I asked you who your son is, you would say the name of your child or children, if you have them. But Paul says that the real sons of Abraham are not those who can theoretically trace a DNA paternity test to Abraham, but the sons of Abraham's promise, which can be tested only by faith in the promise. Abraham's children do not bear his physical characteristics but his spiritual character of faith. If I asked you who were the true sons of George Washington, you probably wouldn't seek out paternity tests, but you would think of people who displayed Washington's principles of democracy. This argument is a bit like that: you're a son of Abraham if you believe like Abraham believed.

If you believe in the God of the Bible revealed in Jesus Christ and have put your faith in him for his perfect righteousness, I've got a wonderful message for you: you are a son of Abraham; you are in his lineage. You believe as he did—against all odds, leaving home, trusting God. You are a true child of Abraham as you evidence his spiritual DNA. Consider Abraham, his righteousness by faith, which means that those who believe are Abraham's children.

Abraham's Gospel

Third, Abraham's gospel was justification by faith to all nations: "The Scripture, foreseeing that God would justify the Gentiles by faith, preached the gospel beforehand to Abraham, saying, 'In you shall all the nations be blessed'" (v. 8). This is a very remarkable verse for two subsidiary reasons, as well as for its main point.

Along the way, we find the expression "the Scripture foreseeing that God . . . " This implies that the Bible is so closely identified with the foresight of God that, without bibliolatry, the Bible is here described in a way that personifies God. What God says is not only what the Bible says, but there is a living, breathing, divine association with the words as revealed in the Word incarnate. We also find here that the gospel was pre-announced in the Old Testament, and therefore the gospel is what the whole Bible is about. But at its heart, this verse teaches us that the gospel is for all nations.

Imagine that you are going to a wedding. A friend of yours is getting married and you're happy to be there. You don't know his family particularly well, and when you arrive, you are told that the family is sitting in one area of the church and friends in another. You start to make your way toward the designated seating for friends when the groom spots you and says, "Oh, no, you're family," and he ushers you to sit with his family. Like that, the family blessing that came to Abraham is extended to all the families or nations of the world through a faith friendship with the groom Jesus.

If you don't feel a part of a church family, this is good news for you. Through friendship with Jesus by faith in God's Word, you can be a part of the family. If you have joined the family, this is the good news that we have to offer. We want not just to welcome people to the church family but to make church a place where it is easy for other believers in Jesus to join. We want coming to church not to be like going to a family wedding where you are welcome but are aware that you are not family, but instead to be like becoming part of the family and being one of us. We have a message for all the nations and families of the world.

As we consider Abraham, then, we find righteousness by faith and, therefore, that believers are true children of Abraham, which means that this is the gospel for all nations.

Abraham's Blessing

Fourth, Abraham's blessing comes to those who believe: "So then, those who are of faith are blessed along with Abraham, the man of faith"

(v. 9). Abraham's blessing is righteousness, and this blessing comes to all who believe as Abraham believed.

Something that most people know about Abraham is that he was very wealthy. He may have been a nomad, but he had servants, and flocks, and herds, and many possessions with silver and gold in abundance. But this material wealth was not the promised blessing of God. That blessing was God's righteousness: God was going to make righteous all the nations, telling Abraham that this was the blessing that all nations would receive through him. Now Paul says that this blessing will come to all who believe like Abraham. The blessing is righteousness, not wealth, received by faith.

When we illustrate that spiritual blessing is more important than materialism, we sometimes do so by stories of very wealthy people who are not happy. "How much money is enough?" John Paul Getty was reportedly asked. "Just a bit more," he replied. We compare people who are wealthy but not happy to those who are of more modest means but are happy as a way to show that true blessing is more than money. But here, instead, we have in Abraham a man who was rich and blessed yet still realized that the blessing of righteousness from God was the far greater blessing. It is striking to find a poor man who is happy and knows he is blessed by his righteousness through faith in Jesus. It is striking to find a rich man who is not happy despite his great wealth. It is perhaps even more striking to find a rich man who holds his wealth loosely and knows that the real blessing of God is not his money but God's righteousness. It illustrates that righteousness is a far greater blessing than even lots of happy money. If someone gave you ten million dollars, you might feel blessed; but if someone were to ask you how you've been blessed by God, and you were to think like Abraham, you would say, "My relationship with God." Such a man was Abraham, and the blessing he received (righteousness from God), greater and more precious than any amount of money and may be ours through faith.

That's the blessing we are to seek—the blessing of a peaceful conscience, of a heart without guilt, of confidence before our Maker—the blessing of Abraham that comes through faith in the promise of Abraham fulfilled in Jesus Christ the Lord.

So consider Abraham. Consider Abraham's righteousness that

comes by faith, which means that Abraham's children are those who believe, and that Abraham's gospel is that of righteousness by faith to all nations, and that Abraham's blessing of righteousness by faith comes to those who believe in Jesus Christ.

Whose father *is* Abraham? He is the father of those who believe. His spiritual DNA is righteousness by faith, a gospel that reaches out to the four corners of the globe, the blessing which means no guilt, and all of this comes through the promise given by God to Abraham, the gospel which the Scriptures declared in advance and fulfilled in Jesus Christ. Abraham is the father of those who believe in Jesus.

If you believe in Jesus, rejoice at the ancient lineage of your faith. Take Abraham as an example of a man who walked with God by faith and, through your uncertainties and trials, trust God as Abraham did. If you don't yet believe in Jesus, perhaps that is because Christianity seems parochial. It seems Western. It seems relatively recent. According to the Bible, the faith of Abraham, the oldest monotheism in the world, is found by faith in the fulfillment of Abraham's promise in the person of Jesus. That faith has extended around the globe, even to where you are now, and is offered to you this moment.

17

The Gospel and Legalism

For all who rely on works of the law are under a curse; for it is written, "Cursed be everyone who does not abide by all things written in the Book of the Law, and do them." Now it is evident that no one is justified before God by the law, for "The righteous shall live by faith." But the law is not of faith, rather "The one who does them shall live by them." Christ redeemed us from the curse of the law by becoming a curse for us—for it is written, "Cursed is everyone who is hanged on a tree"—so that in Christ Jesus the blessing of Abraham might come to the Gentiles, so that we might receive the promised Spirit through faith.

GALATIANS 3:10–14

In 1999 the painkiller Vioxx was approved by the FDA. In 2004 Vioxx was withdrawn. While it was on the market, FDA analysts estimated that Vioxx caused between 88,000 and 139,000 heart attacks.[1] Getting your medicine right matters, but it is even more important to get your theology right. In Galatians 3:10–14 we are presented with blessings and curses, a blessing that will last for eternity and a curse that will do so likewise. How do I get right with God?

Some parts of this are complex, as one would expect from such a great matter. Yet these verses illustrate that in many ways the most significant thing to understand about Paul's letter to the Galatians is simply that it was written to Christians. We tend to think of the letter as written to explain the gospel to people who were fairly ignorant of the basics of the Christian faith, when actually these Galatians were converts; they were part of the church, and the level of theological sophistication with which Paul engages them is really very high. He plucks texts from the

[1]http://www.npr.org/templates/story/story.php?storyId=4054991; Ben Goldacre, *Bad Science* (New York: Harper Perennial, 2009), 218–19.

Old Testament out of the air as if his hearers will immediately know where they come from and will know the wider context of Habakkuk and Leviticus and Deuteronomy. There's a level of debate going on here that would be not only totally out of the reach of the average unchurched person, but also most likely quite a stretch for many inside a modern church.

That means that we are not dealing with an evangelistic tract that those of us who have been Christians for a long time can smile about, and reminisce how we became Christians all those years ago, or perhaps hope that our neighbor who is newer to Christian things will be reading this book closely. Galatians was originally written to Christians, biblically learned Christians. Of course, the Galatians were relatively new Christians, despite their high level of biblical literacy, and this has much to say to us too, if we are newer Christians.

After all, the great concern that many have with the church today is that it is rather legalistic. For those of us on the inside, that comes as something of a surprise, but a frequent contemporary criticism is that we are too quick to judge and presumptuously occupy the high moral ground, when really all is not right in our own house. So, if you are new to Christian things, this is for you as well. It helps you see what Christianity should be about even if it doesn't always reach its ideals. Legalistic judgmentalism is not the spirit of Christ; in fact, an entire book of the Bible was written to make sure that Christianity doesn't go down that road.

You might raise an ironic eyebrow at that and wonder why Christianity is the kind of religion that has to have a book in its canon written to stop Pharisaism; but Pharisaism comes in many forms, some of them religious, many of them not. In fact, it is the default mode of humanity. We all tend to want to justify ourselves, even if we do it by insisting that we are above all that religious nonsense, which is another form of self-justification, just a secular version of the same thing. If you listen carefully to the language of children throughout the world, you'll realize that we are all hardwired legalists: "I didn't do it . . . it was her fault . . . you made me . . . you never told me not to do that." We all at times naturally put the blame on someone else in order to assert our righteousness, whether that righteousness is circumcision or environmentalism, or being against fornication for fear it might lead to dancing. We tend to strain at a gnat and swallow a camel, as Jesus memorably quipped about the whole issue (Matt. 23:24).

Paul picks up a theological machete to hack through this legalistic jungle. He says, "Not by law but by faith," and he says it quite forthrightly because he believes this gospel of law is a genetic mutation that will destroy the whole body of the church if it is not clearly identified and removed.

A Stark Contrast

To hack through this jungle Paul first takes a big swipe at the idea that the law completes what faith began. Instead, he says, law and faith are in stark contrast. They are like oil and water. You have faith on the one side, and you have law on the other. They have different purposes and are not to be confused; to do so is like pairing Jane Austen's *Pride and Prejudice* with zombies—you can do it, you might make some money out of it, but it's hardly the original purpose of the author.[2]

This stark contrast between law and faith is particularly apparent in verses 11 and 12. "Now it is evident that no one is justified before God by the law," Paul says (v. 11), because instead we are justified or made righteous by faith. These two—faith and law—are in contrast. If I were to say to you that you cannot get to a certain town by train because there are no train tracks there, but you can get there by car, you would know that I am contrasting the merits of trains and cars. You can't go by train and car at the same time; you can't start by car and then complete it by train; you can only get there by car.

This contrast between faith and law is even stronger in verse 12: "But the law is not of faith, rather 'The one who does them shall live by them.'" The law is not by faith because the law is about doing, not believing. The Galatians were being told that having received Christ by faith, they now needed to add the Law of Moses. Paul said they were making a category error. Trying to get right before God by the law is like trying to get to that certain town by reading a book. There's nothing wrong with reading books; in fact, lots of good things happen when you read books. But however many book you read, it won't get you to

---

[2] Seth Grahame-Smith, *Pride and Prejudice and Zombies* (Philadelphia: Quirk, 2009).

that town. You need to get in your car and drive there. The law has a purpose, as books have a purpose. The law, as he will explain later more fully, is to make us aware of our need of being saved by Christ. But it is Christ who saves, and we receive that salvation by faith, not by law.

Now we can begin to see what was so pernicious about the confusion the Galatian visitors were spreading. By insisting the Galatians had to have the law to be really good Christians, they were effectively denying the sufficiency of Christ. Adding something, whatever it is, to Jesus detracts from Jesus because then Jesus is no longer sufficient. Jesus has become a stage on one's spiritual development; he is no longer the destination.

Of course, we don't want to say that Christians don't need to make moral effort. There's nothing wrong with reading books, but if you think reading books is going to get you to that town you have a problem, and if you think going to prayer meetings or wearing the right clothes, or not drinking, or not swearing, or reading the right books, or having the right spiritual preacher heroes is necessary to be an acceptable Christian to God, you have a problem. The legalist and licentious have this in common: they both in their own way undervalue the seriousness of sin and the sufficiency of Christ. The one attempts to do what only Jesus can do, and the other acts as if Jesus didn't need to do it. Instead, we are to realize that it is all Christ, and therefore it is all by faith. When we do, we're actually going to make a lot more moral effort, for we won't be frustrated that however many books we read, we're not getting any closer to that town, as it were. Making this category error is part of what creates legalism. Paul therefore wants us to see the stark contrast between faith and law.

He also wants us to understand why it is not law that makes us acceptable Christians, so he says shockingly in verse 10 that anyone who relies on the law is under a curse, because if you don't do everything written in the book of the law you will be cursed. The law pronounced blessings for obedience and curses for disobedience. In a way, that would have deeply shocked the Galatian visitors. Surely, they would have thought, the law can be a blessing if you keep it; after all, it is *God's* law. That divine sanction was the rhetorical weight behind the Galatian visitors' teaching. But Paul says if you rely on the law, you are under the curse, not the blessing, for three reasons.

1) *No one* can actually keep everything written in God's law because of the fallen inability of the entire human species (which Paul explains in greater detail in Romans 3). Is it theoretically possible to be accepted by God by keeping the law? Yes. Does anyone ever manage it? No. Therefore trying to do so will place you under the curse of not keeping it, because you will not keep it.

2) Paul emphasizes the general principle that we sinners can never live up to God's moral standards by our efforts, by picking the most holy thing he can find—*God's* law—and showing thereby that absolutely anything other than Jesus (even God's own law) is inadequate. If you wanted to persuade people that a certain object was far too heavy to lift, you wouldn't pick the weakest person you could find as an example to prove that. You would pick the strongest and have him try to lift the object in front of everyone, and when he failed, it would be evident that the object was too heavy to lift. If *he* couldn't lift it, then certainly no one else could. If by God's law we cannot live in fellowship with God, then certainly we cannot by any human means or moral effort.

3) Trusting in the law of God to make us acceptable (a purpose for which it was not designed) is not only misguided, but it is a form of natural human pride, which is the source of the strange perennial attraction of legalism in all its forms. We attempt to self-justify and build a ladder to heaven out of a rope of sand, a ridiculous enterprise that we would all quickly avoid if we were not tempted by its appeal to make ourselves look good. Theoretically, being made right before God by the law is an option, but none of us keep it.

Finally, Paul shows us why it is by faith. If verse 10 is shocking, verses 13 and 14 are even more so: "Christ redeemed us from the curse of the law by becoming a curse for us—for it is written, 'Cursed is everyone who is hanged on a tree'—so that in Christ Jesus the blessing of Abraham might come to the Gentiles, so that we might receive the promised Spirit through faith." Christ became a *curse* for us. It is familiar religious language perhaps, but you have to think about what is really being said. The quotation from the Old Testament was originally used of criminals who were hung on a tree after they had been executed. In New Testament times it came to refer to the horrible practice of Roman execution by crucifixion; hence "hanged on a tree."

When the early Christians preached Christ crucified, it was totally countercultural, for the cross was the place of cursing, and how could Christ be victorious at the cross? Their antagonists would say, "No, Jesus is not Lord; he is 'cursed,'" and hence that denigration of Christ became a mark of someone who was not a Christian in early times (1 Cor. 12:3). But here Paul takes that theological machete and smashes it down on the terrible bondage of legalism and says that Christ was cursed for you. We would not dare say it if it was not in our Bibles. Christ became a curse. He took all the judgment of God in himself. Let the words ring with the sound of freedom from legalism. All that we have done, all that was wrong in us, all the curse of generations of malaise, all the pain and suffering of the universe, the curse of the fallen world, which groans with mud slides in Taiwan, cancer, fighting and biting in houses around the globe from dawn to dusk, the quiet desperation of the man who buttons on his Sunday best knowing that he has not kept the rules. Of course not! Cursed is anyone who relies on the law. But look! Cursed is Christ, and so it is by faith.

Many a confusing treatise has been written about faith, and the media love to call believers simpletons because we rely on faith. But faith is not make-believe; faith is the simple trust in a reliable person or thing. When you sit in your chair, you trust it to hold your weight. When you shake hands with a colleague on a deal, you extend trust. Trust is only as strong as the thing or person trusted. Trust has no power in itself; it is simply the relational glue that attaches us to Christ. We do not make him real by trusting him; we accept the gospel fact by trusting him. The curse that was due to us as lawbreakers was taken in Christ when he died in our place, thereby taking God's curse for us.

We receive this blessing, then, by faith (v. 14), a three-part blessing. We have the blessing of justification; that is, a right standing and a right relationship with God. We have the blessing of life; that is, "eternal life, that they know you the only true God, and Jesus Christ whom you have sent" (John 17:3). We have the blessing of the promised Holy Spirit; that is, the person of God with us and within us in the new birth and walking in the new life by the Spirit. I want to apply all this matter of faith and law very directly.

If, as Christians of long standing, we find that our joy has gone or that we are campaigning for some minor matter while insisting it is major, if we are making our human rules to be of divine origin, if we are, in other words, drifting close to the shores of legalism, then come back. Legalism is a many-headed hydra monster, and it can take many different forms, but all are equally deadly to the life of the Spirit. Be people who pray, read their Bible, and serve those around them because in Christ and by the Spirit they now can please God. But not because they must. The difference is hard to describe, but I know it when I see it. It's the difference between the real thing and a cardboard cutout. It's the difference between a person who loves because he is loved and one who does everything he can to avoid keeping the rules because he feels judged. It's the wife who will do anything for the husband who loves her, or the soldier who will do anything for his captain whom he knows would take a bullet for him.

If we are simply trusting Christ, we must not let anyone say that that faith is simplistic. There are few things more profound than living by faith and walking in the Spirit. If you're someone new to Christian things, don't be surprised! Christianity is really not about culture, or law, or pressure groups, or ideology. In fact, it is not religion at all. Christianity is really only and always about Christ. That should be of great encouragement to you, for I find that when people truly meet Jesus, they end up following him.

18

Gospel and Covenant

*To give a human example, brothers: even with a man-made covenant,
no one annuls it or adds to it once it has been ratified. Now the
promises were made to Abraham and to his offspring. It does not say,
"And to offsprings," referring to many, but referring to one, "And to
your offspring," who is Christ. This is what I mean: the law, which
came 430 years afterward, does not annul a covenant previously
ratified by God, so as to make the promise void. For if the inheritance
comes by the law, it no longer comes by promise; but God gave it to
Abraham by a promise.*

GALATIANS 3:15–18

For the first time in the letter Paul introduces a term that is of great
importance to Christians—*covenant*. It governs our verses here. Paul
uses a human example to explain it, and then he looks in detail at what
the covenant says. Then he asks when it was written in relation to the
law, and then he shows by its very nature that it is by grace, not by
law, for law is not by promise. This is his whole case. He introduces it
here because the Galatians, for all Paul's talk about being justified by
faith, might have been tempted to think that faith was something that
they did.

That's a frequent temptation for us. If it is by faith (not by works),
we can still look at that faith as something we need to drum up or make
happen. We see that tendency down through the ages of the church, and
in many ways it is what the world thinks is what we mean by faith. It
thinks that faith is something we do. It is a projection, a castle in the air
that we imagine. Faith healing is another form of this idea.

That is far from the biblical idea of faith, and Paul now introduces
this topic of the covenant to make sure that we understand that. Faith is
not something we do; it is something that God has done. When you go

to a bank and draw a cashier's check for a certain amount of money and give it to someone, you do not say to the recipient, "What great faith you have," though I suppose in a certain economic climate you might. No, in general you say, "You're just taking money."

A Human Argument

That is a human argument, and Paul is actually using a human argument, though it is a very specific one. The word *covenant* in the Greek translation of the Old Testament was also used for a secular last will and testament. The two words are close in our own language too, but they were identical in that language and culture. So Paul is playing on that, and he uses a human example.

He is asking us to imagine a scene concerning a will. This is quite important because people have often felt that Paul's argument here is very weak. They feel the same about his arguments in the next two verses, but actually his argument here is not weak at all. People say, however, that of course you can add to a human will. People do it all the time. Someone makes a will, then there is a new circumstance, so he changes his will accordingly. It's all quite normal. So, some say, Paul's argument doesn't work.

But that is ridiculous. In fact, people have gone to astonishing lengths to find out whether in Hebrew or Greek culture, wills once made could not be changed. One man has discovered a certain form of will that he thinks could not be changed. He may be right, but all that is quite unnecessary. All we need to realize is what Paul meant when he writes that the last will and testament has been ratified. To my mind, this means the person is dead. You can have the will legally established before you die—in fact, you should if you want to avoid a great burden on others— but it is not until you actually die that the will is sealed, as we would say.

Who changes a will once it is duly established in that sense? The answer is no one. It doesn't matter if you don't like what is in the will. Perhaps you wish you had gotten the porcelain vase. You don't add it in afterwards; that would be quite ridiculous. Perhaps you wish you hadn't got the porcelain vase, but you don't take it out either. It is in the will. A will is one of the most sacred legal documents of the human culture right across all cultures. Paul makes an argument from the minor to the major. He says if that sort of will is sacred, how much more is God's last will and testament to us? We don't need to pretend that he is referring to Jesus' death. I don't think he is. It's an argument by analogy.

Understanding Faith

How does that help us understand what Paul means by "faith"? It tells us that faith is not anything we contribute. It is all of God. It is not works. It is not law. It is God's promise. It cannot be added to or taken away from. That should be of deep encouragement to us. If you are a Christian, your status before God is as certain as the distribution of a person's will after he or she has died. It is not going to change; it cannot change. God has promised. But Paul goes further than that. He notes in verse 16 what specifically is in this will. That's a question worth asking—what does the will actually say? What Paul tells us is that the covenant actually says "Christ." It's not our name on the covenant; it is Christ's name. Christ is the seed.

That goes back to a big part of his argument in terms of what faith is and why it matters. It is not faith plus law but just faith alone. Christ is the recipient of the promise. He is the seed. This means that faith unites us to Christ. Again, it is not our work; it is Christ's work, his death on the cross, his perfect life. We just bind ourselves to him by faith. At the end of the chapter Paul will return to this seed, showing that we are in him and that therefore we are also the seed, but only because we believe in Jesus who is the seed, the promised one.

People misunderstand this when they say that Paul misuses a certain form of grammar called a "collective noun" when he makes a distinction between seed and seeds. Paul understood collective nouns; he used them himself, and he even used this particular collective noun in a more collective sense in various places. They also misunderstand Paul when they think that he doesn't understand that the immediate promise to Abraham was fulfilled in the Promised Land. Of course Paul understood that; he was a Jew, a man of the Promised Land, but he also knew that the full extent of God's promise to Abraham—that all nations through him would be blessed—had never been and could never be fulfilled in the physical land. It was all really about Jesus, through whom salvation would go to the ends of the earth.

An Argument from History

That brings us to Paul's argument from history (v. 17). The promise came before the law; therefore it is by promise, not by law. He is not saying that the law has no purpose; he will go on after verse 19 to explain very clearly what the purpose of the law is, as we shall see. No, he is just saying that promise came first. This is important because it shows that God did not first ask his people to try to be good to win his favor. No, God first gave his favor and then encouraged them to be good. This is always the pattern of salvation.

God comes, saves, and rescues, then the law comes along, and he encourages us to live in a pure relationship with him. But it is not first by law. It is by grace through faith. That is the standard pattern. Paul is also saying by this means that our relationship in the covenant is not conditional upon our obedience to the law. Of course not! The promise came first. The rescue came first. It is conditional on God's promise, not on our works. We are in because God said we are and promised us in. We are not in because we do good things. That would be to turn the whole message of the Bible upside down. It is first by promise, and the promise is salvation, fulfilled in Christ in whom we believe. My salvation now is as certain as Christ's presence in heaven. He is the seed, and I through faith am in him, and therefore if Christ cannot be taken out of heaven, then I cannot either.

Radical Consequences

This is radical stuff, and Paul will answer all the objections that naturally come to our minds about whether that means we can do anything we like. He will answer simply by saying that we are free, but not free to indulge the sinful flesh. We are free to follow God. The unregenerate mind does not understand that distinction, but the person who has been born again does. Unregenerate minds think that sin is freedom. They think that having this grace frees them to do whatever they want, and what they want is to sin against the holy God. But the regenerate person knows far better. That is not freedom; it is bondage. I am not free when I am addicted to drugs, and I am not free when I am addicted to sin. It is a terrible bondage. But Christ has set us free, and we are in him, and therefore by his Spirit who dwells within us, we are able to live a life like his, the fruit of his Spirit. It is all wonderful and glorious, and Paul is just beginning to lay it out here, but I show you the horizon lest you think Paul is saying something which he is not.

Very simply in verse 18 Paul says that the promise and law are mutually exclusive; it cannot be both. No one comes along and says that you don't need faith. They just say it's not faith alone. But if it's not faith alone, then it is faith plus law; and if it is by law, then it is no longer by promise; then it is no longer by faith. The message of faith and works is really a message of work; it is simply legalism. People won't put it like that because it is not attractive, but that was the subtle message of the false teachers who had come to the churches in Galatia, and it is very often the same sort of message preached today, though it takes different forms. Paul just uses logic. If law, then not promise; it can't be both. It is grace; it is a gift.

All this is to make sure they understand what faith is about. Faith is not a work. It is not a combination of faith plus works. It is the covenant, it is the promise, it is God's will. Our faith is not something we magic up, any more than we magic up a million dollars if we just believe it hard enough. Faith is simply accepting that inheritance gratefully and living a changed life as a result.

I want you to see how wonderful it is to live as people of the covenant. Perhaps you do not. Perhaps you are religious but have never understood that it is not by works. So many Christians from good Christian homes spend their lives living as if it is a work, a moral effort, that will get them to heaven. George Whitefield once cried, "Works, Works! A man as soon would get to the moon by a rope of sand as get to heaven by works!" He was always one for creative metaphors, but his point stands. Not only is it impossible, but it is not necessary; it is not how God designed things. He has a will, and the seed of that will is Christ, and if we believe in Christ, then we are the recipients of all that promised blessing.

Perhaps you are a real Christian believer and are looking at the next few months and weeks with trepidation. Some great new challenge is ahead of you, and you're not sure that you are up to it. Well, remember God's covenant with you: "He who calls you is faithful; he will surely do it" (1 Thess. 5:24). I am not saying that Christians never struggle, but I am saying that whatever the struggles may be, every Christian has a perspective on life because of this covenant that frees from the sting of all the troubles in the world. They can walk through fire and not be burned; they can run and not grow weary. It is not fanciful; it is a matter of the Spirit revealing through the Word the real state of affairs. Christ is God's promised seed, I am in Christ, and, therefore, what do I have to worry about? Jeremiah Burroughs put it like this in his reflections on Christian contentment:

> It is no trouble that troubles, but discontent; it is not the water without the ship, but the water that gets within the leak, which drowns it; it is not outward affliction that can make the life of a Christian sad; a contented mind would sail above these waters.

We all have our troubles and fears, but the Christian can float above them and smile at adversity, all because of this covenant and his relationship to Christ, the seed of the covenant.

It is a matter of awesome majesty, this will of God. He has bound himself in Christ to rescue a sinful people. It is a matter of such grandeur and beauty that if we could but touch a tithe of it, it would change our lives and give us such a fresh view of the universe that we would, as it were, walk on air and give our lives with sacrificial joy to all that God has for us. We are a covenant people, we Christians—covenanted, promised, guaranteed, and willed by God himself. All the way back to Abraham, all those thousands of years ago. We are no new creation of the moment, we are not a speck of dust on modernity. We are born in the will of God, and to him be all praise for ever and ever.

19

Gospel and Law

Why then the law? It was added because of transgressions,
until the offspring should come to whom the promise had been made,
and it was put in place through angels by an intermediary.
Now an intermediary implies more than one, but God is one.
Is the law then contrary to the promises of God? Certainly not!
For if a law had been given that could give life, then righteousness
would indeed be by the law. But the Scripture imprisoned everything
under sin, so that the promise by faith in Jesus Christ might be given
to those who believe.

GALATIANS 3:19–22

I used to feel special when someone wanted to be my friend, until I joined Facebook. Now I compare my paltry few hundred with others' thousands. Of course, a true friend *is* special, whether "friended" on Facebook or befriended by more traditional means. A friend has particular permission to point out your faults, because you trust that when he says you have halitosis, it is for your benefit. In the spiritual realm, the straight-talking role of a good friend used to be fulfilled by the local church.

But not so often any more. Themes such as our moral inadequacy before a holy God or our deserved condemnation are noticeable by their absence in the church today. The law of God—moral, ceremonial—revealed in Scripture, as well as revealed generally in our conscience, has been replaced by feel-good preaching with a practical how-to list. Nowadays the message is, to misquote the Black Eyed Peas, "I gotta feeling, this *morning's* gonna be a good *morning*, a *good* morning, a good morning, a good morning," or words to that effect. While growing up I heard sermons on sin from time to time, but I would guess that many of us never, or only occasionally, have done so in the more recent past.

The reasons for that are not hard to guess. Declaring our moral falli-
bility seems offensive; we are told we must be attractive in order to bring
people into the church, so we preach other themes. Ironically, however,
this soft-focus Christianity is producing exactly the reverse effect, and
if you are new to Christian things, you probably know what I mean.
Instead of making the church more attractive, not preaching sin has led
many to associate church with a kind of bumper-sticker cheesiness—or
worse, a moral hypocrisy—which means that while some churches may
be momentarily impressively large, much of the up-and-coming generation associates real moral righteousness more with the Green movement,
or humanitarian nonprofits and the like, instead of with a Bible teaching
church.

Certainly preaching the law can be done legalistically, and to correct that Paul writes to the Galatians. But legalism (the wrong use of the
law) is very different from not preaching for conviction of sin, which
Paul does. More recently we have offered a cheap grace, which has led
to a cheapened Christianity, and—irony piling upon irony—has caused
some to respond with indignation to this cheesy Christianity by preaching the law as the *foundation* for our *salvation*, the exact same misuse
of the law that Paul was correcting in the Galatian churches.

Just as we should not preach the law without preaching the gospel, so we cannot rightly preach the gospel without also preaching for
conviction of sin. The good news has no cache until people understand
the bad news; the remedy is pointless unless there is conviction that the
diagnosis is accurate. As the old graffiti under the poster "Jesus is the
answer" puts it: "but what is the question?"

I once asked some Azerbaijani Christians their technique for their
great evangelistic success. They said this: "We preach to people that
they are sinners *until they believe it*, and then we preach to them that
Christ died for their sins." In contrast, a Western evangelical today
might answer that same question about the secret of outreach success
with "good programs and a large parking lot." Few would talk about
sin, and some shamefully might not mention the cross at all.

So we are left with a generation that has little or no sense of the
value of Christianity. They live as if it *were* cheap, and they are more
likely to give their lives for a trust fund or, somewhat better I suppose,

a humanitarian organization, but rarely for the sacrificial work of the gospel locally and globally.

Paul's Two Questions

All this is addressed by Galatians 3:19–22, as we continue working our way through this most profound of letters. This part of the letter has two questions. I am going to walk us through these two questions, and then we'll see what Paul's answers mean for us today. The two questions are (1) "Why then the law?" (v. 19); and (2) "Is the law then contrary to the promises of God?" (v. 21).

Paul is, as it were, playing devil's advocate. He dramatically puts himself on the interview hot seat of a *60 Minutes* broadcast, or in front of the Larry King desk, and he asks himself rhetorically two questions criticizing what he has been teaching. Paul has been saying that the promise given to Abraham was fulfilled in Christ, and the law does not change that in any way. The question criticizing that, as the Galatian false teachers would have wanted a Larry King to ask, is "What's the point of the law then? You've skipped over Moses, Paul! He's kind of important in the Bible, don't you think?" Paul replies that the law has a different role. It is "because of transgressions," which enigmatic phrase he interprets in verse 22 by saying that Scripture shows we are imprisoned under sin. The law is not for salvation; that is the promise. The law's role is for conviction of sin.

The second hot-seat question follows inevitably from Paul's reply to the first question, which is that the law has a different role from the promise. "If the law has a different role from the promise," a Larry King might ask—and the Galatian false teachers certainly would have— "surely this means that the law *opposes* the promise?" If the role of law is to convict of sin, but the role of the promise is to save, then God appears double-minded. Paul replies with indignation, "Certainly not!" There is one purpose, which is our salvation, but the law and the promise play different *roles* in that one purpose.

To use a crass example, the law is a hammer, not a toothbrush, and hammers are useful things, but you wouldn't be advised to brush your teeth with one. So the law is to show us our sins, while the promise of God's grace through faith in Christ is to save us. Each is important; each

serves the overall purpose of God, but it's essential we use each in its
fitting role: a hammer for hammering in the nail of conviction, and the
promise of the gospel for salvation through faith in Jesus.

Some parts of these verses need further explanation. I do not
apologize for taking a moment to explore this with you, for while some
advertisements assume we are a people who want no context, substance,
or explanation, actually we all know that not everything can be communicated in a "tweet" of 140 characters or less. The second half of
verse 19 and verse 20 are, as one commentator put it, "acknowledged
to be difficult"! After all, who is the mediator? Why does Paul suddenly
say "but God is one" (v. 20) and then not, it seems, finish the sentence?

My take on these difficult few words is that they are underlining
the *subsidiary* role of the law to God's overall salvation purpose. The
mediator here is most probably Moses, who was at the mountain when
the law was given and would otherwise be the elephant in the room of
any discussion of the law. As Bishop Stephen Neil said, Paul is telling us
that the law came "third-hand": from God, through the angels, through
Moses, to us. This underlines the comparison with the promise, which
came directly from God to Abraham. "God is one," Paul then says,
appealing to a central teaching of the Old Testament and showing that
in the law and the promise God has one purpose of salvation, as he is
one. It may even be that Paul, in this way, is counteracting a rhetoric
of the Galatian false teachers. "Look," they might have said, "the law
came by angels," to which Paul replies, "Yes, it did, and through an
intermediary as well, whereas God's promise was given directly to
Abraham and fulfilled in God himself in Christ."

That's how I understand it, but if you interpret these few words in
a slightly different way, be encouraged that a commentator in the nine-
teenth century estimated that even by that time there were 350 or so
different interpretations! It doesn't make much difference to the overall
meaning of the passage as long as we see the point, which is that Paul
is answering these critical questions by saying that the law does not
change the promise, because the role of the law is different from that of
the promise, and so God's overall purpose for our salvation ("God is
one") is consistent.

Those are his two hot-seat questions and his two compelling

answers, which emphasize the overall consistent purpose of God throughout. To use another analogy, say you were driving along a road after a storm, and the stoplights were broken. A policeman would come and gesticulate to beckon traffic. You need him there, you might say, "because of transgressions." We are a people, because of the storm of the fall, who will transgress and bump into each other and cannot and will not keep the rules before a holy God. Therefore, we need the policeman of the law. But that is not the final purpose. The fact that the policeman is there tells us that someone is coming to fix the lights. It's an analogy that certainly isn't perfect, but it gets at the point of the different roles of the law and the promise that Paul is explaining here by means of his two hot-seat questions and his two compelling answers.

We have listened to Paul getting grilled by the Galatian false teachers' version of Jay Leno or Larry King or Diane Sawyer, but this is not really an intellectual fight club sparring debate. Now it's more like a friend coming alongside us and speaking personally and straightforwardly, for our benefit, about what this means for us today. First, it means something for how we look at ourselves. Second, it means something for how we look at God. Third, it means something for how we do church. Those are the three areas the "friend" wants us to see in the light of this teaching about the distinct role of the law in God's overall salvation purpose.

How We Look at Ourselves

The friend tells us to look in the mirror, for it is clear that the Bible's view of humanity is vastly different from man's contemporary view. The Bible is not trying to make us feel bad or give us a sense of psychological inadequacy that, however good we try to be, we can never be good enough. It is not fostering a psychological condition of atelophobia, the fear of imperfection. The Bible recognizes we are wonderful, full of great worth, made in the image of God, of enough value to God that he shed his blood for us. The doctrine of total depravity is not an excuse for control-freak preachers to manipulate their congregations, nor is it a Freudian super-ego fostered by a great-parent myth to inhibit our true natural desires. It is simply the state of things as they are; our sinful condition does not mean things are as bad as they could possibly be, but even the good things are terribly tainted.

Humans can do the most wonderful activities. They can build skyscrapers and foster communities, but each and every one of even the best of our endeavors is riven with a fault line as large as the San Andreas Fault. Each Tower of Babel is a testimony not only to our divine image but also to our fallen pride. Yet we are largely oblivious to this. Ours is not the first age, and it will not be the last, should the good Lord tarry, to have lived in glorious and blissful ignorance of the true state of things. Part of our condition is not only that we are not good but *that we think we are.*

That is why the law is preached. Ours is a medical condition that is not obvious. It has some symptoms, but those symptoms could indicate a less serious condition, so our condition requires an X-ray diagnosis, a CT scan—the law—by the work of the Spirit to reveal just how far short of God's standards we are.

A man who came to Christ told me that the start for him was the realization that he did not live up to his own standards. When we began to look at God's standards, he realized more deeply the condition of the human heart. According to a recent poll, half of all Americans believe they are good enough to go to heaven. I am surprised it is such a small figure, and in fact I would suspect that deep down most of us feel that we are good enough for heaven. The curse of the fall of Adam is not just to be shut out of Eden but to believe that we have the right to determine good and evil.

You may say that religion is no solution, for the church has done wicked things at times, and who would I be to deny it? But then so have atheistic regimes such as the Nazis, and what the history of the world teaches us is that under the guise of good and bad philosophies, the human condition remains the same. We are jokers trying to play Hamlet, we are Lady Macbeth tortured not by fake guilt but by real.

That is the condition of our humanity, and it is important to preach that from every pulpit, for as Dietrich Bonhoeffer said, "It is only when one submits to the law that one can speak of grace. . . . I don't think it is Christian to want to get to the New Testament too soon and too directly." Galatians was written to *Christians*, so the point of this is not just to bring us to Christ for the first time but to make us realize that the ground of our salvation is such a sweet thing that we would taste it as one who has before been feeding on pig husks. It will lead us to live a life of renewed praise to God, in service and devotion, in children's ministries, in mission, in pastoral labor for God—all our gifts at the service of our heavenly Father.

How We Look at God

The friend tells us that the distinction between law and promise in God's overall salvation purpose also tells us something about God. God is a saving God. His purpose throughout time, throughout the Bible— through Abraham and Moses to Jesus Christ—is to rescue those who believe. God is self-sufficient; he needs nothing and depends on no one. In him we live and move and have our being, and by him the universe was created and has its constancy. He is big enough for the taste of a world-renowned cosmologist and small enough for a hovel in the jungle. This God has designed all of life so that we who believe might be righteous, saved. Is this the God we worship, the God who died for us? We do not have a false god who doesn't care about us. Give the God of the Bible renewed thanks and praise today.

How We Look at Church

This brings us (the friend says) to how we do church. We need to learn much from Paul today. Paul brings together the whole of Scripture, from Abraham, to Moses, to Christ, under one heading—namely, salvation— and says it all leads to faith in Jesus Christ. That is a grand vision of the purpose of the Bible, which we are to preach and believe and teach. He unashamedly proclaims the message of Bible by means of the law. He imprisons under sin that we might be freed from that prison by faith. We are to preach that too. We are not to heal God's people too lightly, as the false prophets did, but to expose our wound that the sweet salve of God's healing oil might bind up the brokenhearted. We are not to cry "peace, peace" where there is no peace, but to say "flee from the wrath to come" and "hide yourself in Jesus."

Our churches, as our Bibles, are not to be about any other agenda but Christ, salvation, and faith. In short, we are to counteract the great tendency toward cheap grace and cheesy Christianity by being people who stare at the wounds of Christ and the cross and say, "It was for my sins that he hung there," and then rejoice that he is risen. In his resurrection power we are to live a life in the Spirit that authenticates God's purpose in Christ that we might be saved by faith, not by law.

Cities are a blur of human light; when we look at the night sky from within a city we see a vague orange tinge. But turn down the lights. Let me paint the human condition as black as it is. I am not just talking about concentration camps and torture chambers, or abduction of eleven-year-old girls and murder, but about our self-hate, the vicious snide remarks that we make and realize we did it because we liked it. We heap up our resources while others starve. Let me turn down the lights. Come away with me from the human fluorescent glow of our selfish ambition and our petty greed. Cut the power of human shining. Come out to the desert. Come out to the trees where it is so black you cannot see the hand in front of your face. This is the purpose of the law. Then look up, look up at the night sky, and see the myriad stars shining with the promise of Abraham and know that the light of God's grace in Christ is shining on you—if you believe.

20

Living in the Light of the Gospel

Now before faith came, we were held captive under the law,
imprisoned until the coming faith would be revealed. So then,
the law was our guardian until Christ came, in order that we might be
justified by faith. But now that faith has come, we are no longer under
a guardian, for in Christ Jesus you are all sons of God, through faith.
For as many of you as were baptized into Christ have put on Christ.
There is neither Jew nor Greek, there is neither slave nor free,
there is no male and female, for you are all one in Christ Jesus.
And if you are Christ's, then you are Abraham's offspring, heirs
according to promise.

GALATIANS 3:23–29

The day came when Michael Jackson was finally buried. In retrospect, the King of Pop, as he became known, not only wrote famous hit songs such as *Thriller* but also sparked controversy, accusation, and speculation. Even friendly interviewers such as Michael Bashir wondered, as they questioned the unique phenomenon that was Michael Jackson, whether his abbreviated and traumatic childhood had led him to be a lifelong Peter Pan, to be unhealthily fixated on childhood and children. Surely, some apparently felt, it was no accident that Jackson's massive theme park and personal ranch was called *Neverland*, Peter Pan's home for the boy who never grew up.

In Galatians 3:23–29 Paul encourages the Galatians to live in the light of *mature* spiritual reality. He wants them to grow into the realization of what has *already* taken place with Christ's death and resurrection. Before Christ (or BC), under the Law of Moses, life was a certain way. Now, after Christ (or what our calendar calls AD) things have changed. Paul says that the Galatians are not to live BC, or under Moses, but AD, in the light of the coming of Jesus Christ.

I was alerted to the way in which we humans sometimes find it hard to catch up with a new reality, when reading through the autobiography of the former director of the FBI, Louis Freeh. One of the points Freeh makes in his book *My FBI* is that prior to 9/11 we lived as if the terrorist threat was not that serious when in fact all the evidence, he believed, showed that it was very much a real and present danger. Humans seem to have the capacity to live in the past experientially, even though that past is gone; the human mind allows us to live as if things were not that are, and as if things are that are not. Paul says that a big change in salvation history has taken place: you are no longer a child, you have grown up; therefore, let live that way. This is post 9/11, not pre 9/11; we must not do our accounting as if Enron never took place. In the same way, we don't live under Moses (BC) but in Christ (AD).

Of course, this is a call for those of us who do not yet follow Jesus to enter in to AD, but amazingly, even as Christians in a Christian community, it is possible to live in some respects as if we were BC. Christ has come, but the Galatian Christians were still leaning toward living BC, not AD, and, in fact, their resident false teachers seemed to think that living BC was the solution to the Galatians' present spiritual ails. So the message from this passage is to live AD, not BC. We are going to look first at what life is like BC and then at what life is like AD. The passage is structured around a massive shift that has taken place. Verse 23 to the first part of verse 24 is BC, and the second half of verse 24 all the way to verse 29 is AD.

BC

"Now before faith came, we were held captive under the law, imprisoned until the coming faith would be revealed. So then, the law was our guardian until Christ came" (vv. 23–24a). Living BC, then, is living under the law, which, Paul says, is like being "imprisoned" and like having the law guard us. Those are his two pictures of what it is like to live BC, being a prisoner and having someone else as guardian over us.

The first picture is familiar to modern eyes. Paul talks of being "held captive," which refers to being a prisoner. But having the law as a "guardian" is one of those ancient phrases that has no direct equivalent in the English language, so it is hard to get the picture. This phrase adds to the sense of imprisonment in another way: relating the role of the law broadly to discipline in ancient schooling. A *paidagogus* was a slave whose job it was to make sure that a schoolboy got to and from his lessons and behaved properly. A *paidagogus* was, then, a disciplinarian, usually depicted in the ancient world carrying a rod or a stick, and was capable of being very strict or even cruel. Once a child had grown up, a *paidagogus* was no longer necessary. A *paidagogus* was for the childhood season of life, for schooldays. He was not the teacher or the tutor but the disciplinarian. The closest concept in modern life (but by no means a direct equivalent) that I can come up with is that of school security. School security personnel are sometimes there to provide discipline at schools, and at least in that regard they were similar to the harsh discipline of a *paidagogus*, though I am sure school security is rather more sophisticated today.

To get the picture crystal clear, it is worth knowing that Paul uses the same word in 1 Corinthians 4:15: "For though you have countless guides [*paidagogus*] in Christ, you do not have many fathers. For I became your father in Christ Jesus through the gospel." The word there, whether translated "guide," "tutor," or "guardian," is the same. Paul says that even though the Corinthian Christians have ten thousand people to discipline them, they have only him as a father to love and nurture them. He then carries the same picture on to further clarity: "What do you wish? Shall I come to you with a rod [that is, like a *paidagogus*], or with love in a spirit of gentleness [that is, like a father]?" (1 Cor. 4:21).

So being under the law, living BC, is like being in prison and being disciplined by school security, or literally by the *paidagogus*. BC is to be in jail and whipped by your *paidagogus*. Why is living under the law like this? It is because the law tells us how we should live as well as what the penalties are for our disobedience. We have all disobeyed, so we are under its just condemnation, in prison and having the law put in charge of us. BC reality, then, is like a jailer throwing us into prison and like a *paidagogus* rebuking and punishing us for our misdeeds.

Living under the law is living in prison and under judgment. We do it to ourselves, and then we do it to others. We whip ourselves for our imperfections and failures, making ourselves feel bad. Then, with the inner turmoil boiling, we judge others for their children or spouses, for their tastes or their talents. It was never meant to be thus. Living as a godly Israelite in Old Testament times was not legalistic; salvation was always by faith because the promise came first. But trying to live BC, under Moses, when Christ has arrived is legalism, for it is trying to use the law to save when it was meant to prepare for Christ's coming. When we use the law that way, we are spiritual adults reverting to Peter Pan in *Neverland*. We strain at a gnat while swallowing the camel of being judgmental, because we ourselves feel judged. It can lead to pathetic frustration, caricatured on television by Pastor Lovejoy of *The Simpsons*, who feels anything but love or joy, goes through the motions, and is constantly frustrated by the sickly piety of Ned Flanders. It is not freedom; it is prison. It does not make people good; it beats them up.

AD

An AD community, on the other hand, is quite different, for it lives in the light of the coming of Christ. The Galatians passage tells us that the law leads us to Christ "in order that we might be justified by faith. But now that faith has come, we are no longer under a guardian, for in Christ Jesus you are all sons of God, through faith. For as many of you as were baptized into Christ have put on Christ. There is neither Jew nor Greek, there is neither slave nor free, there is no male and female, for you are all one in Christ Jesus. And if you are Christ's, then you are Abraham's offspring, heirs according to promise" (vv. 24b–29).

Living AD, in Christ, gives us a new relationship with God, and because of this new relationship, we have a new relationship to the law and a new relationship to each other. The mature Christian life is relational, not legal. The new relationship doesn't mean we must sing what some disparage as "Jesus is my boyfriend" songs; rather, it means the difference between having to be made to do something and doing something because we want to. The law convicts, controls, and delivers the righteous judgment of God against us. But in Christ we are sons. We are in a family relationship with God now. We live freely to please God, not feeling forced to do what we do not want to do. Paul describes this new relationship with God that we have in Christ, and therefore our new relationship to the law and the new relationship we have to each other.

We have a new relationship with God, Paul says, because we are justified by faith. Justification was always by faith, for, as Galatians 3:6 tells us, Abraham believed God and it was credited to him (or imputed to him) as righteousness. In that sense it is not new. But now that Christ has arrived, the operation of this justification by faith (or by Christ, for the word faith is used interchangeably with Christ here) has been revealed. The cross works backward and forward in history. Abraham was saved by faith through the cross, though he looked forward to it, and we are saved by faith through the cross though we look back to it. The law tells us we deserve to die. Christ died our death. Therefore we are saved by Christ, or justified by faith, which is the same thing.

Justification by faith alone is simply another way of saying that Jesus saves us. We now enjoy God as our Father, and we are sons and inheritors of his promised blessing fulfilled in Jesus. The Bible does not teach the doctrine of the universal fatherhood of God so that everyone can rightly call God father. Only if we are in Christ then is God truly our Father. We have this new relationship with God.

Because of that, we also have a new relationship to the law. We are no longer under the *paidagogus*, the guardian, of the law. Not being under the law does not mean that we are not held responsible to God's moral standards. It means that because the Spirit has come, we now have a new, inner (mature) desire to please God, a new heart and spirit. The law says, "You must," but we find we cannot. Christ says, "With me you can," and we find that by his Spirit we do and we want to do. Christians still sin, but they no longer like their sin, and if they are really in Christ, they gradually become more like him and follow his moral standards increasingly. That is why the most miserable person on the face of the planet is a sinning Christian; a pagan enjoys his sin, but a Christian does not, and it leaves him in an inner battle. Because of our new relationship to God as our Father through faith alone in Christ, we have a new relationship to the law.

We also have a new relationship to each other, Paul explains profoundly (vv. 26–29). We are now all one in Christ, we are "heirs" and "sons," with the full rights of those in the ancient world who could inherit all the blessings of the father. These verses are full of Christ. Baptism is a sign that we are *in Christ*. We are sons and therefore heirs because we are Abraham's seed, and we are Abraham's seed because we

are *in Christ*, who is Abraham's seed. We are all *in Christ* irrespective
of race, gender, and status. Paul is not saying that race, gender, and status no longer exist, which would be plainly untrue. There are different
races, and there are different genders. He says that in Christ they no
longer matter. Male nor female, slave nor free, Jew nor Greek—none is
a barrier to fellowship in Christ.

Paul is not talking about our different roles, which he addresses
elsewhere in the Bible, but about our equal value in Christ irrespective
of different roles. Galatians 3:28 does not overturn the creation order
of Genesis 1 and 2, but it does redeem the fallen state of Genesis 3. It is
against male misogynism as well as female clawing, it is against employers abusing their employees and employees abusing their employers.
Within the fixed realities of gender, status, and race, it is calling us to a
deeper and higher reality whereby we look at each other as all equally
one in Christ irrespective of the differences of race, gender, or status.

So, living in the AD reality of Christ's death and resurrection means
to live as sons of a heavenly Father, with a desire to please him in every
way, and with a fellowship unbroken by the barriers we construct
between each other, whether gender wars, racial tension, or class distinction. We, in Christ, are one. Paul says there has been this big change in
salvation history from BC to AD, and therefore the Galatians are not to
live BC when now they are in AD. BC is prison; BC is beating up yourself and others. It is living legalistically under the law. AD is freedom;
it is a new relationship to God, a new desire to please him, and a new
fellowship with others.

Of course, sometimes living AD is easier said than done. Chicago has
the "L" and New York the subway, so London has the Underground or
the Tube. One of the characteristic sounds of the London Underground
is the voice over the public address system, which, when the train stops
at a station, says, "Mind the gap," meaning, "Watch out for the small
space between the train and the platform." My guess is that most of us
do not live BC, but then I would also guess that few of us live fully AD
either. Perhaps what we most need to do is mind the gap.

In the gap we can say the right things and feel the wrong things. We
live with the shadow of self-criticism and judgment and pass on those
same feelings to others. We do not live fully in the freedom of the gospel

of Jesus Christ. My intuition is that too often we are like the Galatians, who were planted by the apostle Paul himself and surely well taught, yet tempted to add law to faith as a solution to the feelings that we are not sufficiently moral. We hear of evangelical leaders who compromise, and statistics seem to suggest that we are not much more moral than anyone else, so we add rules or structure, or speak prophetically against individualism, or come up with a system for church that will effectively control behavior. Appropriate in their place as those may on occasion be, perhaps what we really need to do is mind the gap. To live more fully AD, we do not need more Moses but to go through Moses to Christ.

When we don't do that, when we exist in the in-between world that reverts to the law from Christ rather than goes through the law to Christ, we tend to draw the line in the wrong places. We might keep our distance from the "Greeks," or the socioeconomic class that feels uncomfortable to us, perhaps less as a conscious choice but more as a matter of habit. We righteously frown on beer, but we suffer creative speculation on the doctrine of the Trinity; we legislate against smoking, but we play with the core doctrine of justification; we are hard line on inerrancy, but we turn off the lights when the "Greeks" from the other side of the tracks come to play basketball at the church. All along there are even bigger fish to fry. Our children statistically live with higher levels of anxiety than the average child psychiatric patient did in the 1950s, as North Korea tests its nuclear options and the jobless rate rises to a twenty-six-year high.

We keep on looking to Moses for salvation, or at least in the gap, stuck betwixt and between. Instead, we should go through Moses to Christ, and then rest in Jesus. Be one in him. Heirs, sons, no longer living in the past guilt of sins committed long ago but in the present AD reality of Christ and his righteousness. A seismic shift *has* taken place. A new time *has* arrived. It is not Neverland, the home of the boy who never grew up, guarded by security, but Abraham's land, the Promised Land, the place where you can be free. This is the land that, in Christ, you have inherited; it is your home now, your family, and it's time to live AD, not BC.

I spent about ten years studying in Cambridge in the United Kingdom. Cambridge is a unique place. It is filled with dreamy spires, dons (elsewhere known as professors) leaning atop creaking bicycles, gondola-like boats called "punts" drifting down the river Cam, libraries stuffed with books, and villages positively bursting with roses and bonhomie. It is a little idyllic at times. Near my college was one of Cambridge's many expanses of open grass, this one called Parker's Piece. In the middle of Parker's Piece is a lamppost. For some reason, once you get to the other side of Parker's Piece it feels as if you are more on the town side of Cambridge rather than on the university side, certainly no less Cambridge but not an ivory tower anymore. Scratched onto this lamp post, symbolically placed in many people's minds as being between the university and the real life beyond, are the words "Reality Checkpoint." When you pass the lamppost, supposedly, you enter reality.

Real life is usually thought to be worse than our dreams. I suppose that is why fantasies and science fiction are so popular. But what if the reverse were true? What if actually we only felt that we were controlled by hideous machines of fate when the reality—for Christians—is that we are free? Certainly we are not in heaven yet, and so Abraham's land has not yet been fully realized. Christ has come, but he is still to come again. We do not want an over-realized eschatology, in the language of theologians, a rather painful-sounding disease.

Most of us, I would guess, are more like the Galatians who had a sneaking suspicion that reality is *worse* than our dream, when, if we could but go through Reality Checkpoint, we would see a beautiful land, a land flowing with milk and honey—not the "Sounds sticky to me" of Veggie Tales but bursting with life and opportunity. Perhaps our greatest sin is not our petty moral failures, bad as they are, but the murmuring that we internalize as if the Promised Land was not good. We are still to be revealed as the sons we will be in the age to come, yet now, in the here and now, we live in the true reality of a life far more beautiful and filled with awe than any other could be.

We have access to God through faith in Christ. We are forgiven. We are righteous. We are pure. We have no condemnation. We are one, black and white, Jew and Greek, rich and poor, male and female. That's quite a dream, and if you're a Christian, it's the reality.

21

Gospel versus Religion

I mean that the heir, as long as he is a child, is no different from a slave, though he is the owner of everything, but he is under guardians and managers until the date set by his father. In the same way we also, when we were children, were enslaved to the elementary principles of the world. But when the fullness of time had come, God sent forth his Son, born of woman, born under the law, to redeem those who were under the law, so that we might receive adoption as sons. And because you are sons, God has sent the Spirit of his Son into our hearts, crying, "Abba! Father!" So you are no longer a slave, but a son, and if a son, then an heir through God.

GALATIANS 4:1–7

When you first hear the song *Losing My Religion* by R.E.M., you get the sense of someone losing his faith. Mind you, Wikipedia, that source of all Internet knowledge, tells us that the song is really about losing one's temper, but it certainly has become a phrase waved by, for instance, journalist William Lobdell when he wrote a book about his disillusionment with religion.

> That's me in the corner
> That's me in the spotlight
> Losing my religion.

Many people seem to be doing so. In some countries in the West, former churches have become Indian restaurants, bars, bingo halls, even nightclubs. Behind this, of course, are not only well-known proponents of atheism, such as Richard Dawkins and Christopher Hitchens, who are attempting to make full-blown secularism intellectually compelling. There is also a major movement of our society away from the modern and rational, which is viewed as being connected to the age of institutional churches and toward the postmodern and relativistic.

Religion is viewed as the cause of many ills, the source behind many wars, and that which imprisons, even enslaves, and keeps society in a state of evil bondage. But it is surprising to find that the apostle Paul talks about religion in much the same way in our passage. There is a certain form of religion, he writes, that is "enslaved to the elementary principles of the world" (v. 3). In case we think he is just talking about Old Testament religion, itself shocking enough, he uses the same phrase later in verse 9, where he talks about the Galatian Gentiles' former pagan religion. "How can you turn back again," he writes, "to the weak and worthless elementary principles of the world?"

According to the Bible, contrary to what people like Dawkins or Lobdell seem to expect, not all religion is a good thing. In fact, some of it is a terrible thing. There's more than a hint of a suggestion here that Paul views some forms of religion as positively devilish, "enslaved to those that by nature are not gods" (v. 8), and there is more than a possibility that the elemental principles twice referred to are not just basic but are those which are viewed as demonic. The movie *The Golden Compass*, from Pullman's His Dark Materials series of books, could not have characterized religion more negatively, even in the magisterium and all the horrible things it gets up to. Religion—this form of religion, which he defines—is like being a slave, Paul says. It is like being held back in immaturity and not going on to adult spirituality.

Now, obviously, the Bible is *for* some form of religion, but what sort is it? C. S. Lewis described his conversion as moving from Religion A to Religion B. Lewis grew up going to chapel and church regularly. He was religious in an outward sense, but it held no meaning for him. I'm not sure he would have described it as slavery, but as someone who went to a nominal Christian Anglican boarding school, where chapel was mandated every morning, I think some who went through that experience might have objected to the mandatory attendance even as some sort of slavery.

When a journalist returned from being imprisoned by a terrorist organization, he was asked what it had been like, and he replied that compared to being at Eton it was a breeze, no doubt jokingly. There is a kind of numbing that happens to you through overexposure. You can get so used to the cant phrases, good in themselves but killed through misuse, that religion in this sense can become a kind of perfect devil's inoculation against the real thing. When you have been overexposed to Religion A, it can be very difficult to spot Religion B.

If you don't lose your religion, in the sense of giving up on God altogether, you can end up loosening your religious ties. Church becomes something you have to do. God becomes a tool. Ministry becomes a profession. It can all seem a bit, well, like slavery, like having to be immature and not being allowed to grow up. So we begin to look for a way out. We question some of the core doctrines of our faith. We try to reshape our confession to allow us "out," to deal with this postmodern age in which we live. We react against something, and, in all likelihood, that thing is religion, in Paul's sense of that which enslaves. What we need instead is not a loss of faith in God but a true faith in God.

Paul contrasts for the Galatians the difference between religion and Christianity. I can think of no more important matter for the Western church today, and no more important matter for all of us. I, too, am one who, as perhaps in an especial way handles holy things all the time, may become religious-ified rather than more and more Christ-like. We learn the phrases and develop the habits, but that can sometimes lead us further away from the real Christianity that Paul talks about here. Verses 1–3 is religion, which is contrasted with Christianity in verses 4–7.

Religion

Religion is child-like and slave-like: "I mean that the heir, as long as he is a child, is no different from a slave, though he is the owner of everything, but he is under guardians and managers until the date set by his father. In the same way we also, when we were children, were enslaved to the elementary principles of the world" (vv. 1–3). Some will say this is only about what used to be the case in the Old Testament, but that is not Paul's point. Why would he tell them something that had no direct relevance to them? Paul uses the same phrase, "elementary principles," for Old Testament religion as he does for pagan religion (v. 9). No, Paul is not giving the Galatians a history lesson on how things used to be. He says this is a real and present danger.

The Old Testament was revealed by God, and pagan religion is against the true doctrine of God. But Paul's point is that when we use the law for that which it was not intended, it becomes to us just like pagan religion. It may have a different form or different doctrines theoretically, but it actually becomes just another religion. That is, it becomes another attempt to justify ourselves by our moral, religious, or ceremonial activities.

I can take the best thing from God, and in my human pride make it something that offends God. I can take a sermon and feel justified because I preached well. I can take a marriage and feel justified because I have a good marriage. I can take a church and feel justified because I am a member of a church. Those in themselves are good things, but I am using them in a way that, in the most important and essential sense, is no different from the pagan religion that seeks to please the gods by various magic, moral, or ritual activities.

The point here is that we are hardwired legalists, something that goes all the way back to Genesis 3. We assert our own morality and blame others for our sins. This is the very nature of what it means to be outside the favor of God. The person who thinks he is pleasing God by his own efforts, whether or not he thinks they are divinely inspired, is farthest from the grace of God. Martin Luther said, "When the devil cannot ruin people by making them worse, he will ruin them by making them better." The road to hell is not so much paved with good intentions as it is paved with self-justification. "I have not done anything wrong. I'm no worse than anyone else. I have kept the rules."

This is the kind of religion we are meant to lose. The Bible wants us to lose this religion. The purpose of the law was for our minority, to convict us of our sin that we might turn to Christ for his righteousness by faith. This is the religion that causes wars. This religion is an assertion of natural pride. This religion does not care for the poor because it thinks their poverty is always their fault. In contrast, George Whitefield founded an orphanage. In contrast, Charles Spurgeon founded an orphanage. In contrast, the church ministers to the disabled, to the disadvantaged, to people of all races and backgrounds. Religion is like a magnifying glass to the problem of the human condition. It makes it worse. It takes our natural human pride and invests in it religious pride.

It shields us from self-criticism and from our basic natural human compassion; it makes us judgmental and hypercritical of others.

Christianity is nothing like that. Lose your religion. Go ahead, that's you in the corner, the spotlight's on you. Lose it. You have my permission. Put away the idea that your works are necessary for your justification.

Christianity

In contrast there is Christianity:

> But when the fullness of time had come, God sent forth his Son, born of woman, born under the law, to redeem those who were under the law, so that we might receive adoption as sons. And because you are sons, God has sent the Spirit of his Son into our hearts, crying, "Abba! Father!" So you are no longer a slave, but a son, and if a son, then an heir through God. (vv. 4–7)

This is not really religion at all. Religion is child-like; humans tell us what to do. Religion is slave-like; a system tells us what to do. It is the elementary principles of the world. It is basic in the sense of the ABCs, the constituent elements, of the universe, *and* the elemental spirits, the idea of different gods who are not really gods. Very broadly speaking, the phrase has a little of both suggestions in it. That's religion, but look at Christianity!

Christianity is God doing something. Religion starts with man; Christianity starts with God. In some parts of the contemporary church, a program is created for every problem. There's nothing wrong with programs as long as they do not stop us thinking primarily in terms of our communion with God. That means you need to start with God. You start each day with God. You start your decisions with God. You pray. You wait. You listen. God is real. He is speaking. He is here. Christianity is God doing something. It's not a religious philosophy with pragmatic tips for a better life.

It is centered on *Jesus*, "God sent forth his Son" (v. 4). When life is God-centered, it starts with God, and when we become God-centered, it means we are Jesus-centered, for Jesus is whom God sent to redeem us. A sure sign of religion creeping in is the lack of the name of Jesus. Oh, give me Jesus, give me Jesus. A woman from the church I pastored in New Haven was heard constantly saying, "It's all about Jesus, it's all about Jesus," which used to annoy the Yale Divinity School students but was very good for them. It's all about Jesus. You need to ask yourself when visiting a church, "Could all this be done in a synagogue? Where's the name of Jesus, where is the Son?" Is the cross there, and redemption? So much of religion today, even apparently evangelical religion, is marginalizing the cross and Christ. It's all about him. He is sufficient. You need no other.

Christianity gives dignity to adherents. We have adoption as sons; we are heirs, inheritors. Religion dehumanizes. That's how you spot it. When I become more holy, I will not become less human; I will become more human. I now have the full adoption of a son. I am an inheritor of all the blessings of heaven. I can lift my head up high. No more groveling in the ditch. No more false Uriah-Heep kind of self-recriminated human humility that is really self-abasement. I may not have been born to a rich family so as to inherit wealth, but as a Christian I have something far better than that—I have been adopted.

A healthy church, then, constantly treats Christians well. That does not mean we do not sometimes discipline Christians. It means that we do, for we treat them well, with dignity; we love enough to confront. A healthy church has an atmosphere in which the one put to the forefront is not the man with the golden ring and the purple tunic or the one with the connections or the right amount of money. We have spiritual values, and we value Christians for Christ's sake. God does not simply get us to use us for his glory in a manipulative sense; his glory exists in our redemption and in our standing as his sons. He is like a father whose pleasure comes from our blessing, our redemption.

Christianity, as opposed to religion, emphasizes the work of the Spirit. Because we are sons, God sent his Spirit into our hearts, the Spirit who cries out "Abba! Father!" (4:6). There are two sendings here: the sending of the Son to redeem and the sending of the Spirit into the redeemed. There is a magic and a mystery to my personal relationship with God the Father. In our hearts, that is, in the center of our being, who we are as people, as Christians, is the silent calling of the Spirit constantly affirming our special son status and the privilege of being able to have God as our Father. The Spirit is the Spirit of his Son, Jesus, and the Spirit points away from himself to Jesus and calls out from himself to the Father, to whom we have access by the work of Christ.

Christianity, then, as opposed to religion, has intimacy with God as Father. This fact is the great secret of many a successful navigation of painful and problematic moments in our spiritual journeys. My son is autistic. He was diagnosed with autism when he was two, and he is now eight and doing well. I am so pleased with him. He works hard. He's a good helper. He has his moments (we all do), but he has been blessed with an appealing character and a determination to work hard. Yet he is autistic. It is a sadness that never goes away. It is a grief to which you can never say good-bye. There is a very real sense in which, at an emotional level, it would have been easier for my wife, Rochelle, and me to see him die. Instead, we watched a boy's thriving die every day, and then very slowly crawled back bits of him from his prison. To say it has been painful is like saying that running a marathon is hard work, or that gravity means things fall to the ground, or that it's cold in winter in Chicagoland. Of course it's been painful, but the spiritual pain—that's something different altogether. What do you do with it? Where do you put your agony for your son?

The turning point for me came when I got away. I went up into a hill by myself to think and pray. I went to get some quiet and actually got interrupted by a school outing of shouting children. When I was by myself I finally said to the Lord, "You can do anything. If I could do anything, I would heal my son, so why won't you? I would give my right arm to make him better." Then the thought entered my head, as I said those words, that of course what, on the other hand, would it be like to be a father who was able to stop his son from hurting but instead sent his son into the face of harm to redeem someone else. I was talking to a Father. I was a dad talking to a Dad. At some level, I got what he felt, and I knew that he got what I felt. And it made sense.

I'm not suggesting that we're all going to have voices in our heads of what God says—"God told me to do it" is often the ultimate trump card or another way of saying with pseudo-religious double-talk, "I really want to do it"— but I am saying we need to relate to God as Father, to tell him, to hear the father heart of God, and to hear the Spirit calling out within us, "Abba! Father!"

That's Christianity, thoroughly Trinitarian—Father, Son, and Holy Spirit—in action redeeming, sending, and being sent. God at work, us relating to him. A day-by-day journey. It is very different from religion. Perhaps the first step in your re-finding your Christianity will be to lose your religion. I encourage you to do so.

22

The Gospel and Formalism

Formerly, when you did not know God, you were enslaved to those that by nature are not gods. But now that you have come to know God, or rather to be known by God, how can you turn back again to the weak and worthless elementary principles of the world, whose slaves you want to be once more? You observe days and months and seasons and years! I am afraid I may have labored over you in vain. Brothers, I entreat you, become as I am, for I also have become as you are. You did me no wrong. You know it was because of a bodily ailment that I preached the gospel to you at first, and though my condition was a trial to you, you did not scorn or despise me, but received me as an angel of God, as Christ Jesus. What then has become of the blessing you felt? For I testify to you that, if possible, you would have gouged out your eyes and given them to me. Have I then become your enemy by telling you the truth?

GALATIANS 4:8–16

Pain is highly subjective. Your pain is not my pain, and I can never feel your pain. Yet we all know what pain is. Hospitals—particularly for children, but also for adults—have developed diagrammatic scales (one called the face scale or the "oucher") to help communicate a patient's pain to his or her doctor. At one extreme there is a smiley face and at the other is a face with the mouth turned right down and a tear running down the cheek. Is the pain stabbing, throbbing, or burning?

However much we do not like pain, pain is necessary. It indicates that something is wrong. It protects us from seriously burning our hand when we touch something hot. The terrible disease of leprosy tells us that, without fully functioning pain receptors, we end up badly damaging our bodies for lack of the early warning signal that is pain. Pain is a very important diagnostic tool.

In Galatians 4:8–16 Paul is, if you like, using two diagnostic tools to help the Galatians understand their situation. They "observe days and months and seasons and years!" (v. 10). That is one of his diagnostics that something is wrong with them. The other is found in verse 15: "What then has become of the blessing you felt?" Paul is like a pastor with a good medical bedside manner. He is sitting on the bed next to the patient, the Galatian church, and he tells the people that they observe all these days and seasons and months, but they are lacking the joy, that blessing, that they'd had.

Legalism is in some respects a bit like leprosy. Not only is it bad for you, but also it works by taking away the pain that indicates something is wrong. So you need someone like Paul, a good doctor of the soul, to come along and point out the pain. He's bringing the scale of faces and helping them to see that they are in pain; there really is an issue here.

Formalism

The first diagnostic is discussed from verses 8 through 11 and centers on verse 10:

> Formerly, when you did not know God, you were enslaved to those that by nature are not gods. But now that you have come to know God, or rather to be known by God, how can you turn back again to the weak and worthless elementary principles of the world, whose slaves you want to be once more? You observe days and months and seasons and years! I am afraid I may have labored over you in vain.

He is talking about how when we Christians degenerate into being people who observe special religious days and months and years, we emphasize the form. We become formalists. We rely upon the observances of the religious ceremonies, the days, years, and months. This is not just about the Jewish festivals, though it includes those. He is talking about the pagan festivals. These are all, in either case, the weak and miserable principles, the worthless elementary principles of the world. They both have the idea that we are able to get right with God by keeping the moral law, *rather than* that we are made right with God through Christ's death on the cross, and as a result of that we in the power of the

Spirit now want to follow God's moral law and are able increasingly to do so. But how do we know when we're doing that?

One way we know is with this creeping formalism. I suspect most of us tend to think we are not likely to be attracted to it. But a degeneration to an observance of the forms, rather than to an observance of the power of the gospel, is actually very apparent, and a constant possibility for all of us. There's nothing new in this. As a great Puritan preacher said in 1658, "Formalism, formalism, formalism is the great sin of this day, under which the whole country groans. There is more light than there was, but less life; more profession, but less holiness."[1]

Formalism can take many different forms. It can be in the great Catholic cathedral, or in the massive Protestant church. It can be with old hymns and traditional music, and it can be with new songs and electric guitars. By its nature, it is not the form that counts; our gospel is a matter of the Word and of power, of the Holy Spirit and of Christ himself. It is not the form. But we love to degenerate to external forms. We can be enamored by never singing a song newer than 1658; or we can feel it is inauthentic to sing a song any older than 2008. These are the forms. They are not the reality. I can go into a church buzzing with sound and energy and also truth and with spiritual life and worship God there. I can go into a church that is quiet on a windy day in the country and worship God there with the ten farmers gathered. It is the content, the message, and the person of Christ that matter, not the external form.

We love to hang on to the forms, and when we do, it is the first diagnostic of our faith degenerating into a new form of legalism. That we are fascinated by forms is a sign of the degeneracy of the evangelical movement in our times. The worship wars, whichever side we stand on, are forms. Those who long to worship with candles, robes, or ritual response readings—those are forms. We can go to other kinds of more exuberant churches, but their exuberance can be similarly prescribed and dictated to a certain external form. There are many different kinds of forms. It is not the form but the content, the message, and the person of Christ that counts.

When Christianity degenerates to forms, it becomes more like the sort of human religion that we want to invent. Ramadan is a form. I am

---

[1]Thomas Hall, cited in J. C. Ryle, "Formalism," http://www.biblebb.com/files/ryle/PRACT11.TXT.

told that of all the months of the year in predominantly Moslem countries, more food and drink is consumed during the month of Ramadan than at any other time because after the day's fasting comes the night's feasting.

Bishop of Liverpool J. C. Ryle spoke a wonderful sermon on formalism, and in it he said these words: "Formalism may take your hand with a smile, and look like a brother, while sin comes against us with drawn sword, and strikes at us like an enemy. But both have one end in view. Both want to ruin our souls; and of the two, formalism is the one most likely to do it. If we love life, let us beware of formalism in religion."

Let us also beware of not having any form at all. While we should look beyond the forms, that does not mean we do not need them. Just because the forms cannot save does not mean they do not have any use at all. The misuse of a thing is not an argument against its right use. We need to come together; we need to worship together; we need to hear preaching together; we need songs, structure, and organization; we must not run to extremes. We need all this, but we need it for the content and for the person and power of Christ himself to minister to us.

Is there anything wrong with celebrating Christmas and Easter and Sunday as days and months and seasons? No, but we are not to celebrate them formalistically, as things we must do. The Puritans tried to ban Christmas, which itself was something of a marketing mistake for the Puritan movement, and in any case is potentially another form of formalism. We are not to judge ourselves or let others judge us by these days or even by Sabbath days, as Colossians boldly says. J. C. Ryle put it like this in a quaint metaphor: "A painting of a fire cannot warm, and a painted banquet cannot satisfy hunger, and a formal religion cannot bring peace to the soul." He also said, "There is no formalism so dangerous as an Evangelical formalism," going through the motions with our forms, not realizing that they too are purely formalism when not taken to the heart, to the soul, to our relationship with Jesus.

That is the first diagnostic. Of course, the solution to it is true heart religion. It is connection with God through faith. It is the real thing; it is not the painted fire, it is the warmth of the Holy Spirit of Christ himself.

Lacking Joy

This brings us to the second diagnostic, lack of joy, which Paul talks about, especially in verse 14. It is the theme of the passage on the positive side:

> Brothers, I entreat you, become as I am, for I also have become as you are. You did me no wrong. You know it was because of a bodily ailment that I preached the gospel to you at first, and though my condition was a trial to you, you did not scorn or despise me, but received me as an angel of God, as Christ Jesus. What then has become of the blessing you felt? For I testify to you that, if possible, you would have gouged out your eyes and given them to me. Have I then become your enemy by telling you the truth? (vv. 12–16)

This is a matter of such great and sublime importance that it requires the best of our thinking and attention. What is Paul talking about here? What experience is he referring to that they now do not have or feel? In some ways I think this is the key verse of the whole book. Why does Paul call them to their knowledge of God, or rather that they have come to be known by God (Paul cannot resist emphasizing that their relationship with God begins with God)? Why does he remind them of their reception of him, which meant they would have done anything for him, even plucking out their eyes, to, perhaps, supply the good eyesight that Paul's weakness lacked? What is this buzz, this joy, this blessing they felt, about which he now asks? Where is it? Why is it a matter so personal and pertinent, that, as he writes about it, he fears that his confrontation could lead them to not appreciate him and perhaps even look at Paul as their enemy because he tells them the truth?

First, this is not simply the opposite of being dire, or regimented, or overly strict. The man at Cambridge with whom I first studied the Puritans told me as an aside that whenever you meet Puritans, they are always filled with joy. This joy is not simply the opposite of that wonderful caricature of Thomas Gradgrind, the irrepressible stoic, that Charles Dickens paints in his novel *Hard Times*:

> Thomas Gradgrind, sir [Dickens introduces his own self-talk], A man of realities. A man of facts and calculations. A man who proceeds

upon the principle that two and two are four, and nothing over, and who is not to be talked into allowing for anything over. Thomas Gradgrind, sir—peremptorily Thomas—Thomas Gradgrind. With a rule and a pair of scales, and the multiplication table always in his pocket, sir, ready to weigh and measure any parcel of human nature, and tell you exactly what it comes to. It is a mere case of figures, a case of simple arithmetic. You might hope to get some other nonsensical belief into the head of George Gradgrind, or Augustus Gradgrind, or John Gradgrind, or Joseph Gradgrind [all supposititious, non-existent persons], but into the head of Thomas Gradgrind—no, sir!

Paul is not merely arguing against what we think of as Victorian, stoic, non-emotional sensibilities. Nor is he simply, by contrast, advocating an experiential, existentialist blessing, like Søren Kierkegaard, who said, "To know a creed by rote is, quite simply, paganism. This is because Christianity is inwardness."

Paul is not separating what God has joined together—doctrine and emotion, facts and feelings, objectivity and subjectivity, hard reality and wonderful relationship. He is thinking of another matter altogether.

The King James Version of verse 15 is, "Where is the blessing you spake of?" Literally, the verse is simply, "Where is your blessing?" without any mention of feeling or the word *joy*. This noun *blessing* is used only in one other place in the New Testament, in Romans 4:6–9, where Paul is talking about the blessing of justification by faith alone. That, I think, is the same blessing to which he is referring here, and to which he has been referring throughout the letter. "The blessing of the one to whom God counts righteousness apart from works" (Rom. 4:6). The blessing of Abraham in Galatians 3 is the same, though the word "blessing" there is a different word to the one translated "blessing" here, which refers to believing God and having God's righteousness credited to us.

There is certainly feeling here, and joy. Paul records their passion: they would have plucked out their eyes and given them to him if that would have helped Paul see better. There is a wonderful description of Paul's pastoral care for them ("I am afraid"; "I entreat you"), which we will look at more next chapter, where Paul describes that more fully, and their loving, passionate, joyful response to the blessing of the gospel.

The core of this is not their feelings; it is the blessing of God, which led them to those feelings.

Some of us are unlikely to get caught wrong footed by formalism but by a lack of joy. Churchill called his temperament "the black dog" that dogged his footsteps with melancholy. But Paul is not talking about that. He is not talking about temperament. I have met men who will praise the Lord for their cornflakes at 6 AM, loudly blessing their neighbor who might be tempted, as Proverbs says, to curse them for it. I have also met the dire who with a twinkle in his eye is rejoicing. Paul is talking about the reality of God's pronounced blessing. A blessing is always a pronouncement, a declaration. When God blesses us, he is declaring that we are in a blessed state. When we bless God, we are confirming that we see that God is eternally blessed. It's an announcement, a proclamation, a declaration, and when we have that, it leads to this feeling, this joy and passion, this incredible commitment to the gospel and to the apostle of the gospel.

Martyn Lloyd-Jones, the great Welsh preacher, is said to have put it like this: "What matters is not what I feel is true about myself at any moment, but what I know is true about God at every moment." When we look at a star directly, we cannot see it; when we navel gaze at our feelings, they are sure to go. But when we stare at God, when we look at the truth of what God has done in Christ, our feelings follow. There is an old illustration of a faith, facts, feelings train, and another of three men walking on a wall—faith in the middle, facts in front, feelings behind. As long as faith keeps his eyes on facts, feelings follows; but when faith turns around to look at feelings, he falls off the wall.

Keep your eye on the blessing, the blessing of Abraham, the blessing of righteousness credited to you by faith in Christ's death on the cross, and the joy, the passion—the blessing you feel—will follow along with that.

Paul gives two diagnostics, formalism and lack of joy. He gives one solution: Christ. The gospel, justification by faith alone, the blessing of God—from that there is a renewed blessing we feel, a joy beyond circumstances and temperaments. God bless you.

23

True Gospel Zeal

They make much of you, but for no good purpose. They want to shut you out, that you may make much of them. It is always good to be made much of for a good purpose, and not only when I am present with you, my little children, for whom I am again in the anguish of childbirth until Christ is formed in you! I wish I could be present with you now and change my tone, for I am perplexed about you.

GALATIANS 4:17–20

Imagine that you have been asked to write an Agatha Christie detective story, Hercule Poirot, Miss Marple, the butler, the candlestick, and all. Perhaps a teacher at school has given you this assignment in a fiction-writing class. Perhaps you are doing it for sheer fun. Maybe you hope to sell the novel and become a successful writer. Whatever the reason, imagine that you are beginning to write this story. How would you go about constructing an Agatha Christie whodunit? You would set the location, characters, and certain stereotypical events.

If you want to be successful at springing the unexpected surprise that such novels always have—the final denouement when the characters gather to hear how the clever detective figured it all out—then I suggest you need to follow one infallible rule: decide who among your cast is the very *least* likely to have committed the crime and frame that person so that he or she is the guilty party. This nice person will have no apparent motive and was supposedly absent at the time of the crime. For an effective whodunit surprise kicker, this person, the *least* likely to have done it, is the one who did it. An author who knew Agatha Christie claimed that she had told him that this was her actual novel-writing technique.[1]

---

[1]Brian Aldiss, "Desert Island Discs," BBC Radio, January 28, 2007, http://www.bbc.co.uk/radio4/factual/desertislanddiscs_20070128.shtml.

Whether that is true, or whether you are likely to attempt to write a detective story of any kind, this idea of the *least* likely to have done it is relevant to Galatians 4:17–20. The Galatian false teachers were zealous, they were making much of the Galatians, and they were giving them attention. There is behind this appealing behavior, some think, a reference to the ancient method of courting. The Galatian false teachers were buying the Galatians flowers or books and taking them to restaurants or Bible classes; they were giving them a lot of devoted attention. They were showering them with gifts, treating them as beloved friends, and generally acting in a nice and pleasing manner.

We tend to think that false teachers will have a nasty personal demeanor when actually the reverse is usually true. Typically in church history, heretics have been absolutely the last word in charismatic charm; if you're trying to get Christians to buy something other than Jesus, you've got to have a good sales pitch. By contrast, tradition holds that the apostle Paul was ugly in his physical appearance. We know he never came across as any sort of smooth talker; he was often criticized for being unimpressive as a speaker. His false-teaching opponents, however, were well groomed, nicely mannered, zealous, and making much of their disciples. Perhaps they had written some passionate songs to stir up warm feelings, an old trick that was used to propagate false teaching in the ancient sub-apostolic church. Perhaps the false teachers had good credentials; they were rather impressively intellectual. But above all, they acted as if they cared. They were nice, charming, dynamic, and zealous, and they made much of the Galatians. They visited them, wrote them personal cards, and overall gave them a lot of attention as they attempted to woo them away from Paul's preaching and therefore also from Christ. The Galatian false teachers may not have been the *least* likely to have "done it," but they certainly would have appeared extremely *un*likely with all the charm they exuded.

These few verses can help us distinguish between what is good pastoral leadership and what is not; what is appropriate discipleship and what is not; what is the right way to accept shepherding and what is not; how we as Christian brothers and sisters are genuinely to care for others and how we are not to do it in a fake or self-serving way. It applies most directly to the pastoral and discipleship relationship of Christian brother to brother and sister to sister. But it also applies to how we shepherd our children and lead our families, whether that is self-serving or Christ-serving. It gives us discernment to know when we are being manipulated for the manipulator's benefit, but it also gives us a standard of Christian living, loving, discipling, and shepherding to live by and to pray for. It speaks to pastors, and it also speaks to people about the right way to relate to a pastor. It speaks to home, children, parents, and families. Paul is contrasting a bad zeal, or making much of people, with a good zeal.

The Wrong Way

In the first half of the passage, verses 17 and 18, Paul describes the wrong way to go about it, as exemplified by his theological opponents, the Galatian false teachers. That they are in the wrong is a surprising whodunit. They are the dear old lady who never means any harm. They are the bishop with his pastoral way who preaches heresy. They are the smarmy snake oil salesman who wants us to buy his spiritual product. They are Judaizing false teachers with the authority of James. And they are charming! They make much of the Galatians.

Paul points out the Galatian false teachers' motives. He does the same thing in Galatians 6. This issue of motive is important to the book of Galatians as a whole. Heresy is always in the end a heart issue. Those who want to elevate works to a source of salvation do so because they long to justify themselves, or because they are frustrated at the apparent moral ill of others. They are judge, jury, and often charming advocate. In Galatians 6:12 Paul says they are trying to make a good impression outwardly so that they can avoid persecution for the sake of the cross.

Here in Galatians 4 Paul criticizes their motives as being self-serving. They are making much of the Galatians, which seems good, but they are doing it only so that the Galatians can make much of them. It is a classic manipulator's technique. A manipulator makes much of others so that they feel indebted and will in turn make much of him, in this case, the false teachers. They are trying to exclude the Galatians from Paul and from the true gospel in order to build a little group around their personal agenda so that the Galatians will follow them.

This happens all the time in religious circles, and so it is very relevant. There are the cults who "love bomb" us; that is, they throw affection at us so that when we have received all that affection, we feel we owe them and will therefore do what they want. But even in normal circles things like this often happen. People construct a particular teaching. It must be able to have a unique brand identity. It must be distinct from other Christian teaching so that you can gather a movement around it. You raise the barrier high, and then you are zealous for others to join in; you love them, you befriend them, you make them feel special. Gradually they are brought into your particular way of thinking so that they can be zealous and make much of the originators of the novel teaching.

Call me a cynic if you like, but sometimes I feel almost distressed inside when it seems to me that many worthy ministries are formed in this sort of way by this sort of personal manipulation. Paul does not say that loving, being nice, and caring for people is wrong. He says it is good to make much of people, to have zeal, provided the purpose is good. What makes this wrong is that the purpose was really for them, for the teachers, for their own benefit. The text may be about God, but the subtext is for the benefit of the Galatian false teachers.

For us, it is worth saying simply that we are not to be naïve and think that anyone who is nice and kind and religious has a good agenda. Thinking like that may be okay for children, but adults need to realize that just because someone is warm and affectionate, looks and sounds good, has impressive credentials, and is charismatic doesn't mean he has a good purpose.

The Right Way

On the positive side, what is real passion, zeal, and making much of for our children, our families, our churches, our pastors, and our sheep?

Paul wears his heart on his sleeve and gives us an insight into what it means to truly care for someone as Christ cares. There are six aspects of this in verses 19 and 20, five of which are about what it feels like to care for people in this true way, and one of which is the key differential between the Galatian false teachers and Paul as the apostle. Each paints a character of someone who, on the outside, might seem the obvious villain in the whodunit crime piece, but actually has the right agenda and the right heart. This one is the surprising hero of the story.

1) *The attitude of pastoral care.* "My little children, for whom I am

again in the anguish of childbirth until Christ is formed in you!" (v. 19). The attitude here is that of a parent to a child, or particularly (unusually) of a mother to a child. Paul more commonly refers to himself in the image of a father caring for his children, but here and also in 1 Thessalonians 2:7 he talks of himself as a mother caring for her children.

Pastoral care exhibits the attitude of a mother toward a child. It is not the attitude of a showman to an audience. It is not the attitude of an entrepreneur to a market. It is not the attitude of a manager to a corporation. It is the attitude of a mother to child—deeply personal, entirely devoted, and wanting what's best. Not everyone has had a good experience of a mother, perhaps, and none of us has had a perfect mother, but we know that all good mothers have this in common: they are nurturers, giving of themselves to their children to make them grow up to be strong and healthy.

2) *The agony of pastoral care.* Paul describes himself as being in the "anguish of childbirth," not just once but "again." Theologically, Paul wonders whether the Galatians need not just to be taught but to be evangelized again. Are they really born again or does Paul have to go through the "anguish of childbirth" again so that they would truly be born again? Experientially he's in agony. I've never given birth to a child, but I have been present while children are born; is Paul using an over-embellished metaphor, the mothers among us may wonder? He is not talking about physical pain but to spiritual pain. I can think of times when I have watched people under my care sail close to the rocks, and it is agony to care for them and pray for them and hope that they will be all right. These are emotions, but when someone really cares for you, that is what it's like. Caring for someone in this way is not churning out a product or administering a program; it is delivering a baby.

3) *The purpose of pastoral care.* This is the key differential in terms of purpose between the Galatian false teachers and Paul. His purpose is that "Christ is formed in you." Their purpose was that the Galatians would make much of them. Their purpose was self-aggrandizement, that the Galatians would join their movement, copy their style and mannerisms, and be part of their zealous group. Paul's purpose was that Christ be formed in them. This is the key difference.

It is not just a theological point, for no false Christian teacher says that they are not for Christ in some way or another; it is a point about *purpose*. The intention is for the formation of Christ in them, that is, not only would they become more like Christ in their behavior but also that they would have more of Christ in them. Only a true Christian teacher or pastor has this as his summary goal. It is a goal to create people as they really are in relation to Christ, not as cardboard-cutout, cookie-cutter characters just like their leaders. We want people to be themselves with Christ (not us) formed in them.

4) The *longing of pastoral care*. Paul wishes he "could be present with" them (v. 20). He longs for this. He misses them. The heart of a true pastor longs to be with his sheep. He may be shy or socially awkward, but when he sees them in a ditch or knows they are in trouble, he longs to be with them. An engineer does not long to be with a bridge he is building, however much he might want to do his job well; but the engineer who is a parent does long to be with his child. So true ministry is characterized by a desire to be with the people who are being served. This is not about the purely temperamental longing of the party-going type who longs to be with people so as to live off their emotional highs and lows, nor can we infer from this that those who shepherd don't sometimes get fed up with sheep bites. It is about the longing of friendship, of parenting, and of love that runs across personality types and passing circumstances.

5) The *struggle of pastoral care*. Paul wants to change his tone. He wants to be nice. This letter is not a nice letter. He is being very firm with the Galatians, but he doesn't like to be that way. He doesn't enjoy a good, strong, pastoral rebuke. He's not looking for a fight. He's not like someone who puts a humidifier and a dehumidifier in the same room and lets them fight it out for the sheer fun of it. He doesn't enjoy the conflict, but he will do it when necessary. He wants to be personally present so he can see whether his words are having the necessary impact in order to let off the harsh tone and come back to the more warm approach that he prefers with his children.

6) The *confusion of pastoral care*. Paul is "perplexed" about them (v. 20). Did he do something wrong? Did he not preach the gospel clearly enough? Did he not pray long enough? Did he not love enough? What could he have done differently? Why are they being taken in by

these false teachers? Paul is perplexed because he cares. He longs and struggles because of his attitude of mother to child, because of the personal agony of child birth, and most importantly because of his true purpose that Christ—the love of *his* life—would be formed in them.

There is good zeal and bad zeal; good pastoral care and bad ministry manipulation; good parenting and parenting to make the children just like you so you look good and can live your life through them; and good discipleship and bad discipleship that tries to make disciples of you, not of Jesus Christ.

This is a passage that encourages us not to be naïve about false teachers that come with a smile—wolves in sheep's clothing—but instead to look at the true purpose of the teacher. Is his purpose to form Christ in us? It is also a call for us, when we have or do receive that kind of care, to receive it with great joy and confidence. We are not to look on the externals of our elders, deacons, pastors, or small-group leaders. We are not to gather around the teacher who has the brightest smile, the funniest jokes, or the most charismatic personality, one who has this zeal for "making much of." We are to gather around the teacher who asks us to gather around not him but Christ. The reverse is what Dietrich Bonhoeffer called "human absorption."[2]

A strong personality can so dominate a group or an individual that people in the end yield to him and are overcome and drawn into his spell. The primary loyalty is not really to Christ, for he has not worthily been formed. Loyalty is given to the individual, and therefore opposition to that charismatic personality or false teacher, or involvement in the cause, becomes impossible. It's about them; it's not about Jesus.

This is as bad for manipulators as it is for the manipulated. The professional ministerial "ladder climbers" either ruin their family's lives in the process or stay late, get up early, and work for their own career (not ministry) because their home life is unpleasant to begin with. Like Willy Loman in Arthur Miller's *Death of a Salesman*, such folk have all the wrong dreams and never really know who they are, or more importantly who Christ is. The manipulated become the manipulators, those who have been made much of make much of others in turn, and the cycle continues. Instead are Christ and his servants. They have agony.

---

[2]Dietrich Bonhoeffer, *Life Together* (New York: Harper Collins, 1954), 33.

They have a parental attitude, not so that they can keep their disciples hanging onto their apron strings but so that they could help them move on to mature independence in Christ formed in them.

Think of one visit to a hospital, a prayer there, a word of witness. Think of a sermon that feels like casting bread on the waters, trusting it will do its work. Think of the foolishness of preaching Christ crucified. Think of the failure of lives truly devoted to Christ in the world's eyes:

> Poor things! They give their money away, and no one even knows that they did! Poor things! They send their children to the mission field; who is going to care for them when they are old? Poor things! They are serving and caring, and no one even notices. They are like the glass in a greenhouse through whom the sun of Christ's righteousness shines, and the plants grow under their care, but all *they* see is Christ, and they do not even notice the glass through which the light shines hotly. They are disparaged—ugly Paul, short Paul, unimpressive Paul. Their children go off to school and forget all about them. All the while the Galatian false teachers gather their impressive team around them and look good and have others saying how good they are. How much we make of you! How zealous we are for you! They have the plaudits and the cheers. All the while, the engine of the true church is run by people who write a card, sign a check, pray a prayer, preach a sermon, visit a sick man or woman, get on their knees in the quiet of the night when no one is looking and no one knows, and cry out "God have mercy on these children; Jesus form yourself in them." Their scars are unknown, their agonies are unseen, and they seem to have nothing.

That is how the world sees us. But to be cared for by such a one, to care ourselves for people in this way, well, that is the route to having Christ formed in us. I for one, despite all that we leave behind, would rather have Christ than all that this world, even this religious world, with its baubles and temptations, affords. Have zeal, make much of those you work with, and make sure the purpose is good, that it is Christ. *He* is the surprising hero of the story.

24

Gospel Identity

Tell me, you who desire to be under the law, do you not listen to the law? For it is written that Abraham had two sons, one by a slave woman and one by a free woman. But the son of the slave was born according to the flesh, while the son of the free woman was born through promise. Now this may be interpreted allegorically: these women are two covenants. One is from Mount Sinai, bearing children for slavery; she is Hagar. Now Hagar is Mount Sinai in Arabia; she corresponds to the present Jerusalem, for she is in slavery with her children. But the Jerusalem above is free, and she is our mother. For it is written,

> *"Rejoice, O barren one who does not bear;*
> > *break forth and cry aloud, you who are not in labor!*
> *For the children of the desolate one will be more*
> > *than those of the one who has a husband."*

Now you, brothers, like Isaac, are children of promise. But just as at that time he who was born according to the flesh persecuted him who was born according to the Spirit, so also it is now. But what does the Scripture say? "Cast out the slave woman and her son, for the son of the slave woman shall not inherit with the son of the free woman." So, brothers, we are not children of the slave but of the free woman.

GALATIANS 4:21–31

This passage, complex though it may be, is really all about issues of identity. Who are we? What kind of *city* do we identify ourselves with? Where is our motherland? What sort of children were we or are we?

Paul poses a fundamental question at the beginning of the passage to those who wish to live in a religious way, that is, who wish to live "under the law." To people who wish to be religious, Paul explains that at root there is an identity issue that needs to be addressed. There are three choices here—two mothers, two cities, two children—and each choice is binary; in other words, it is this kind of mother, or that kind of mother; this kind of city, or that kind of city; this kind of child, or that kind of child. Each speaks to the relevant issue of identity.

We have become a generation confused about our identity. In the past, people were identified primarily by their family, their nationality, or their birth town. Now that we move around so much and change careers, and our families have become dispersed, these primary identity markers are harder to use. Some of the most popular movies and literature these days deal with identity issues. The talk-show host and psychiatrist Dr. Phil does so in his book *Self Matters*. The postmodern theorist Michel Foucault did so, saying that his text "rejects its identity."[1] Even *Harry Potter* does the same: its theme is an orphan boy who cannot identify himself by his parents, so he looks for identity in his headmaster, or godfather, or friends.

What about your religious identity? Are you a part of the Christian religion? Or are you someone born of the Spirit through faith in Christ? Paul says there is a difference as he outlines in this passage two mothers, two cities, and, finally, two children. Each of these identity markers concerns matters about which we need to make a choice; each reflects the large theological structure of the Bible in terms of the two covenants, Old and New Testaments; and each comes down to some very practical application for what it means to live as children of the promise.

Paul uses an allegory, not fancifully or as a theory of interpretation distinct from interpreting the Bible literally but as a divinely inspired archetypal series of illustrations—like Jesus used parables—that speak to the basic issue of our identity. Paul is solving the Galatians' religious identity crisis.

Two Mothers

Paul recounts the story in verses 22 and 23 that Abraham did not have only one son (Isaac) but two sons (Isaac and Ishmael). The question is not only which is our father, but who is our mother. Jews at Jesus' time

---

[1]Michel Foucault, *The Archaeology of Knowledge and the Discourse on Language* (London: Vintage, 1982), 17.

were proud of their Abrahamic inheritance, and the Judaizers were playing off that theme. They had Abraham as their father. But having Abraham as their father was not enough; there was also a question as to which child one was descended from, and therefore which of the two mothers.

Sarah was the free woman. She was the wife of Abraham. She was the miracle mother of the child of promise born in her advanced old age. She certainly had issues in her life and was not perfect, but she stands for the one who received God's promise and bore Isaac.

Hagar, on the other hand, was the concubine. She was chosen by Abraham and Sarah because they doubted God's promise to provide a child. They thought they could help God along a little bit by giving Abraham the chance to sire a child through Sarah's handmaid. Hagar stands for our doubt. She stands for our tendency not to fully believe God but to help that faith along with our own flesh, in our own power, and by our own will. Hagar, Paul says—in a series of associations still shocking, when you think about it—is representative of Mount Sinai, where God's Law was delivered, and of the physical Jerusalem that was in captivity under a foreign power. There is much debate over the exact meaning of the beginning of verse 25, but basically Paul says that Hagar stands for a law that was delivered outside of the geographical Promised Land, which is symbolic of trying to be religious apart from God's promise.

The Galatians must have felt like spiritual orphans. Since they had a pagan background, they felt they were outside the great stream of God's people as fathered by Abraham. How could they get closer to that? What would they need to do? Well, the Judaizers came and said that they could become fully integrated into Israel by behaving and acting as Israelites, practicing circumcision and the law. Paul countered that their orphan feeling—cut off, lonely, motherless—would be fulfilled not in living under the law but in Sarah as their mother, who had received the promise by faith through the work of the Spirit, not through works.

Perhaps you are not too sure about your own spiritual identity. Perhaps you find the conservative church rather masculine, even patriarchal, in its rhetoric. The question is not just "Who is your father?" but "Who is your mother?" Abraham had two sons, but only one was born to Sarah. To be in the line of that promise, of that home, is to be children of faith born of the Spirit.

Two Cities

Paul pushes the series of metaphors. There is Jerusalem, which is in slavery, and there is Jerusalem above, which is, carrying his allegory to another level, our mother. Paul says that just being from the physical Jerusalem doesn't mean anything. In fact the physical Jerusalem was under the pagan control of the Roman Empire. What mattered was being connected to the spiritual Jerusalem, that is, to the Christian church.

Verse 27 is not about Hagar and Sarah. He quotes from Isaiah about Jerusalem in exile, saying that many children will come from it. How has that been fulfilled? Well, it has been fulfilled in "the Jerusalem above," that is, in the Christian church.

This allegory is important also because many under forty want to be urbane and sophisticated, to be city dwellers. But what sort of city are we seeking to be a part of: the physical or the spiritual? The Jerusalem that we are to identify ourselves with spiritually is the Jerusalem above, not the present city of Jerusalem, as Paul puts it. Our city is the city of God, as Augustine put it. This reminds me of how Charles Dickens began his novel *A Tale of Two Cities*: "It was the best of times it was the worst of times." We are not to make our home here. We are to be urbane in the spiritual Jerusalem.

Our identity is to be with the church. That is perhaps the most telling application of this part of Paul's allegory. Nowhere in the New Testament is there a Christian who is not committed to a local church. We are to be part of this spiritual Jerusalem, our mother, the Jerusalem that is above. Historically, some have manipulated the importance of the spiritual connection with the church, making salvation dependent upon the church. That is the physical Jerusalem, if you like. We are to be connected to the spiritual Jerusalem, members of the body of Christ, the church.

People sometimes ask me why local church membership is important. I tend to answer that membership in a local church is a formal expression of an already existing organic reality. You are members of the body of Christ. Well, if you are, if the Jerusalem above is your mother, then express it formally. That formal expression of membership matters. Men of my father's generation did not wear wedding rings, but men of my generation tend to. It's only a formal expression, but it matters. If you saw a man going into a bar and surreptitiously slipping off his wedding ring, you would know what was up. You don't just live with the church or date the church; you become committed to the church, formally, in a kind of marriage covenant.

Which is your city? Is it the physical city of urbane sophistication, coffee bars, the latest music and fashion, and the connectivity through the Web? Or is yours the spiritual city above, the church? Is the community of God's people your Jerusalem? Christians, I think, often struggle with identity issues because they are not really committed to a local church. *If you don't like this Jerusalem, there's another one down the road.* If you are a member of the body of Christ, you must express that commitment. It is this "our mother" who bears many children as we identify ourselves with the spiritual Jerusalem, the church, through all its strengths and weaknesses.

Two Children

This is the heart of it. The younger-brother type, we think, is extroverted and reckless; the older-brother type is conscientious and hardworking; the middle-brother type is peacemaking and hard to settle down. All these characterizations and "scripts" of identity that we bear into adulthood need to be replaced with a fundamentally more accurate spiritual sibling choice. Are we Ishmael, the child who was sent away, or are we Isaac, the child born by the promise of the Spirit? It is a fundamental identity issue. Are we those who help God to do what he has promised by living under the law? Or are we those who in the power of the Spirit serve and commit and get involved by the promise and faith in that promise? How do you know the difference?

Here's how you know the difference: are you being opposed or are you the one opposing the work of the gospel? That's the fundamental, foundational distinction in practice: "But just as at that time he who was born according to the flesh persecuted him who was born according to the Spirit, *so also it is now*" (v. 29). How do you know? You know because you are either the one doing the persecuting or the one being persecuted for the sake of the gospel.

Maybe you think this happens only in third-world countries where people persecute Christians. It certainly does happen there. But the greatest persecution in the world has not been by non-Christians, for when they hear the gospel they either receive it or ignore it, on the whole. The persecution of gospel Christians tends to come from nominal Christians. Isaac gets persecuted by Ishmael. It happened then. It happened with Christ. Who were his biggest bugbears? The Pharisees, who really knew their Bibles but wanted to live under the law. It happened with Paul. Those who persecuted him were the nominal believers, those wanting to live under the law. All his difficulty came from there. It happened in the ancient church. Certainly there was persecution from the pagan empire, but once that had been evangelized, the persecution came from nominal believers. The Reformers were opposed by the established church, and the evangelical leaders of the Great Awakening by the Old Lights. Today it is the same. "So also it is now."

If you are being persecuted for being a child of the promise, it is a telling marker that you are his. It describes who you are. It assures you that you are his. This is how you know your identity ultimately. Perhaps you are a pastor or in ministry of some kind. If so, be encouraged when you are opposed. Don't deliberately stir up a fight in order to feel encouraged; 99 percent of the times that pastors are persecuted, it is because they preach the gospel. Nominal Christians don't like it because it means they don't get saved by the law, which means they are not as good as they think they are, which means that unless the Spirit humbles them to come under grace, they're going to get really annoyed. It happens all the time.

We don't know exactly what Ishmael did to Isaac, but we are told that he mocked him in some way. Perhaps that is happening to you. Perhaps there is someone where you work who claims to be a Christian or "religious" and thinks you're too keen because you go to church every Sunday and serve in children's ministries. You might be called "holy Joe," "religious freak," or "fundamentalist." Perhaps a fellow student sees you getting up early to get to church on Sunday and sneers at you for your zeal. Be encouraged. It is an identity marker. It shows who you are—who you really are in Christ. It means you are doing what's right.

That is not to say that the children of promise just sit back and take it. What do they do? They go eat their lunch at a different table (v. 30). They say, "If you don't like this, I'm going to shake the dust off my sandals and go somewhere else. You don't want to be my friend; I'll find someone who does." They don't just sit there and get pummeled, nor do they take revenge and pummel back. They move on. Sometimes churches need to do that too. There are times when churches will ask someone to leave because he or she is causing much trouble. That's a good thing. You want to be a part of a church that would kick you out if you behaved badly enough for long enough and didn't repent.

Two mothers, two cities, two children. What is all this really about? Paul is just using picture language. He's not being fanciful. He is not being like Philo or the Alexandrian school of hermeneutics or taking a medieval course in exegesis; he's using his right brain. He's being imaginative, which is okay. But when being imaginative, one must do it correctly. You've got to do it based on several chapters of hardline, straightforward exegesis, which is what Paul has already established. We do have a right brain as a well as a left, and using the creative side is good. Jesus spoke in parables and allegories, and so did Paul sometimes. To do it correctly, you've got to have your doctrine correct so that the imaginative becomes an illustration of what Paul has been saying all along in a more prosaic fashion.

He is saying that we don't live in the old covenant anymore. These three choices, each binary—this mother or that; this child or that; this city or that—point to the theological matter of the old covenant and the new covenant. Paul is saying that sometimes Christians, who are New Testament believers, start to live as if they were still Old Testament people. That's a problem. The old covenant says, "You *must* do this," but in Christ by faith, Jesus says, "In the power of my Spirit you *will* do this." That's the teaching still to come of the fruit of the Spirit. Paul isn't saying that moral obedience doesn't matter. It does. He's saying, "Israel tried to live under the law but failed to keep the conditions of the law. Now that Christ has come, the fulfillment of the promise to Abraham, we might receive salvation by faith and live that out in the power of the

Spirit." The letter of Galatians is as much about regeneration as it is about justification, in some ways.

Be new-covenant people. That means that we are free—not free to do what we want in our natural sinful selves, but free to do what is really best for us and the most fun and enjoyable, which is to become more like Christ. If you think becoming more like Christ is not really what's most fun and enjoyable, but rather catching the football game tonight, or getting a nice latte from Starbucks, or whatever it is, then you haven't really understood what Jesus is about. He is here to set you free, even you religious people.

Who is your mother, which is your kind of city, what sort of child are you? These are archetypal identity markers. We think, *he's a typical younger child*. Or, *he comes from good stock—like mother, like son*. Or we think, *yep, that's a Chicago person*. But ultimately our spiritual identity is that of a child of promise by faith as expressed in the local Christian community of the church. If we're struggling with identity—who we are, where we're going, the point of our life—then probably one or other of those is out of joint. Either you are trying to live under the law, not by grace through faith, or trying to do it as a solo Christian, not as a part of the spiritual Jerusalem.

In *The Lord of the Rings*, Gandalf rides up to see Saruman. The storm is gathering. He comes looking for counsel. They talk, they walk, and they stand together in the great chamber, locked high up in the tower of Orthanc. Saruman puts to Gandalf a terrible choice. "Against the power that rises in the east there is no victory. The Dark Lord Sauron will win. We must join with him, Gandalf; it would be wise."

"Tell me, Saruman," Gandalf replies, "when did you exchange wisdom for folly?" So the choice is made. He escapes off the roof prison and joins himself with a struggling band of hobbits, an alliance of middle earth against the might of Sauron.

We too have to choose, as did the Galatians. Judaism was the dominant religion. It would be wise to join them. They have grandfathered status in the Roman Empire. If you identify yourself with them, you will escape persecution, and besides, Abraham is their father. But who is their mother? And which city are you talking about, and which child are you?

In every life, there comes a moment when fundamental identity questions come to the fore. Certain developmental stages—teen years, midlife, retirement. Certain circumstances spring it upon us: losing a job, a sick child. Who are we really? What is life truly about? There come moments in history when nations and peoples have to make similar choices. Are we going to merge with the dominant postmodern culture? Are we going to change our interpretation of the Bible to suit the taste of the postmodern thought police, on matters of sexuality, gender, and relativism? It would be wise, my friend. Against the power that rises in the east there is no victory. Join with them. Identify with them. Go with the flow.

But sometimes a hobbit or two, a church or two, one or two of God's people, who stand as Isaac (not Ishmael), Sarah (not Hagar), the Jerusalem above (not the Jerusalem below), can go on a walk together and defeat all the hordes of Mordor. Sometimes what matters is the identification, the initial choice: whose are we? If we are with God, well, we and God make a majority, don't you think? Even if we fail in this life, even if this institution or that job, this sickness or that opportunity, is lost, the great news is that by identification with Christ, we cannot lose. However much Ishmael persecutes, we have already won. We have the inheritance. We have heaven. We have Christ. That is worth an identity crisis to discover.

25

Maintaining the Freedom of the Gospel

For freedom Christ has set us free; stand firm therefore, and do not submit again to a yoke of slavery. Look: I, Paul, say to you that if you accept circumcision, Christ will be of no advantage to you.
I testify again to every man who accepts circumcision that he is obligated to keep the whole law. You are severed from Christ,
you who would be justified by the law; you have fallen away from grace. For through the Spirit, by faith, we ourselves eagerly wait for the hope of righteousness. For in Christ Jesus neither circumcision nor uncircumcision counts for anything, but only faith working through love.

GALATIANS 5:1–6

What does it really mean to be free? My guess is that most of us want to be free, and probably most of us think that in some sense we are free. After all, many of us live in a free country, where once we come of age we have the right to vote. Yet have we attained full liberty simply by exercising an appropriate role within the constitutionally established democratic process? Can we live in a democratic country, be free in that sense politically, and yet inherently still be deeply enslaved?

Terminology makes the discussion even more convoluted. What's the difference between being free, having liberty, being a liberal, or advocating libertarianism? Many people might want to have liberty but not be a liberal, or be liberal with their time but not with their morals.

For some people, freedom is more akin to opportunity. I am free in some sense if I am resident in a democracy, but I only really have freedom if I am able to actualize my full potential as a human being. Freedom then becomes associated with means, capital, education, and conversely with responsibility and achievement, even public service. But great achievements can leave one feeling restricted and restrained. The man or woman at the top of the corporate ladder may have great freedom in one sense, but he is bound by all sorts of responsibilities, not to mention by long hours at the office.

Others have carefully defined true freedom in a more philosophical sense. For them what counts is not simply political freedom or the freedom to achieve great things, but the freedom within. We are encouraged to be not masters of the external universe but of the internal. So in Hans Sachs' play *Diogenes*, the Greek philosopher tells Alexander the Great that while he has conquered much of the external world, he has not conquered his fear, his lust, or his anger—the internal world which the philosopher claims to have mastered. "You are," he says, "*my* servants' servant," because, while externally successful, Alexander is enslaved to his inner passions. This stoic ideal of individual freedom still informs our contemporary philosophies, combined with the political freedom, and influences movies from *Braveheart* to *Gladiator* to Luke Skywalker's ideal or battle with his inner nemesis to overcome the dark side.

This seems to be getting closer, in some ways, to the Christian idea of freedom but still some distance from it. While modern people take for granted the underlying assumptions of Rousseau's Enlightenment philosophy—that "man was born free but is everywhere in chains," that external social forces restrict us, and if we can be educated enough, or provide the right cultural environment, we will be free—the Bible teaches us that we were naturally born in chains and need to be actively set free. What's more, that freedom is not primarily a freedom to be ourselves, or even a freedom from social or political restraints, but a freedom from the judgment of God. The message of the Bible, the gospel, is intended to show us how to get free from condemnation, to have our conscience set free, to be justified before the holy God—not just forgiven but declared righteous.

That is freedom, biblically, and all other freedoms are either expressions of it (when appropriate) or distractions from it, and frequently are vain attempts to find freedom in things, people, opportunity, or systems that will in the end disappoint, for they are still part of our chains, our slavery.

So, when we come to this passage in front of us, we find that the heart of it is in verses 4 and 5, where Paul teaches us that freedom is not trying to be justified by the law but being justified by faith. However, that statement will make very little sense if we import into it our typical assumptions in modern society that freedom is about being politically free, or socially free, or economically free, or existentially free, or even morally free, as in not restrained and part of the libertarian society. Paul is talking about freedom theologically. He says that the fundamental freedom we all need, far more important than all the others, is the basic certainty that we are justified before God. He says that the only way to have that freedom is to ensure that we are not trying to be justified before God by the law but by faith. He wants us to stand in this, and to do so, there are ways in which we actively and deliberately need to stand firm to ensure that we are and continue to be free.

Assert the Principle of Freedom

First, we need to maintain our freedom, to stand firm in it, and resist theological or spiritual slavery by simply, though strongly, asserting the principle itself. This is often overlooked, but it is terribly important. Paul asserts the principle: "For freedom Christ has set us free" (v. 1a). Jesus did not save us to enslave us; he saved us to set us free. Having given us this principle, Paul encourages us to assert it in our own lives: "Stand firm therefore, and do not submit again to a yoke of slavery" (v. 1b).

I believe in the entire sovereignty of God, his overruling power, and his ability to get done what we cannot do, his constant upholding of everything by his almighty hand. Yet we, you and I, need to assert this principle—actively, deliberately, and strongly—ourselves. We must actively "not submit" to being burdened again by a yoke of slavery. We must assert the principle that "for freedom Christ has set us free." We need to do this in three ways.

First, in our apologetics we need to explain to those who are not yet convinced of biblical Christianity that true freedom comes from following Jesus. Perhaps you are not yet a Christian, or you are unconvinced that Bible-believing Christianity is anything other than restrictive fundamentalism, or lots of men wearing black suits with rules longer than their frowns. If, as someone quipped, Puritanism is the sneaking suspicion that someone somewhere is having some fun, then I'm not sure I want to put the fun back in fundamentalism, but we do need to assert the freedom that is in biblical Christianity.

Theologian Gary Badcock put it like this: "Freedom has become the dominant issue in virtually all aspects of our lives." Therefore, he suggests, "the most basic problem we face in modern theology is to find a way to reconstruct an understanding of human nature in which the relation with God has central place."[1] To put it in other terms, because the human engine was made to run on worshiping God, any other ideal or passion is idolatrous and becomes destructive. Religion, money, relationships, or anything or anyone other than God at the center cannot hold our freedom. A radical assertion of God's power does not diminish our freedom. It alone can be a bulwark against the encroachments of fatalistic slavery and human dictatorship.

In our morality, we need to explain that holiness, the sweetness of becoming more like Christ day by day—the theme that Galatians is beginning to transition toward—is actually freedom. We tend to talk of holiness as a discipline, which it is. We tend to talk of holiness as self-denial, which it is. We rarely talk of holiness as freedom, which it also is. Christian, as you survey your temptations to lust, pornography, anger, jealousy, or greed, and each time the Bible calls you to love your wife as you love yourself, to not sin in your anger, to give so that you may receive bountifully, know that this is God's purpose—to set you free gradually as you have been set free. For freedom Christ has set you free.

Reject the Jesus-Plus Gospel

Second, we must reject the Jesus-plus gospel. Paul asserts the principle of freedom and encourages us to do likewise by deliberately rejecting the false gospel, which in Galatia was connected to the issue of circumcision, but it is any Jesus-plus gospel, anything that tells us that Jesus is not a sufficient means by which to be justified. In verses 2 through 4 he specifically rejects the Jesus-plus gospel.

Paul says basically that this is an *either-or*. You cannot have both

---

[1] Peter Jensen, *The Revelation of God*, Contours of Christian Theology, ed. Gerald Bray (Downers Grove, IL: IVP Academic, 2002), 255.

circumcision and Jesus. If you accept circumcision, Christ will be of no value to you (v. 2). If you rely on circumcision, then you have to obey the whole law to get saved. No one does obey the whole law, so we are in serious spiritual trouble (v. 3). An attempt to be justified by the law means that you are separated from Christ, you are cut off from grace (v. 4). It is an either-or, not a *both-and*. You cannot have both. Lest they thought that Paul really cared about circumcision itself, which he did not, he says, "Neither circumcision nor uncircumcision counts for anything" (v. 6). Anything that gets inserted into justification, any law or work that says you've got to have me to be justified, is a rejection of Christ and leads away from grace.

I am fully aware that this either-or logic Paul uses here is radical, and I think we all need to take that seriously. There are many who believe that justification is by faith *and* works. Paul did not, nor did Jesus, whose salvation comes to whoever believes. Other religions basically think that salvation comes through good works of one kind or another, plus a faith system of one kind or another. But Paul says it is either-or. On the one hand there is all human-made religion, which, in our pride, always involves our pretended ability to keep the moral law, and on the other there is God's grace, his Son's sacrifice for us on the cross, and our reception of that by faith.

I am tempted immediately to ameliorate that and soft-pedal the implications, but let Paul speak for himself: "Every man who accepts circumcision . . . is obligated to keep the whole law. You are severed from Christ, you who would be justified by the law; you have fallen away from grace" (vv. 3–4). Not all religion is good religion, not every church is a true church, and just because something is ancient doesn't make it right. Paul, we have maintained, is not talking just about circumcision, for circumcision is itself nothing to him. Paul is talking about the attempt to self-justify before God through one religious law or another versus the wonderful free grace of God that is received through faith as a gift.

Assert the Spiritual Vitality of Faith

The third and final way that Paul maintains and urges us to maintain Christian freedom is by asserting the spiritual vitality of faith. You'll find this in verse 5 and in the second half of verse 6. Everyone immediately claims that if we are justified by faith without the law, does that not mean that we can do what we like? It really depends on what you mean by *faith*. If by *faith* you mean a notional faith, that is, a faith that simply believes God exists and Jesus died for our sins, that kind of faith is not what the Bible means by *faith*. Even the Devil believes in God in that sense, and shudders. Faith in the Bible sense is what we call "trust."

An old illustration is perhaps best here. Charles Blondin was a tightrope walker. In the mid-nineteenth century he performed the amazing feat of walking on a tightrope across Niagara Falls. He then did a backwards somersault on the rope, and then he did it blindfolded. He did it while pushing a wheelbarrow. He did it on stilts. One time, he stopped halfway across and cooked an omelet on a portable stove. But one day, apparently, he turned to the crowd and asked, "Do you believe I can carry someone across the rope on my back?" They, of course, having seen his tricks before, roared back that yes, they did believe it. Then Blondin asked for a volunteer. No one came forward. He pointed at one man nearby who refused to risk his life. He then pointed at another man who accepted the challenge and stepped forward in faith. "Will you trust me?" Blondin asked. "I will," the man said. Unknown to the crowd, the man was Blondin's manager, who had had ample time to observe Blondin's technique and to be able to trust him. Perhaps also he had some vested interest in the success of the amazing performance.

Notional or nominal faith is answering the question, "Do you believe that he can cross Niagara Falls?" with a yes but leaving it there. Actual faith, trust, is sitting on the back of the tightrope walker and letting him carry you across.

This is the faith found in our passage: "Through the Spirit, by faith, we ourselves eagerly wait for the hope of righteousness" (v. 5). Verse 5, if you like, is justification that we receive by faith. Verse 6, then, is sanctification: "For in Christ Jesus neither circumcision nor uncircumcision counts for anything, but only faith working through love." Paul is not making love the ground of our justification, but he is saying that real faith, faith that trusts and works itself out in love, actually gets on the back of the tightrope walker and is carried across. Martin Luther puts it like this: Paul "makes love the tool through which faith works."

It all goes back to freedom. We need to assert the principle strongly. We need to reject the Jesus-plus gospel, using the either-or logic that Paul employs here. We also need to assert the spiritual vitality of faith. True faith is trust, and it works itself out through love. There is a spiritual dynamic to it; it is by the Spirit that we are born again. As new creations we begin to bear the fruit of the Spirit. Consider this example from the Gospel of Luke:

> One of the Pharisees asked him to eat with him, and he went into the Pharisee's house and took his place at the table. And behold, a woman of the city, who was a sinner, when she learned that he was reclining at table in the Pharisee's house, brought an alabaster flask of ointment, and standing behind him at his feet, weeping, she began to wet his feet with her tears and wiped them with the hair of her head and kissed his feet and anointed them with the ointment. Now when the Pharisee who had invited him saw this, he said to himself, "If this man were a prophet, he would have known who and what sort of woman this is who is touching him, for she is a sinner." And Jesus answering said to him, "Simon, I have something to say to you." And he answered, "Say it, Teacher." "A certain moneylender had two debtors. One owed five hundred denarii, and the other fifty. When they could not pay, he cancelled the debt of both. Now which of them will love him more?" Simon answered, "The one, I suppose, for whom he cancelled the larger debt." And he said to him, "You have judged rightly." Then turning toward the woman he said to Simon, "Do you see this woman? I entered your house; you gave me no water for my feet, but she has wet my feet with her tears and wiped them with her hair. You gave me no kiss, but from the time I came in she has not ceased to kiss my feet. You did not anoint my head with oil, but she has anointed my feet with ointment. Therefore I tell you, her sins, which are many, are forgiven—for she loved much. But he who is forgiven little, loves little." And he said to her, "Your sins are forgiven." Then those who were at table with him began to say among themselves, "Who is this, who even forgives sins?" And he said to the woman, "Your faith has saved you; go in peace." (Luke 7:36–50)

There is Jesus, surrounded by many religious Pharisees. They have kept the law, at least externally. A woman came in. She had already repented of her sins, no doubt, for otherwise she would not have come to Jesus to express her devotion. She came and began to weep, and she broke an expensive jar of perfume, an annual salary stored in this ancient method of investment, poured out on Jesus. This woman, who had lived a sinful life, wet Jesus' feet with her tears and wiped them with her hair and kissed them.

The tongues began to wag around the Pharisees' table. Surely if Jesus was such a great spiritual leader he would know who she was, a sinner. He did know, and he welcomed her. "Simon, I have something to teach you," he said, and he told the parable about debts. The woman was a visual aid for the Pharisees and Simon, and for us. Her love was not the ground of her forgiveness but the evidence. The ground, the basis of her salvation, Jesus declares: "Your faith has saved you; go in peace" (v. 50).

We are all sinners. We all have much that needs to be forgiven, and we are invited to come to the feet of Jesus. We are invited to express our love in pouring out the oil of our worship to him. We are invited to believe in him. We are invited away from the condemnation of legalism, of works righteousness, of Pharisaic self-justification.

Weep the tears of joy, for it is for freedom that Christ has set you free. Do not be burdened again by a yoke of slavery.

26

Defending the Gospel

*You were running well. Who hindered you from obeying the truth?
This persuasion is not from him who calls you. A little leaven leavens
the whole lump. I have confidence in the Lord that you will take no
other view than mine, and the one who is troubling you will bear the
penalty, whoever he is. But if I, brothers, still preach circumcision,
why am I still being persecuted? In that case the offense of the cross
has been removed. I wish those who unsettle you would emasculate
themselves!*

GALATIANS 5:7–12

There is a long history of great leaders being rude to other people.
Winston Churchill did it frequently: "My opponent is a humble man
with a lot to be humble about." And Lady Astor to Churchill: "Sir, if
you were my husband I would give you poison"; "Madam, if you were
my wife I would take it." Even Gandhi got in on the act. When asked
what he thought of Western civilization, he replied, "I think it's a good
idea." But it's a little surprising to find—apparently—the same sort of
thing advocated in the Bible.

Paul, of course, was never one to mince his words; he is, to use a
football analogy, your original gun-slinging quarterback apostle. Still,
the frankness with which he concludes this paragraph—"I wish those
who unsettle you would emasculate themselves"—is so shocking that
at various times scholars have suggested that perhaps he did not really
say what he appears to have said. Perhaps when he talks about "cutting
off," he means "cutting off from the assembly," a wish for excommuni-
cation. Perhaps he is talking relationally rather than physically, cutting
off interpersonal contact with the Galatians. It is certainly true that in
the Old Testament, a physical crushing, cutting, or dismemberment
could lead to being barred from the assembly, ritually speaking. Despite

these understandable exegetical questions, found more in the Latin tradition than in the Greek, most contemporary exegetes conclude that Paul really said what he seems to have said. The context of circumcision makes that almost beyond dispute. Paul is wishing that the knife would slip a little.

This is not your normal Sunday morning language, nor is it the common language of our politically correct age. It is colorful and racy, and it verges on being downright offensive. I am sure it would have been offensive to the Galatian agitators! Even if Paul was talking only about cutting off from the community, that does not make his wish any less grueling; in fact, it is along the same line as his formal declaration of separation at the beginning of the letter where he says about anyone preaching a different gospel, "Let him be accursed" (1:8–9). Paul has not volcanically erupted and blown his top in some intemperate rant here. This is part of his ongoing, public declaration against the false teaching, even here with what is maybe a bit of caustic humor.

Certainly we shouldn't be quick to cast curses on our theological opponents, nor should we readily spring to bar-room humor to dismiss them. *Those Baptists—I wish they'd go all the way and drown themselves!* But is there a time to use powerful language to make clear the seriousness of issues at stake? We can find other places in the Bible where the same sort of communication occurs from time to time. The imprecatory psalms do it: "When he is tried, let him come forth guilty. . . . May another take his office!" (Ps. 109:7–8). In Acts 8 Peter wishes that the money of Simon, who had tried to buy the gift of the Holy Spirit, would perish with him for his blasphemous intention. Jesus is, well, damning with his language toward some of the Pharisees. He describes them as unmarked graves that people walk over without knowing and as whitewashed walls that are about to topple over even though they've been given a lick of paint to make them look good. He frequently called them hypocrites.

We are not David, nor are we apostles, and we're certainly not Jesus. But when did we last contend earnestly for the faith (Jude 3)? Jude advises that in some situations we need to do that, but it almost never happens these days. It isn't because there aren't matters of faith for which to contend; perhaps it's because we are too politically correct.

No longer do we have problems; we have "issues." We are taught to be tolerant and never say that anyone's opinion is wrong. We are taught to have an open mind, but some people's minds have been open so long that their brains have fallen out. We wouldn't call anyone a heretic, and we wouldn't describe anything as wrong, bad, or evil. We certainly wouldn't tell a church that the false teaching within it is so bad that, if they believe it, they will go to hell and that those who preach it are going to hell; nor would we wish that those who preach it would dismember the most private part of their anatomy. For such things as this, you get kicked out of denominations not lauded as "valiant for truth" today.

But God, as C. S. Lewis implied, is no tame lion. We need not to defend Paul but to let God's Word roar. With five growls leading to a full blown sixth roar, Paul confronts theological or doctrinal error in six points from which we can discover how to stand up for truth today.

Contradiction

First, Paul shows how this human persuasion to turn from the truth *contradicts* the call of God. "You were running well. Who hindered you from obeying the truth? This persuasion is not from him who calls you" (vv. 7–8). The Galatian agitators were trying to persuade the Galatians to add religious works to the gospel, and Paul responds by exposing that persuasion as a contradiction. If works are necessary for our justification, that contradicts God's call; therefore, it cannot be from "him who calls you." The gospel is about God's calling us, not about our earning our way to heaven; it is a call of grace. For the Galatian false teachers to claim that the Galatians needed to be circumcised, to obey the whole Law of Moses, in order to be justified made about as much sense as being drafted into the army and then telling the sergeant he should be grateful that you volunteered. It makes as much sense as coming down on Christmas morning and being told that you have to pay for your presents. An atheistic character in a Douglas Adams book found himself in a bad situation and prayed and hoped that there was no afterlife. He then realized that was a contradiction in terms, so he just hoped. You can't get called by grace and then be persuaded that you need works if you think about how you were called. It would be like stopping at a stop sign and waiting for it to say go.

They were "running well" and "obeying the truth." Actually, "obeying" is used to smooth out Paul's staccato series of six one-liner theological putdowns and to explain the connection between cutting and "persuading no to truth," as it is more literally. They were doing just fine, all by grace. That's the first way Paul confronts the error: he points to conversion, to how one becomes a Christian. People get taken in by legalism because they forget how they got converted.

I've come across people with stunning, dramatic, Spirit-filled, sit-up-and-shout-hallelujah conversions who end up getting all legalistic because they don't think about how they were born again. If all this justification talk confuses you, just think how you got called as a Christian. If you're not a Christian, the good news is that it's by grace, not works. That doesn't mean that you don't walk the walk; it means you do obey because you are born again. If you're a fisherman, you fish, if you're a painter, you paint, if you're a Christian, you follow Jesus. Getting saved is not like people who try to get physically fit by buying an expensive gym membership and then never going to the gym. It's like people who fall in love with Jesus because he first called out to them in love.

Just a Bit Off

The second way to stand up for truth and confront error is to realize that being a little bit off on the gospel matters massively: "A little leaven leavens the whole lump" (v. 9). Behind this well-known saying is the exodus story about when God's people were asked to make unleavened bread, bread without yeast, in order to be ready to leave quickly. Paul uses the saying again in 1 Corinthians 5:6: "Do you not know that a little leaven leavens the whole lump?" Yeast stands for the malevolent influence not ready to leave Egypt and get saved. The point of the pithy saying is that only a bit of yeast (evil) in the church or in an individual trying to get away with a bit of private sin impacts the whole batch of dough.

Going a bit off on the gospel is like having only a bit of the flu virus. Small, but very bad. One person comments: "One of the most serious things about evil and error is that they spread." A virus is tiny, but it infects cells and spreads, even as just a few small granules of false gospel yeast. Calling the Galatian false teachers' message "leavened bread" is a bit like Mozart, who apparently once walked out of an opera and said, "I liked your opera. Perhaps I will set it to music." The Galatians were talking generally about God, but they'd so badly messed up their doctrine that it had mutated to an infectious disease.

Small mistakes on gospel DNA matter big time. Our biblical knowledge has become in some places sufficiently unsophisticated that some think that if Jesus is just mentioned, then everything is fine. In contrast, our society is full of well-educated consumers who can confidently take the Pepsi Challenge or spot brand-name Levi imitations. Jesus, yes, we want Jesus. But *which* Jesus? The Jesus of Mormons, or of Jehovah's Witnesses, or of liberals, or the Jesus of the Bible? The Trinity, yes, but can we read through a doctrinal statement from a non-Trinitarian group and tell the difference?

I'm still dumbfounded by someone I spoke with who went to a Roman Catholic church from an evangelical megachurch. I asked him about the differences, and he said, 'The Catholic church is a bit more somber," and when I asked him if he'd heard of justification by faith alone, he replied, "No, what's that?" It's only the heart of the gospel and the means of your salvation, brother.

Our commitment to the Jesus of the Bible does not mean that we go around excommunicating people who have slightly different views of the creation or of the precise dating of the second coming, or how hot hell is, or how happy heaven will be. It does mean that on the primary matters of salvation, a few granules of yeast will impact the whole batch of dough. The same is true for moral matters. We are not going to distance ourselves from people who sound a little grumpy when we call them at 6 AM, but when it comes to basic Christian morality— sexuality, anger, hate, lust, greed—these things need to be addressed. However, we do so with gospel compassion, not legalistic judgmentalism, because a little yeast goes through the whole batch. So the second way to stand up for truth and confront error is to make a big deal of the central matters of the gospel but not a big deal of the secondary matters.

No Intimidation

The third way to stand up for truth and confront error is not to be intimidated. Paul prevents the Galatians from feeling intimidated by the impressive false teachers by communicating his confidence in the

Galatians: "I have confidence in the Lord that you will take no other view than mine" (v. 10a). Paul knows the Galatians are real Christians; therefore, with the doctrine of the preservation of the saints, Paul is confident that they will take no other view and will come around in the end.

When we are in a difficult situation, we need that confidence. We need to know that Jesus did not lie when he said, "I give them eternal life, and they will never perish, and no one will snatch them out of my hand" (John 10:28). We need a pastor who will come to us and say, "This is bad, but you're going to make it, because God hasn't changed his mind about you, and he promised he'd never leave you nor forsake you." That's justification. That's the doctrine that Paul has been teaching all along applied to this pastoral situation. He's confident in them because he's confident in the gospel and in the God of the gospel, who has promised that they are his people eternally.

The Repercussions

The fourth way to stand up for truth and confront error is to declare at times the repercussions for deliberately misleading God's people: "The one who is troubling you will bear the penalty, whoever he is" (v. 10b). There will be a penalty, and it will be paid.

"Not many of you should become teachers, my brothers, for you know that we who teach will be judged with greater strictness" (James 3:1). When you stand behind the pulpit, or the lectern, or with the Bible open on your knee in a Bible study group, when you talk with authority over coffee afterwards about some theological matter, when you have roast pastor for lunch, when you write books that are creative and innovative—realize that there is a judgment for what we teach. That is why my main advice to teachers of God's Word is to be just that. Do not be a teacher of your own agenda, but be an expositor, an explainer of God's Word. Hide behind it and declare it, and let God do with it as he wills.

Paul brings in the eternal perspective, and if there is a greater need in the church today, I have not discerned it. You can make jokes about death as Woody Allen did: "I don't mind dying; I just don't want to be there when it happens." Oscar Wilde planned to say to his wife on his death bed, "Either that wall paper goes or I do." But I have never heard someone laugh about the separation of the sheep from the goats, of the final judgment they will bear. People don't like us talking about the penalties of hell or confidence in future of all true Christians. I guess that's because they don't believe in it. But no one objects to crying "Fire! Fire!" as loud as possible when a building is burning down. *Please, don't be so impolite, don't try to frighten people, don't get so loud, calm down; if you have to mention it, hide it in the footnotes of your doctrinal statement but don't actually declare it from your pulpits or write it in your letters and e-mails and books.* No one who believes that the house is burning down would say that, and we do believe it. So we need to proclaim it as loudly and as clearly as possible. In the same way we must proclaim the eternal security of those who are running the race of the Christian life and obeying the truth.

False Accusation

The fifth way to stand up for truth and confront error is to stand up against false accusation. Paul defends himself against false accusation, which all leaders need to do occasionally. George Bernard Shaw wrote to Churchill, "Am reserving two tickets for you for my premiere. Come and bring a friend—if you have one," to which Churchill defended himself, "Impossible to be present for the first performance. Will attend second—if there is one."

For some reason, the agitators had been saying that Paul was on their side, which must have really riled him up, much as the band of Meatloaf would feel if they were made poster boys for country music. "But if I, brothers, still preach circumcision, why am I still being persecuted? In that case the offense of the cross has been removed" (v. 11). "Paul is still preaching circumcision," the Galatian agitators said, meaning that Paul was still advocating the law as necessary for justification, just as they were. In reality, Paul had always taught justification by faith and that the Law of Moses was intended to underline our need for that justification and point to Christ as the fulfillment of the law.

False accusation against Christian leaders happens frequently. Sometimes, as here, people who want to persuade us of some new idea will claim a great forebear, or current famed leader, as being on their side. As a Jonathan Edwards scholar, I see this happening often.

Whatever the theological issue of the day, someone will claim Edwards for their side. Edwards is a bit like Michael Jordan—with him on your team, you are more likely to slam-dunk your theological opponents.

Sometimes people make merry with what you do not say to get you to mean something you would never agree to, which is a bit like saying that because a NASA scientist never explicitly denies the existence of alien remains in Area 51 of the Nevada desert, they must exist. Perhaps the agitators had heard that Paul had circumcised Timothy, though that would put this letter a little later in the chronology of Acts than where I put it. Paul had circumcised Timothy for the purpose of contextualizing evangelism, not because he thought Timothy needed to be justified. Perhaps they used the fact that Paul himself, as a former Pharisee, was circumcised. Whatever the circumstance, they made much ado about nothing.

It's important to defend Christian leaders against false accusation. One of the ways the Devil tries to undermine the teaching of the gospel is by undermining those who teach it. Support your elders. Support your pastors. How does Paul defend himself? He doesn't go into great detail; he just points out the logical impossibility. Paul was being persecuted for preaching the cross; if he had still been preaching circumcision, he would not have been persecuted. The logic of this is a little lost on us now, but at the time, because Judaism was the grandfathered religion of the Jewish people, it was given acceptable legal status within the Roman Empire. The newfangled religion called Christianity, however, which was all about Jesus' death on the cross for our sins, did not have that privileged status and around this time was beginning to suffer persecution because of it. So, Paul says, if he were preaching circumcision, he wouldn't be getting persecuted. They hadn't just lost the plot; they'd lost the whole library.

So, a key sign of our faithfulness to the gospel is that we get beaten up a little by nominal Christians or by the world. If we do not experience any friction with this current age, then it's probably a sign that we're on autopilot spiritually, floating downstream rather than upstream. Don't pray for opposition, and don't seek it, but remember that only dead salmon float downstream. Living faith swims upstream, against the flow, and there will normally be some friction from the opposing current of the world. If you never sense friction with the world, perhaps it is time to find a deeper recommitment to Christ and the church.

Paul's Verbal Putdown

Sixth, and finally, we come to where we started, which is with Paul's eye-popping verbal putdown of the Galatian agitators, the roar of verse 12: "I wish those who unsettle you would emasculate themselves!" There may have been a touch of rakish irony to it. As David Niven said of his friend Errol Flynn, "You always knew precisely where you stood with him because he always let you down." But, like Shakespeare's humor, "Better a witty fool than a foolish wit," Paul's putdown had a serious point.

We would have said, "I wish they'd quiet down a little bit," or, "I wish they'd get off their hobbyhorse." More likely, we wouldn't have said anything about them at all for fear of offense. With verse 12, Paul lets the Bible roar. I am reminded of the wisdom of Paul in taking a stand, an unpopular stand, even with a verbal putdown, against prevalent evil, by the famous words on the holocaust memorial in Boston:

> They came first for the Communists,
>> and I didn't speak up because I wasn't a Communist.
> Then they came for the Jews,
>> and I didn't speak up because I wasn't a Jew.
> Then they came for the trade unionists,
>> and I didn't speak up because I wasn't a trade unionist.
> Then they came for the Catholics,
>> and I didn't speak up because I was a Protestant.
> Then they came for me,
>> and by that time no one was left to speak up.[1]

I am also reminded of the even more famous words, often attributed to Edmund Burke, "All that is necessary for evil to triumph is for good men to do nothing."

Good men and women, children, students, old and young, we live in great pleasure and splendid ease, many of us. Some of us have hard

---

[1] Attributed to Martin Niemöeller (1892–1984).

battles to fight to provide and live another day. If you're not yet a Christian, I want to tell you that this gospel that saves is so important that it is worth taking a stand for. It is something to live for. If you are a Christian, I want to remind you of that. "Like a muddied spring or a polluted fountain is a righteous man who gives way before the wicked" (Prov. 25:26). You and I must not be a generation that future generations will look back to and say, "They went quietly into the night." We must stand up for the one hope for all mankind, the gospel of Jesus Christ. Even if it means not being nice.

27

The Use of Gospel Freedom

For you were called to freedom, brothers. Only do not use your freedom as an opportunity for the flesh, but through love serve one another. For the whole law is fulfilled in one word: "You shall love your neighbor as yourself." But if you bite and devour one another, watch out that you are not consumed by one another.

GALATIANS 5:13–15

A man is drenched wet with rain. His face is white, sick looking, and he has a raking cough. He stumbles into the expansive estate of his friends to convalesce from his illness. Each night he wakes with haunted dreams of the slave trade, of his failure at this point to have it abolished, and of his ongoing drive, passion, and calling to set slaves free. William Wilberforce was that man, and he did in the end prevail in abolishing the slave trade, but not without considerable personal cost.

Another man sits at his luxurious resort in Jamaica, counting his millions as he pumps out fiction novel after fiction novel and watches them turn into bestselling movies. At the same time, he's in the midst of an adulterous affair, which culminates in a marriage and a son, who later commits suicide. This man is Ian Fleming, the author of the James Bond saga, who died in his mid-fifties of a heart attack after years of excessive drinking.

The one man is enslaved by an overruling love to set his fellow man free and is himself free to rise to true human greatness. The other man is freely dissolute with endless worldly possibilities, and his life ends prematurely and his child's in tragedy.

Freedom is the desire of the human race. As Abraham Lincoln said, "Freedom is the last, best hope of earth." Even if the cynics say freedom is just chaos with better lighting, we still want it.[1] But is freedom fol-

---

[1] Alan Dean Foster.

lowing your natural desires, or is freedom giving yourself in service to others? If the latter, is that just moral duty, or is there something more to the process of becoming holy than dogged determination?

Paul returns to the theme of freedom with which he opened Galatians 5. There is actually a delightful, teasing contrast between that opening verse and the passage we are looking at now, which indicates the profundity of what Paul is teaching. In verse 1, Paul says don't let anyone take away the freedom of justification by faith alone, which would be a return to the yoke of slavery. In verse 13, Paul says make sure that freedom issues in service, which, in apparently paradoxical symmetry, is the same word for "slavery."

Paul is not what theologians call "antinomian," that the moral law has no authority in the Christian life. He and the Galatian agitators are united in their belief that Christians must live like Christians, like God's people, holy as he is holy. The difference between them is that while the Galatian agitators thought that we live good lives by the law, Paul says we live good lives "by the Spirit" (v. 16). The Spirit is not only for becoming born again but also for living as born-again people. This is one of the great teachings of the Bible but frequently missed.

These verses tell us that *true freedom is loving service.* First, we have to fight for true freedom. Second, loving, mutual service is the way to win that internal battle. Third, watch out for fake freedom, because it enslaves.

Fight for True Freedom

First, *we have to fight for true freedom.* "You were called to freedom, brothers. Only do not use your freedom as an opportunity for the flesh" (v. 13a). There are two words in the verse that Paul uses in a specific sense, which, if you don't get, can lead you to completely misunderstand everything he's saying about holiness. One of those words is "flesh." The "flesh" or "sinful nature" is not just the body or our physical nature. It is the tendency we all have in every aspect of our lives to do what Paul describes in verses 19 through 21, a litany of self-destructive and God-denying attitudes and actions. Paul is not a gnostic, who believes that the body is bad and the spirit is good. He is a Christian, who believes that everything about us is naturally in rebellion against God. This is the flesh or sinful nature.

The other word here that he uses in a specific sense is the word "opportunity." That word has the sense of a base camp for a military operation. Paul, then, says that the flesh, our sinful human nature—us in our continuing sinful state this side of heaven—sees the freedom of the gospel and wants to use that as a base, a military base, for a warfare campaign to take us toward what is sinful. That is why we have to fight for true freedom. Paul writes, "For the desires of the flesh are against the Spirit, and the desires of the Spirit are against the flesh, for these are opposed to each other" (v. 17). There is a battle going on; and the flesh wishes to take our freedom in Christ as a base camp to do what it wants.

Paul wants us to realize that whenever the gospel of free grace is preached, where our sins are forgiven for the asking and we are declared eternally right with God, our great temptation is to abuse that freedom to sin. It might be pride, or jealousy, or the idea that somehow Jesus' death means that we can do whatever we like and that there will be no accounting for our moral actions. That idea has found its time, but Jesus is not the Savior *of* our sins so that we might sin more but the Savior *from* our sins so that we might sin less. We are a slave to whatever masters us, so, having been set free, we must resist a new slavery to idolatries and addictions and maintain and develop our gospel freedom. We are in an ongoing, pitched battle to take the freedom of the gospel and use it for God and the gospel, and not for self-indulgence. We live on a battlefield. As the old saying puts it, "You can't stop the birds flying over your head, but you can stop them nesting in your hair." Or, as the child with computers on his mind prayed with unwitting humor, "Lead us not into temptation but deliver us from e-mail." We have to fight for true freedom, but how do we win that battle?

Winning the Battle

Second, *loving, mutual service is the way to win this battle*. Paul continues, "But through love serve one another. For the whole law is fulfilled in one word: 'You shall love your neighbor as yourself'" (vv. 13b–14). This is far more than just the standard idea of duty. When we look at verses like this one, we tend toward natural ideas like George Bernard

Shaw's saying, "Liberty means responsibility. That is why most men dread it." Yes, liberty does carry with it a certain responsibility, but Paul is saying far more than that we need to take responsibility and do our civic duty.

Notice that Paul does not give a summary of the entire law. When Jesus was asked to summarize the law, he said, love the Lord your God and then love your neighbor as yourself. In a passage parallel to this one in Galatians, Paul does the same thing: he quotes only the second part of Jesus' summary of the whole law (Rom. 13:9). This is the entire law summed up, but it is only the entire law of what theologians, for convenience, sometimes call the "second table" of the Ten Commandments, those commandments which are about our relationship to those around us. The "first table" contains commandments about our relationship to God.

Notice also how Paul suddenly introduces love: "But through love serve one another." Paul says that the freedom to which we are called establishes the relationship represented by the first table, the love toward God. We are now in a free, loving relationship with God. We are right with God. Paul says that *with this love* we can love each other through practical service.

A rugby movie starring Morgan Freeman and Matt Damon explored the relationship between Nelson Mandela's historic presidency of South Africa and the Springboks' 1995 winning of the Rugby World Cup. Race and rugby in South Africa have long had a, well, colorful relationship, and Mandela symbolically and deliberately shared the celebrations of the winning Springbok team. Mandela, of course, was formed by his time in prison. Before that, he was a freedom fighter; some said he was a terrorist. After many years in prison he came out a changed man with a new vision for South Africa. I am not saying the gospel setting us free from prison is exactly like that, of course, but it does seem to me that in a somewhat similar way, the set-us-free call of God from our prison of sin, that love with which he first loved us, functions not only as a motivator but also as a character-changing event. If you were in jail, and someone came along and set you free, would you wander aimlessly back to jail? Don't. Use the inspiration of that person who set you free to change the course of your life. You are free now, and that set-free love is the inspiration for your service to those around you, to set them free.

Specifically, Paul says the law is "fulfilled in one word," which is important because "fulfilled" is Paul's standard way of expressing the Christian's relation to the law, and "word" relates to the *word* of the Ten Commandments, as they are described in Deuteronomy. Jesus' death was, "in order that the righteous requirement of the law might be fulfilled in us, who walk not according to the flesh but according to the Spirit" (Rom. 8:4). Paul's practice is not to quote a law and simply say, "Christian, you need to do that." He says that the law is fulfilled in those who are in Christ. In a sense, we fulfill the law. So, in us this law is now fulfilled. We are free, we have been gospel loved, and therefore we love and serve others as Christ's love serves us.

Some common misunderstandings of what Paul says here can then be addressed. The misunderstanding of the so-called new morality that Robinson represented in his book *Honest to God* or that the Beatles tipped their hat to with "All You Need Is Love" is now terribly old-fashioned. Paul does not mean that we can do whatever we like as long as we do it in love. He is saying that if we love, we will love our neighbors and therefore live in a way that is best for our neighbors. We won't defraud them of their possessions, their time, or their relationships. This also corrects the misunderstanding that the old Protestant interpretation of Paul, the one I take, somehow does not take seriously the idea that we are responsible to fulfill the law. Luther himself, in his great commentary on Galatians, went on for a whole page at this point about those who take the freedom of the gospel and don't use it to serve each other in love but as a base camp for the flesh.[2] He also quoted from the ancient Christian commentator Jerome, who expressed regret about the legalistic monastic movement, because "we punish our bodies with vigils, fasts, and labors; but we neglect love, which is the lord and master of all works."[3] It is the freedom of the call of love that alone leads to neighbor-love service.

How are we going to become holier? We become holier through the gospel. The gospel is not only the means of our being saved, but it is also

---

[2]Martin Luther, *Lectures on Galatians*, Luther's Works, ed. Jaroslav Jan Pelikan (St. Louis, MO: Concordia, 1963), 48.
[3]Ibid., 55.

the mechanism by which we grow in godliness and ongoing holy freedom. We become holy through God's call that sets us free. Like him, we serve. Like him, we die to ourselves to save our neighbor. Our neighbor, of course, is not just the person living next door to us but those whom our actions could influence either positively or negatively. Lord Acton, in the celebrated 1932 case of Donoghue and Stevenson the British House of Lords, which dealt with a snail found in the bottom of a bottle of ginger beer, if you can believe it, defined neighbor like this: "Who then, in law, is my neighbor? The answer seems to be 'persons who are so closely and directly affected by my act that I ought reasonably to have them in contemplation as being so affected when I am directing my mind to the acts or emissions which are called in question.'" Or, as Martin Luther King put it, "the true neighbor will risk his position, his prestige, and even his life for the welfare of others. In dangerous valleys and hazardous pathways, he will lift some bruised and beaten brother to a higher and more noble life."

Christians fulfill the law of neighbor love. This means that Christians will be known for loving their neighbors, in the full sense of the word *neighbor*. Even atheists notice this sometimes. A well-known atheist wrote an article in the Guardian newspaper on his observations about the response to the tragedy of Hurricane Katrina a few years ago. In it he grudgingly admitted that whatever one thought of Christians' beliefs, the people who were down in the ditches, doing the hard work of shelter and providing food and clothes, were the evangelical Christians.[4] "Notable by their absence," he said, were "teams from rationalist societies, free thinkers' clubs, and atheists' associations—the sort of people who scoff at religion's intellectual absurdity." Gospel Christians love their neighbors.

Fake Freedom

Third, *watch out for fake freedom because it enslaves*. Paul concludes these words on freedom with a warning: "If you bite and devour one another, watch out that you are not consumed by one another" (v. 15). This is a verse full of dramatic imagery. If you *bite* and *eat* each other,

---

[4]Roy Hattersley, "Faith Does Breed Charity," September 12, 2005, *Guardian*, http://www.guardian.co.uk/world/2005/sep/12/religion.uk.

watch out or you'll *consume* each other. This is probably an image of the lions or wild animals at the Roman circus games, or perhaps of the slaves that had to fight. Paul is obviously warning the Galatians that if they don't love each other, there will be negative consequences for all. A bit of verbal biting, an occasional character suicide devouring—watch out or you'll destroy each other, like wild animals in the games.

There is an important theological, or exegetical, question behind this: Is Paul describing the consequences of being a legalist or the consequences of immoral license? Is he saying: "This is what will happen if you listen to the Galatian agitators. They think they're going to help you become more holy, but it will really just lead to communal relational breakdown. In fact, it already is going that way. Watch out! Come back to the gospel, because that is how you get holy, and live in love together." Or is Paul saying, "If you use this gospel of freedom as an excuse to sin, then that immoral license, that base camp for the flesh, is going to destroy the community. You might think you're getting some free living, but actually you're no different from wild animals being set free in the amphitheater of the games. They—and you—are just going to end up eating each other completely if you don't stop taking advantage."

I think the answer is probably both, not because Paul can't make his mind up but because of the context of this letter. In the *immediate* context Paul is saying that immoral licentiousness leads to destruction, but in the context of the *whole* letter Paul is saying that legalism also leads to destruction. The first, that licentiousness leads to communal destruction, is probably obvious to us; if we're all selfish, no one's going to be happy. The second, that legalism leads to communal destruction, is perhaps not as obvious.

Legalism potentially leads even to communal destruction because once we start putting secondary things in place of the primacy of the gospel, there is no end to the potential disagreement. It could be baptism that we make primary; it could be eschatology; it could be a certain religious experience; it could be a particular practice or discipline. Only the gospel can hold us together in the Spirit of love. When the true center of Christian community is marginalized, we develop a hydra-headed multitude of alternative centers, even calling each other names in the name of Jesus. The phrase "in essentials unity, in nonessentials diversity, in all things charity" is still not a bad principle (as long as it doesn't lead to theological sloppiness, or an inability to discern new heresies that always mushroom because of our natural sinful flesh this side of glory).

To say that Paul is spiritually insightful in these few verses is an understatement of the order of saying that Michelangelo's Sistine chapel is pretty good art. Paul says that freedom is not the freedom that the flesh wants to take and make a military base camp for sinful patterns of behaving, because that freedom is destructive. Instead, true freedom is loving service. Because of and through the free gospel call of love, serve one another, as we were served in love, and so fulfill the law.

John F. Kennedy visited West Berlin on June 26, 1963, and gave a speech in the shadow of the Berlin wall, which had been built by the East Germans in the fall of 1961. After brief opening comments, he said: "Two thousand years ago the proudest boast was '*civis Romanus sum*' [I am a citizen of Rome]. Today, in the world of *freedom*, the proudest boast is '*Ich bin ein Berliner*' [I am a Berliner]." Technically, Kennedy's comment was correct, but the usage is ambiguous and uncommon. By inserting the word *ein* in front of Berliner, Kennedy, according to many and to others an urban legend, effectively communicated to the large audience, "I am a jelly donut." Evidently a translator stepped in at this point, for after the cheering and laughing died down enough for him to resume, Kennedy said, "I appreciate my interpreter translating my German." The Simpsons had fun with this goof in one of their episodes. The mayor of the program's hometown of Springfield was giving a speech in which he said, "*Ich bin ein Springfielder*," to which Homer Simpson responded, "Mmmmmm. Jelly donuts."

Freedom is often misunderstood. Paul wanted the Galatians not to misunderstand it. He wanted them to further it and to love others as they had been loved, and so in themselves fulfill the law. The challenge to love our neighbor always takes us back to the call of Christ, the gospel, our freedom. Talk of sanctification should always lead us back in humility to our justification, and talk of justification should always lead us in serving, freeing love and zeal for our continued sanctification. In Anthony Trollope's *The Last Chronicle of Barset*, Mr. Crawley, a sort of hero figure and perpetual curate of a poor parish and therefore very poor himself, talks about how we do not have equal sympathy with the sufferings of all people, however rich or poor, important or insignificant. He remarks that to care for all equally would be the act of a god among men. Then he says, "It is in his perfection as a man that we recognize the *divinity* of Christ. It is in the imperfection of men that we recognize our *necessity* for a Christ." So, as this passage in Galatians challenges us to neighbor love, it also draws us back to the one who called us, to Christ, who served us and gave himself for us in love that we might be free.

28

The Gospel and the Spirit

But I say, walk by the Spirit, and you will not gratify the desires of the
flesh. For the desires of the flesh are against the Spirit, and the
desires of the Spirit are against the flesh, for these are opposed to
each other, to keep you from doing the things you want to do.
But if you are led by the Spirit, you are not under the law.

GALATIANS 5:16–18

Some of us like the idea of going for a long walk or hike, loading up our backpack and heading off into the woods for a day trip or even a camping excursion. Others of us drive repeatedly around the car park next to the grocery store trying to find the parking space nearest the entrance. There are those of us who love the Outward Bound experience, and those of us who think there is nothing more lovely than curling up with a good book or in front of a good movie holding a cup of hot chocolate on a cold day. But we all recognize, I suspect, that there is something pleasant, something basic, about going for a walk with a friend or a family member. Perhaps after Thanksgiving we take a turn around the block, if we can still walk after all the turkey.

There is in Galatians 5:16–18 a controlling metaphor or picture, which, for some strange reason, is often noticed but rarely emphasized. But Paul, as he talks about the life of the Spirit, is deliberating using a picture of walking. "Walk by the Spirit" (v. 16). Then again in verse 18 he says, "If you are led by the Spirit . . . ," referring to the experience of being led on a walk. To confirm this as a controlling metaphor, he says, returning to the same picture, "If we live by the Spirit, let us also walk by the Spirit" (v. 25). The word in Greek is different from the one at the start and refers specifically to keeping in step with one with whom you are walking.

This is important because our mental pictures of life in the Spirit are usually rather confused. I suppose, most commonly, we think of the Spirit as a force. "Use the force, Luke," as Obi Wan Kenobi said to Luke Skywalker, might not be explicitly in our mind as a picture of what life in the Spirit is like, but for many people today, the idea of using the Spirit as a sort of force, an inanimate energy to which we can tap in, is the predominant mental picture.

Sometimes we picture the Spirit as a sort of liquid. The Bible does say in Paul's letter to the Ephesians, "be filled with the Spirit" (5:18) but the picture there is not one of needing to fill up with the Spirit as our car needs to fill up with gas, or as a glass needs to be filled with water. The Bible does talk of the Spirit as like the wind, and it tells us to be filled with the Spirit and to drink of the water of life. The Bible has other metaphors for the spiritual life in general, but being filled with the Spirit is more like the way a strong personality can fill a room.

I want you to picture life in the Spirit as Paul does here, as a walk. That will help those of us who find discussion about the Holy Spirit rather scary and wonder whether we're suddenly going to have to do all sorts of weird things. It's also going to help those of us who tend to think of the spiritual life as following a GPS signal with a rather pleasant voice telling us to turn left in 100 yards, in other words, as an essentially passive lifestyle requiring no effort on our part.

Desires of the Flesh

"But I say, walk by the Spirit, and you will not gratify the desires of the flesh" (v. 16). I want you to notice three things about this. First, notice that Paul is clearly balanced in his teaching about holiness, a balance that emphasizes both the active and the passive. What comes into your mind when you think about holiness? Being bored, not doing fun stuff—don't dance, don't chew, don't go with girls that do, being against fornication in case it might lead to dancing, whips and chains, all-night vigils, and depressive moroseness?

Contrarily, Paul has a wonderfully balanced view of the way not to gratify the desires of the flesh. Those desires are listed in verses 19 through 21 and are far more than merely physical but also attitudes of our heart. How do we not get jealous or angry, or not idolize sophisticated intellectual abilities, good looks, or a powerful individual in our lives? The answer is this wonderful balance called "walking by the Spirit." Earlier in the letter Paul wrote, "Are you so foolish? Having begun by the Spirit, are you now being perfected by the flesh?" (3:3). That's one side of the balance. Just as we begin as a Christian with the Spirit, so we become gradually more like Christ by the same Spirit. The other side is that though it is "by the Spirit," it is still a walk with which we need to keep in step.

Second, notice that Paul carries on his picture of the walk in relation to the desires of the sinful nature that we are not to gratify. The word for "gratify" has the sense of fulfilled or complete, the end point of the walk, the destination or destiny. The flesh wants us to end our journey in a ditch, stuck in a bog, drowning in quicksand, run over by a tractor-trailer. It wants us to give full rein to our addictive tendencies, our self-hate, our destruction of those around us, so that we end up alone and friendless—rich maybe, with lots of toys, but with no friends and no one to mourn our departing or cheer our arriving on the other side of the grave. This walk is not just a nice stroll in the park; there are winds and storms and hurricane forces that, by the Spirit, we need to walk through not to end up with the destiny of the flesh.

Third, notice that the way not to gratify the desires of the sinful nature is to walk by the Spirit. How do I look at a woman without letting my eye gradually scan downward? How do I hear a juicy piece of gossip and not "share it for prayer as a matter of concern" to everyone who will listen? How do I say no to another drink? How do I not get jealous when someone younger than I does better? How do I not get angry when I am passed over for a pay raise or lose my job? Paul says, walk by the Spirit.

Expect Conflict

Paul says that walking by the Spirit will bring conflict: "For the desires of the flesh are against the Spirit, and the desires of the Spirit are against the flesh, for these are opposed to each other, to keep you from doing the things you want to do" (v. 17).

On the eve of D-day General George Patton famously addressed the 3rd Army. His speech is dramatized in the 1970 movie. Patton was a controversial figure and the archetypal fighter. In the speech, peppered with colorful language, he said things like, "My men don't surrender, and I don't want to hear of any man under my command being captured unless he has been hit." He told the story of a man with a bullet in his lung and a gun to his chest who fought back using the helmet off his head.

War speeches are not for church, or are they? Well, here in Galatians Paul describes a war, a conflict, if you prefer the sanitized language, but the same word is used for Jesus' opponents, for the opposition of false doctrine, and even for the opponent the Devil himself.[1]

How do we walk by the Spirit? This is no walk through a country meadow with birds singing and flowers gently bending in the wind. It is a walk through a minefield with bombs whistling overhead and the graves of the unwary, roughly dug, littering the ground around us. We are in conflict, and the flesh is warring against the Spirit.

To walk by the Spirit is to act as if we are marching in a war zone, spiritually speaking. We don't come to church thinking, *I'm going to sing a few songs, and pray a little prayer, and hear a little sermon with, if I'm lucky, a nice story or two, and then go home and watch football on television.* We come to church thinking, *My Lord and my God, if I don't walk by the Spirit today, I'm going to do what I don't want; I'm going to give into the lust of the flesh.* We don't pick up our Bible, dust it off the shelf, and think, *I'll read a thought for the day and off I go to work.* We think, *My Lord and my God, I need the sword of the Spirit, which is the Word of God, or I'm going to give into the lust of the flesh.* We don't think, *I've been a Christian for forty years, so now I'm safe.* We don't think, *I go to a Christian college, so now I'm safe.* We realize that inside us D-day is being fought and that there is a battle raging for our souls, and we live that way.

We don't look at our neighbors and say, "They live nice quiet lives; let's not disturb them by talking to them about Jesus." We don't say, "This church is doing fine; let's just get along." We look at the millions needing the gospel; we act, in short, not as in peace time but as in a time of conflict. We draw up strategies to see people come to Jesus; we burn the midnight oil and set the alarm before dawn; we work our socks off, knowing that we are in a conflict and that it is real. That's what it means

[1]See Luke 13:17; 21:15; 1 Cor. 16:9; Phil. 1:28; 2 Thess. 2:4; 1 Tim. 5:14.

to walk in the Spirit—not to go for a pleasant, Sunday-afternoon stroll, but to march into battle.

Paul's words can sound intimidating: "Keep you from doing the things you want to do." Is there no hope of victory? Certainly, yes. There is the reality of the fight, but Paul's teaching of the walk of the Spirit is not only that the way is a walk into spiritual war but also that we do it with great confidence of final victory, with a peaceful conscience and without condemnation.

No Condemnation

"If you are led by the Spirit, you are not under law" (v. 18). We are back to walking again, though this time the emphasis is not upon our effort but upon the one doing the leading, the Spirit. In order to explain why it is so important that we get this right, I want to give you a theological framework to understand what Paul is saying here and then some examples and applications as we conclude where Paul concludes.

Justification is a technical term that means "being declared right before God." *Sanctification* is a technical term that means "the process of gradually becoming more holy." Paul says, in terms of a theological framework, that our sanctification comes *after* our justification, and it is connected to it. When I am justified before God, I receive his Holy Spirit, and at the moment of justification I begin the process of sanctification. I have the Holy Spirit, and having begun by the Spirit, I am now to continue to make progress in sanctification by the same Spirit. We are led by the Spirit, Paul says, which means we are not under law. Paul doesn't mean that the Christian does not need to behave morally; Paul is telling us that we do. In fact, God's purpose is that we would be holy, as he is holy. This is the law of Christ (6:2), but we are not "under the law," meaning that we know we are justified. We are no longer condemned by the law. So when Paul says, "If you are led by the Spirit, you are not under law," he is explaining that, as Christians, we have the Spirit, and therefore we are led by the Spirit, and that means we are not under law, which means we are not under condemnation. That is the theological framework.

The examples I want to give are from some of the holiest people in history, typically so-thought, and I want you to see how little they thought of themselves and how confident they were in their relationship with Jesus. John Bradford, said by his colleagues to be the most saintly of the English Reformers, constantly signed his letters as "hard-hearted sinner." One Puritan in his last illness said, "Never did I so feel my need of the blood of Christ—and never was able to make such good use of it." John Wesley on his deathbed was supposedly heard to whisper, "No way into the holiest but by the blood of Jesus." Or take the attitude of Paul, who seems only to have grown in his sense of his own shortcomings, as well as of Christ's mercy. In about 54 AD he called himself "the least of the apostles" (1 Cor. 15:9); in about 61 AD he called himself "the very least of all the saints (Eph. 3:8); and in about 65 AD he considered himself the foremost of all sinners (1 Tim. 1:15).[2]

Being led by the Spirit, not the law, in no way means that we end up feeling good about ourselves for our achievements. It means that we are increasingly aware of our shortcomings but also even more increasingly aware of the sufficient sacrifice of Christ. As we began by grace, so we continue by grace; as we get closer to the light, we are more aware of our spots and blemishes—like a man who looks in a well-lit mirror can see every wrinkle and divot—but that only makes us take our attention back to him to be lost in the light of his love and to wonder and praise at his mercy.

One author asks these searching application questions about whether we are living in a state of condemnation ("under the law"): "Do you relate to God as if you were on a kind of permanent probation, suspecting that at any moment He may haul you back into the jail cell of His disfavor?"[3] We are not under the law. "When you come to worship, do you maintain a 'respectful distance' from God, as if He were a fascinating but ill-tempered celebrity known for lashing out at his fans?"[4] We are not under the law. "When you read Scripture, does it reveal the boundless love of the Savior or merely intensify your condemnation?"[5] We are not under the law. "Are you more aware of your sin than you are of God's grace, given to you through the cross?"[6] We are not under the law.

[2]J. I. Packer, *Keep in Step with the Spirit: Finding Fullness in Our Walk with God* (Grand Rapids, MI: Revell, 1987).
[3]C. J. Mahaney, *Living the Cross-Centered Life: Keeping the Gospel the Main Thing* (Sisters, OR: Multnomah, 2006), 125.
[4]Ibid.
[5]Ibid.
[6]Ibid.

Walk by the Spirit and there will be no condemnation. Being led by the Spirit means not being under the condemnation of the law. Yes, you become more aware of your sin; but in doing so, you become even more grateful and glad and free in the overwhelmingly sufficient sacrifice of Christ for that sin. Having begun with the Spirit, you continue with the Spirit, walking actively by the Spirit, depending upon the moral leading of the Spirit. He is real, he is here, he is with us. He does not nudge and guide us like a GPS navigation device or by helping us make the right decisions about which color shirt to wear today; he takes the initiative in asserting his "gentle pressure" upon us against the desires of the flesh, and we are to yield to his control:

> And His that gentle voice we hear,
> Soft as the breath of even,
> That checks each fault, that calms each fear,
> and speaks of Heaven.
> For every virtue we possess,
> And every victory won,
> and every thought of holiness,
> are His alone.[7]

Let's go for a walk. Let's take a turn together around the block. Let's talk about the things of life. Let's discuss whatever is on your mind. Let's walk. Let's step out into the battle. Hear the war cries of the flesh. See the sights of conflict. But let's walk on by the Spirit, depending on him, determining with all his power to live holy lives, make a difference in the world for Christ and for the gospel, and build his church and his kingdom. Let's walk by the Spirit.

---

[7]John R. W. Stott, *The Message of Galatians* (Downers Grove, IL: InterVarsity, 1984), 152–53.

29

Walk by the Spirit

Now the works of the flesh are evident: sexual immorality, impurity, sensuality, idolatry, sorcery, enmity, strife, jealousy, fits of anger, rivalries, dissensions, divisions, envy, drunkenness, orgies, and things like these. I warn you, as I warned you before, that those who do such things will not inherit the kingdom of God. But the fruit of the Spirit is love, joy, peace, patience, kindness, goodness, faithfulness, gentleness, self-control; against such things there is no law. And those who belong to Christ Jesus have crucified the flesh with its passions and desires. If we live by the Spirit, let us also walk by the Spirit. Let us not become conceited, provoking one another, envying one another.

GALATIANS 5:19–26

When Christians think of how to get more holy—how to live lives more akin to the godliness described as normative for the Christian life in Scripture—we tend to fear that this call to godliness is going to be legalistic. Or we tend to feel that it is all going to magically happen without any form of stringent effort, even spiritual effort, on our part. Paul, though, describes, in this famous passage, a method of attaining godliness that is distinctly spiritual yet also by no means passive. It is based upon the active desires of the regenerate Christian nature. It is a walk by the Spirit that causes us to bear the fruit of the Spirit.

This subject of true gospel holiness is of great importance today because we live in a world surrounded by advertising slogans designed to sell stuff, the content of which slogans we know is not, strictly speaking, true. You can't always "just do it," catchy as the Nike phrase may be; the new Starbucks instant coffee "Via" is probably not going to "change your life," as its new promotional booklet proclaims; and few of us, I suspect, believe that by eating good breakfast cereal you can "power yourself with the limitless possibilities of Quaker instant oatmeal." Limitless, I tell you.

Christianity, however, promises much—joy, peace, love—and those with the Spirit *are* able to deliver on the promise. So, in this passage, we are going to learn how to bear the fruit of the Spirit and how not to do the acts of the sinful nature. Paul begins by describing the acts of the sinful nature. He warns us that continuing to live like that means we do not inherit the eternal kingdom of God. Paul then describes the fruit of the Spirit. He tells us that bearing this fruit requires a mixture of passive dependence on God ("we live by the Spirit") as well as active determination ("Let us also walk by the Spirit").

Learning how to bear the fruit of the Spirit and not do the acts of the sinful nature are of great importance today because many people feel that Christianity is becoming one giant non sequitur. They think we talk a good game but do not walk the talk; we do not live up to the promise more than a sort of religious equivalent of the limitless possibilities of a certain oatmeal.

Commonly cited examples of this non-sequitur assumption are not hard to find in day-to-day conversation. Someone mentions a televangelist who embezzles funds. Another, the Roman Catholic priest who is sent to jail for abusing children. Then, there is the person down the road who says he is a Christian but never goes to church, much less behaves like a Christian. Our task is to learn how to have joy, love, and all the fruit of the Spirit and not do the acts of the sinful nature, thereby avoiding the religious non sequitur of advertising something but not delivering it.

What we're going to find is that Christian holiness is achieved not by the law, not by rules and regulations and judgmental condemnation, but by the Spirit: "If you are led by the Spirit, you are not under the law" (v. 18). There are two parts to Paul's teaching here about how to bear the fruit of the Spirit: stop kidding yourself, then start denying yourself.

Don't Kid Yourself

"Now the works of the flesh are evident: sexual immorality, impurity, sensuality, idolatry, sorcery, enmity, strife, jealousy, fits of anger, rivalries, dissensions, divisions, envy, drunkenness, orgies, and things like these. I warn you, as I warned you before, that those who do such things will not inherit the kingdom of God" (vv. 19–21). The Galatians were kidding themselves if they thought they could behave like this and still go to heaven. We are kidding ourselves today if we think we can do the deeds of the flesh and still inherit the kingdom of God.

Stopping kidding yourself means *stop thinking no one will notice.* Paul says the acts of the sinful nature are "evident." They are obvious to God. He sees and knows all. They are obvious to other people. We are not omniscient, unlike God, but most of us are very good at spotting fakes a mile away, whether the fakery is more subtle envy or less subtle immorality.

Stopping kidding yourself means *stop thinking it will do you any good.* Paul goes through the list of vices and then tails off with "and things like these." This list does not go anywhere, produce anything, or lead to any good result. It is very different from the lovely ordered fruit of the Spirit, which we will consider next. The acts of the sinful nature are more like rotting vegetables or decomposing fleshy meat. There is a continual, increasing, dissolution, disorder, and destruction. Sexual immorality may give momentary pleasure but at the cost of lasting disappointment. Idolizing your career can give financial rewards, but it destroys your family. Getting angry may let off steam, but the hot steam burns those who happen to be around at the time, like collateral damage. Drunkenness might make you forget your pain, but you remember it with a double dose the next morning. Stop kidding yourself that these will do any good.

Stopping kidding yourself means to *stop thinking you can get away with it.* Paul had warned them earlier that those going to heaven must have heaven in them now. Paul warns them again. This is a somber warning, but it is God's Word. The point is that those in the kingdom of God bear the characteristics of the citizens of the king, or they are not really in the kingdom.

This is not to say that the way to get into the kingdom is by doing good works; it is all by the free grace of Christ. But if we have received the free grace of Christ, then we will show forth the fruit of his Spirit. Jesus used the same illustration about fruit: a bad tree bears bad fruit; a good tree good fruit (Matt. 7:17).

Fruit of the Spirit

"But the fruit of the Spirit is love, joy, peace, patience, kindness, goodness, faithfulness, gentleness, self-control; against such things there is
no law. And those who belong to Christ Jesus have crucified the flesh
with its passions and desires. If we live by the Spirit, let us also walk by
the Spirit." (vv. 22–26). We move from the stinking, rotting vegetables
and decomposing flesh of the acts of the sinful nature to the sweet-
tasting fruit of the Spirit, from dissolution and chaos ("and things like
these") to clear structure and creativity. The promised fruit of the Spirit
is delivered with maximum sweetness, unlike the false promises of the
flesh and the mistaken promises of some marketing campaigns. As we
turn now to these famous words about the fruit of the Spirit, notice two
things about how the advertised promise of God's Spirit is truly fulfilled
in Christians' lives.

First, notice the *characteristics* of the fruit. To be in the kingdom
means bearing the characteristics of the king; to have the Spirit means to
bear the fruit of the Spirit. But what is that fruit; what are those characteristics? The "fruit of the Spirit" is characterized as a single unit. There
are not really *fruits* of the Spirit but only *fruit*. The difference between
the singular and the plural is more than grammatical: the Bible is telling
us that all the fruits of the Spirit are interconnected. I may have more joy
than patience, but as a Christian in the kingdom of God with the fruit of
the Spirit, I will have some of all, or none of any. The term for this concept of connection is *concatenation*, which is an old word but precise.
The fruit of the Spirit is a concatenation; that is, each of the components
of the fruit are connected by a chain to the others. If you have one, then
you have others. They are different aspects of one whole fruit.

This one fruit of the Spirit with nine aspects is interconnected along
the three-axis dimensions of *upward, outward, and inward*. Love, joy,
and peace are directed upward. These traits concern our relationship
with God. Part of walking a godly life is experiencing the peace of
assurance, the joy of intimacy, and the abundant love of an intimate,
strong relationship with the Lord. This triad is not merely for our private experience; it also overflows into the next triad of virtues, which
is outward: patience, kindness, and goodness. When we walk in the
Spirit, we not only experience a strong and vibrant personal relationship

with God but also have patience and kindness and demonstrate acts of goodness toward those around us. There is also an inward aspect, which includes faithfulness, gentleness, and self-control. This triad characterizes the people of God in their basic disposition: they are faithful, they are gentle, and they have self-control.

So, the fruit of the Spirit is characterized as one fruit, interconnected, a "concatenation," that is upward, outward, and inward. While none of us have the characteristics of the fruit in perfect measure, all of us in the kingdom have them in some measure. These characteristics are sweet fruit and greatly to be desired. I want you to desire them and to see them as lovely, and to be moved by the Spirit in your life to long for this fruit.

Second, notice the right way to bear much of this desirable fruit. Paul tells us that it is not by the law but by the cross, and it does take effort on our part. "Against such things there is no law" (v. 23b). The law convicts us of our need of Christ and shows us what holiness is meant to be; but holiness is achieved by the Spirit, not by the law. It is achieved by the cross: "Those who belong to Christ Jesus have crucified the flesh with its passions and desires" (v. 24). Compare this verse with Galatians 2:20: "I have been crucified with Christ. It is no longer I who live." There, the crucifixion is done to us. Here, where Paul is addressing living as a Christian as opposed to becoming a Christian, the crucifixion is something we do: "If we live by the Spirit, let us also walk by the Spirit" (v. 25).

Deny Yourself

The way to bear much fruit is not by the law but by the cross. It is to start denying yourself. John Stott applies it this way:

> So widely is this biblical teaching neglected, that it needs to be further enforced. The first great secret of holiness lies in the degree and decisiveness of our repentance. If besetting sins persistently plague us, it is either because we have never truly repented, or because, having repented, we have not maintained our repentance. It is as if, having nailed our old nature to the cross, we keep wistfully returning to the scene of its execution. We begin to fondle it, to caress it, to long for

its release, even to try to take it down again from the cross. We need to learn to leave it there. When some jealous, or proud, or malicious, or impure thought invades our mind we must kick it out at once. It is fatal to begin to examine it and consider whether we are going to give in to it or not. We have declared war on it; we are not going to resume negotiations. We have settled the issue for good; we are not going to re-open it. We have crucified the flesh; we are never going to draw the nails.[1]

The way, then, to bear the fruit of the Spirit is to start denying yourself. We are to *stop kidding ourselves* that deeds of the flesh go unnoticed, for they are obvious, or will go unaddressed, for they are incongruous to the kingdom and unacceptable to the King of the kingdom. We are to start denying ourselves so that the cross becomes not just our message but our lifestyle.

We've already seen that commercials reveal our tendency to think that the advertised promise is bigger than the fulfillment. Of course commercials are meant to sell us things, and harmless enough at that. You may or may not believe that Kentucky Fried Chicken is "Finger Lickin' Good," but that's probably a better tagline than, "It's quite nice, really, if you're into that sort of thing." We are used to a sort of selling-ourselves inflation. I came across a résumé that, under "Skills," listed: "strong work ethic, attention to detail, team player, self-motivated, *attention to detail*." When the Bible says we are to bear the fruit of the Spirit, is it exaggerating for effect? When it says that we may not live in a consistent lifestyle of the acts of the sinful nature, is it putting the speed limit at 30 just hoping that we don't go 40? Or does Paul mean what he says? Is it acceptable to live non-sequitur lives, to sing songs about "not a mite would I withhold," as if it were like saying that Starbucks Via instant coffee will change your life, a pardonable hyperbole not to be taken seriously? Or are we really to walk the talk?

When a politician promises the earth, we don't really expect much more than an occasional molehill, if we're lucky. But when God promises us heaven, do we begin to live with the Spirit of heaven in us, or are we satisfied with an occasional heavenly song or sermon?

Other people notice. In days gone by, Christians organized them-

[1]John R. W. Stott, *The Message of Galatians* (Downers Grove, IL: InterVarsity, 1984), 151–52.

selves to counter criticisms of the Bible by attempting to outthink their most stringent intellectual critiques. Today, people come to church and see the building and hear the words, but they are looking for us not only to outthink our critics but to outlive them. They come for a taste of heaven, especially today in a society used to promises that aren't worth much. They come to experience the sweetness of the fruit of the Spirit. They are looking for the real deal.

Our task, as Jesus put it, is to deny ourselves, take up our cross, and follow him. Or, as Paul said, to walk by the Spirit. When we do that, we all get to enjoy the fruit.

30

Gospel and Community

Brothers, if anyone is caught in any transgression, you who are
spiritual should restore him in a spirit of gentleness. Keep watch on
yourself, lest you too be tempted. Bear one another's burdens, and so
fulfill the law of Christ. For if anyone thinks he is something, when he
is nothing, he deceives himself. But let each one test his own work,
and then his reason to boast will be in himself alone and not in his
neighbor. For each will have to bear his own load.

GALATIANS 6:1–5

When I was waiting for our third child to be delivered in the hospital, I
happened to notice the laminated cards entitled "Birth Affirmations." A
preacher is always on the lookout for application and illustration from
real life, so I asked the nurse if I could keep them. Here they are:

> There is no need to hurry.
> I am one of thousands today.
> My body grows the perfect size baby for me.
> I am relaxed as I feel the power of my contractions.
> My body knows exactly what to do.
> I feel the love of those who are helping me.
> I experience one contraction at a time.
> My body is strong and knows what to do.
> Untapped sources of strength are available to me.
> I am open to the energy of birth.
> I am giving our baby the very best start in life.
> I easily complete all my important tasks.
> Childbirth is a normal healthy event.
> I can connect to whatever belief system I have faith in.

There you have the philosophy of relativistic, pragmatic pluralism with a
smattering of commonsense niceness applied to real life, and you don't get

much more *real life* than in the delivery room. What we believe impacts everything we do, from birth all the way to death, and every part in between.

In Galatians 6 Paul applies his teaching about the gospel to the real life of communal interaction in the local church. The first and last word of chapter 6 (not including the final "Amen") is the word "brothers." Everything from start to finish in this chapter is about how we interact as brothers and sisters in the family of the local church.

I used to think that these final verses of the teaching in Galatians were just helpful, practical instruction, but actually they are what the gospel looks like in community. And they are by contrast what legalism looks like. Paul is saying that a grace-filled community is a restorative community, whereas a legalistic community is a judgmental community.

A Restorative Community

A grace-filled community is a restorative community. This principle of restoration is found throughout the passage but introduced in the first two verses: "Brothers, if anyone is caught in any transgression, you who are spiritual should restore him in a spirit of gentleness. Keep watch on yourself, lest you too be tempted. Bear one another's burdens, and so fulfill the love of Christ" (vv. 1–2). I want you to notice three things about how a grace-filled community is a restorative community.

1) *A grace-filled community is quick to extenuate, not exaggerate, the sins of those in the community.* The word translated "transgression" is a gentle or kind word. It has the sense of a misstep. Paul is perhaps carrying on the metaphor of walking in the Spirit: "If anyone missteps." This is extenuating language for failure, not condemnatory language. It doesn't exaggerate the fault but makes less of it. We find the same attitude of extenuation rather than exaggeration of others' sins in a grace-filled community where Paul says, "Keep watch on yourself, lest you too be tempted."

A grace-filled community is full of grace-filled individuals who realize that any sin in anyone else is something that they too could easily fall into. "There but for the grace of God go I" is a phrase than any spiritual man or woman must have frequently on their lips and in their hearts when they look at others' sins, however distasteful they may appear to us naturally. Spiritually, we know that we are sinners too, and that we are just as liable to a misstep.

This is very different from a legalistic community, which judges, condemns, and exaggerates the missteps of those around, making them worse, not better, exaggerating them, not extenuating them. Our spiritual maturity in church will be indicated not so much by the number of books we have on our shelves but by our attitude toward those who fail.

2) *A grace-filled community is restorative.* "You who are spiritual should *restore* him [or her] in a spirit of gentleness." Paul chooses a word for "restore" that, in secular Greek, was a medical term employed for setting a broken bone or mending a fracture.

How different is a legalistic community! A legalistic community breaks and hurts; a grace-filled community is in the business of bringing healing to people who make missteps. What a relief! If this is the case, we don't need to wear a mask. We all have made missteps, we all will make missteps. Only in a grace-filled community can we take off the mask and be open and honest with each other, because a grace-filled community is restorative.

Sunday is a funny day,
It starts with lots of noise,
Mummy rushes around with socks,
And Daddy shouts, "You boys!"

Then Mummy says, "Now don't blame them,
You know you're just as bad,
You've only just got out of bed,
It really makes me mad!"

And when we get to church at last,
It's really very strange,
'Cos Mum and Dad stop arguing,
And suddenly they change.

At church my mum and dad are friends,
They get on very well,
But no one knows they've had a row,
And I'm not gonna tell.

Daddy loves the meetings,
He's always at them all,
He's learning how to understand
The letters of St. Paul.

But Mummy says, "I'm stuck at home
To lead my Christian life,
It's just as well for Paul
He didn't have a wife."

I once heard my mummy say
She'd walk out of his life,
I once heard Daddy say to her
He'd picked a rotten wife.

They really love each other,
I really think they do.
I think the people in the church
Would help them—if they knew.

Contrary to a legalistic community, where we need to hide for fear of being judged, a grace-filled community is a place where broken bones get healed and souls get fully restored.

3) *A grace-filled community rightly understands and applies what it means to be spiritual.* There are those who are spiritual, as opposed to those making a misstep (caught in a sin), but that sense of the spiritual is seen in those who gently restore others, bearing the fruit of the Spirit that Paul has recently described, including the trait of gentleness, and in this way fulfilling the law of Christ, which is to love your neighbor as yourself. To have the Holy Spirit in us and filling us means to be spiritual, which means to be acting as Christ did, he who did not come to condemn the world, but to save it, who did not come to be served but to serve and give his life as a ransom for many (John 3:17; Mark 10:45).

Paul says here that a grace-filled community is a restorative community, but he is also comparing that with what happens when a community embodies instead the legalistic teaching of his opponents who were telling the Galatians that their moral lifestyle would save them. So a grace-filled community is a restorative community, whereas a legalistic community is a judgmental community.

A Legalistic Community

Paul contrasts a grace-filled community with a legalistic community: "For if anyone thinks he is something, when he is nothing, he deceives himself. But let each one test his own work, and then his reason to boast will be in himself alone and not in his neighbor. For each will have to bear his own load." (vv. 3–5)

In 2008, Hal Niedzvicki wrote a *New York Times Magazine* article explaining his experience with the community of Facebook. He had accumulated seven hundred "friends" but found he was actually having fewer real-life interactions with people. So he decided he would ask his Facebook friends to meet up with him for a party. Of his seven hundred friends, fifteen said they would show up, and sixty said they might. When the evening came, one person showed up, and he didn't even know her; she was a friend of a friend. After some embarrassed moments of small talk, this friend of a friend made excuses and left. Hal waited till midnight. No one else came. Seven hundred friends, he concluded in his article, and all alone.[1]

I was amused to discover that Facebook issued a cease and desist order against the website *uSocial* because it was offering a service through which one could buy targeted packages of up to five thousand "friends."[2] This strange modern reality of being surrounded by people yet lonely is not only a result of contemporary technology but also the consistent result of legalistic community, whatever the technology used.

Legalistic community makes you think you are "something" (v. 3). Instead of carrying each other's burdens, legalism doesn't make you think "there but for the grace of God go I" but makes you pray like the Pharisee, "I thank you that I am not like other men" (Luke 18:11) but better than they. When we believe that our moral performance—being born in a Christian home, living a proper moral life, doing the right things, saying the right things, brushing our teeth twice a day, wearing nice clothes, not swearing, being intelligent, looking nice on the out-

---

[1] Hal Niedzviecki, "Facebook in a Crowd," *New York Times Magazine,* October 26, 2008.
[2] Http://news.bbc.co.uk/2/hi/technology/8370302.stm.

side—is what makes us right with God, then we think we are something (when really, because we are all naturally sinners, we are all nothing), and we are self-deceived. It creates a community of fakery, distance, and judgmentalism rather than restoration, because we are looking down our long noses at other people who dare to make mistakes.

Legalistic community always makes comparisons to other people (v. 4). Paul uses a surprising expression—"his reason to boast will be in himself"—but he is talking about appropriate self-confidence. As one commentator says, "[Boasting] is in itself a less opprobrious term than the English word 'boast,' referring rather to exultation, gratulation, without the implication of the English word that it is excessive or unjustified."[3] All our works are Christ's work in us, so when we see ourselves reaching out, restoring, loving, we can have an appropriate confidence in ourselves. It is really a confidence in Christ, for it is his work through us. This releases us from the continual tendency to compare ourselves with each other. Who is better? Who has the nicer car or the better house? Who is prettier, who is smarter—the intellectual fashion parade of academia? We are instead, as the French say, to be "happy in our own skin."

Legalistic community is very different from that. It constantly jostles for position. If I am saved by what I do, I will constantly be asking myself whether I am doing more than others; but if I am saved by what Christ has done, then I need only observe whether I am bearing the fruit of the Spirit, and if I am, then I boast in myself, which is really a boasting in Christ. I have an appropriate self-confidence, which is really Christ-confidence.

Legalistic community does not serve (v. 5). It may seem counterintuitive, but the more secure we are in grace, the more we will carry our own load. Paul uses different nouns in verse 5 from those he used in verse 2, where he says that we should carry each other's burdens, but he used the same verb. Paul is saying that we are to carry our own load, that is, the load of carrying each other's burdens, reaching out in restoration to others. There is a balance here between corporate responsibility and individual responsibility. When a grace-filled community is a serving community, I can carry my own load of serving and reaching

---

[3]Richard N. Longenecker, *Galatians*, Word Biblical Commentary (Nashville, TN: Nelson, 1990), 277.

out to others, because I am secure in my relationship with God, secure in my own skin. I can give my time and emotional energy to serving and helping others.

I'm going to conclude with five statements of application comparing a legalistic community with a grace-filled one.

1) A grace-filled community seeks to restore those who make a misstep, whereas a legalistic community condemns them.

2) In a grace-filled community the mature (the "spiritual") are those who, like Jesus, reach out to restore and save, whereas in a legalistic community those held up for honor are, like the Pharisees, seemingly able to achieve more personal, if superficial, moral attainment than others.

3) A grace-filled community encourages individuals who are secure and have an appropriate self-confidence, which is really a confidence in what God is doing in their lives through faith in Christ, whereas a legalistic community encourages insecure individuals to try to prove their worth by being better than others.

4) A grace-filled community is full of individuals who think very little of themselves, not because they do not have self-worth but because they are thinking of others and how they can help them, whereas a legalistic community is full of individuals who think highly of themselves and thus are self-deceived. Anything good comes from God, for naturally none of us is good.

5) A grace-filled community is full of energy, service, and outreach. Each one carries his own load of restoration, other people's burdens, whereas a legalistic community is full of individuals who do very little, for they are always wondering about whether they have done enough to be saved. Rather than focusing on what God has done, they are focused on what they need to do.

The Wemmicks

In the well-known story of the Wemmicks, Punchinello lives among a village of wooden creatures all made by Eli, a carpenter up on a hill, and these wooden creatures give each other stars if they approve and dots if they disapprove. Punchinello is covered in dots. His paint is peeling, his joints are creaking, and all the other Wemmicks disapprove of him. One day he notices another Wemmick who has neither dots nor stars.

Fascinated, he follows her to the carpenter, their creator. Once in his presence Punchinello begins to understand that what matters is not what the other Wemmicks think about him but what God thinks.

"The stickers only stick if they matter to you. The more you trust my love, the less you care about the stickers."

"I'm not sure I understand."

"You will, but it will take time. You've got a lot of marks. For now, just come to see me every day and let me remind you how much I care."

Eli lifted Punchinello off the bench and set him on the ground. "Remember," Eli said as the Wemmick walked out the door, "you are special because I made you. And I don't make mistakes."

Punchinello didn't stop, but in his heart he thought, "I think he really means it." And when he did, a dot fell to the ground.

It is a well-crafted story with a lot of emotional punch that has been helpful to many, but amazingly Paul has something even more profound and compelling to communicate. Yes, we are made by God and therefore in his image and of great value—a wonderful truth to be reflected upon. But the reason we can live in a grace-filled community, restoring and being restored, rather than in a legalistic community, judging and being judged, is not just that we are all made by God and therefore special. It is because we are saved by God and therefore righteous. We are, in other words, brothers and sisters.

Underneath the word *brothers*, which begins and ends Galatians 6, there is, as the old commentator Bengel put it, "a whole theology." That is, we are united in our fallenness, covered with dots and marks, but also now united in our reception of grace. Until we realize just how bad, scarred, broken, and in need of restoration we all are, and just how much grace we have received. If we are Christians, we will tempted to judge each other with stars and dots and the occasional finger wag or "Tut, tut," writing letters of judgment, and leaving little anonymous notes of self-righteousness.

The Christian community, rightly and truly understood and experienced, is an outpost of heaven on earth, where we are all brethren with a common Father, all restored by a common Savior, and all seeking to restore each other. May we be increasingly a part of, and foster, a grace-filled community.

31

The Gospel Harvest

One who is taught the word must share all good things with the one who teaches. Do not be deceived: God is not mocked, for whatever one sows, that will he also reap. For the one who sows to his own flesh will from the flesh reap corruption, but the one who sows to the Spirit will from the Spirit reap eternal life. And let us not grow weary of doing good, for in due season we will reap, if we do not give up. So then, as we have opportunity, let us do good to everyone, and especially to those who are of the household of faith.

GALATIANS 6:6–10

When we read the Bible, it is very easy to feel that it is largely a matter of theory. Not only is it an old book, but also it deals with matters which we know that many people ignore yet seem to live perfectly prosperous lives. Many of the greatest heroes of modern life, from movie stars to celebrity CEOs, do not live exemplary biblical lives, so when we find the Bible urging us not to do certain things, to do other things, and to believe in various matters, it is easy to think about it in largely theoretical terms.

The Bible says "do good," but who will really notice if we do not? The Bible says God is real, but what of it, when there are respected atheists who say he is not? The Bible says Jesus is the only way to heaven, but what of it, when there are millions who believe he is not? We don't quite treat the Bible as Charles Dickens's *A Christmas Carol*, nor do we quite treat God like "Santa Claus," but it is very easy for us, when we read the Bible, to treat it as theory, as a series of ideals that, if we largely ignore in the practical day-to-day reality, will have little consequence to our lives.

That's what Paul addresses in Galatians 6:6–10. One reason why people move away from the gospel to a more works-orientated message is that the works-orientated message appears more practical. When we say we are saved by faith alone, it can appear as the ultimate theory: "I just have to believe it; I don't have to do anything about it." So Paul introduces an analogy to help us see that the gospel of the Bible is not a matter of theory but has very practical results. That analogy is one of *harvest*. He refers to the well-known process of sowing seeds and then reaping harvest. When we sow certain kinds of seeds, we get a certain kind of harvest; as we have sown, so we reap. He is walking us through a wheat field bending in the summer sun and reminding us that the wheat is there because the seed was first sown. He walks us past a harvest table of fruit and vegetables and reminds us that the harvest is there because the seed was first sown. He says this is very much what it's like in our daily, practical lives: what we reap is what we have sown.

In other words, Paul is in a way addressing the same thing that the comedian Fred Allen joked about when he remarked, "Most of us spend the first six days of each week sowing wild oats, then we go to church on Sunday and pray for a crop failure." This is the principle of the harvest, and Paul introduces it to us in three areas.

Share All Good Things

Paul says that the principle of harvest applies to the way we treat our Bible teachers: "One who is taught the word must share all good things with the one who teaches" (v. 6). At first glance, all the remarks in verses 6 to 10 appear somewhat unrelated, but when we inspect more closely the principle of the harvest—the analogy that Paul is using—we see that it is the connecting theme throughout each of the three areas. So, the Word is the seed and the sharing is the harvest. The principle of the harvest applies to Christian ministry.

Those who sow the Word may expect from that sowing to experience a harvest; and those who receive the Word and so receive a harvest are to share that bountiful harvest with those who do the sowing. The ideal of paying people to preach the gospel and teach the Bible is not a modern invention; it goes back to biblical times. When Jesus commissioned the seventy-two to their work of teaching the Word, he told them that they were to receive support from those they taught, saying, "The laborer deserves his wages" (Luke 10:7). Likewise we are reminded, "The Lord commanded that those who proclaim the gospel should get their living by the gospel" (1 Cor. 9:14). This is a basic harvest principle, a principle of sowing the Word and then sharing the harvest. Paul rather unflatteringly reminds us about those whose work is preaching and teaching: "The Scripture says, 'You shall not muzzle an ox when it treads out the grain,' and, 'The laborer deserves his wages'" (1 Tim. 5:18). Paul is quoting from Deuteronomy and from Jesus in Luke's Gospel. The reason for all this is quite practical. As Martin Luther said about it, "It is impossible for one man both to labor day and night to get a living, and at the same time to give himself to the study of sacred learning as the preaching office requireth."

We don't need to emphasize the point any more than Paul does, but it is worth making two observations from Paul's words in Galatians 6:6.

1) *It is worth observing that the analogy Paul uses is a motivation to excellence, hard work, devotion, and faithful Christian Word ministry.* Those who teach God's Word are to be motivated by the principle of sowing and harvest and to realize that they are to be diligent in their teaching. There is no liberty for the supported to be lazy about their work but rather, like the hard-working farmer, give themselves diligently—early in the morning, late at night—to the work of sowing, knowing that this will mean not only a sharing in the harvest in terms of support, but also—much more—a sharing in the harvest in terms of eternal life.

2) *It is worth observing that the analogy Paul uses is also a motivation to excellent and committed support to those who are in faithful Christian Word ministry.* Those who receive instruction in God's Word primarily from their pastors have a motivation to look after their pastors well, by this analogy of harvest. Many other factors can come into play, but a major cause of congregational health and growth in experiencing the harvest is connected to the seed that is sown, which is connected to the faithfulness of the sowing and the support for the sowers, or the oxen, as Paul unflatteringly also calls them. This is not simply a payment but an expression of the *koinonia*, the sharing, the fellowship that we together as brothers and sisters have in the gospel.

If you want a good harvest, pray that the Lord of the harvest would send more workers into the harvest field. Those workers work zealously sowing the Word, so keep those workers well-fueled so they can keep on sowing.

Personal Godliness

The analogy of the harvest is applied to our personal godliness: "Do not be deceived: God is not mocked, for whatever one sows, that will he also reap. For the one who sows to his own flesh will from the flesh reap corruption, but the one who sows to the Spirit will from the Spirit reap eternal life" (vv. 7–8).

Paul takes his teaching about the flesh and the Spirit from chapter 5 and superimposes upon it this same analogy of the harvest. Instead of the picture being that of two elements at war, there are now two fields in which we may sow either fleshy deeds or Spirit-filled deeds. We may sow the acts of the flesh—sexual immorality, impurity, idolatry, jealousy, and the like—or we may sow to please the Spirit—love, joy, peace, patience, kindness. The harvest will depend on what we sow. The flesh will reap destruction, a corruption of the rotting acts of the sinful nature. The Spirit will reap eternal life. Do not be deceived: God cannot be mocked.

It is important to see this analogy of seed and harvest in relation to our personal godliness, because it is tempting to think that what we do does not matter much in real life. I remember a famous story told of President Coolidge, who after hearing a particular preacher, was asked what he had preached about, and Coolidge replied, "Sin," and when asked what the preacher had said about sin, Coolidge replied, "He was against it." This fails the test of practicality that G. K. Chesterton, in typical wit, exposed when asked what book he would bring if he were stranded on a desert island. He said, "Thomas's practical guide to ship-building." We need to know not just that we should be against sin, but also why we are against it. The answer is, "because there is a harvest coming."

Picture that field. See the harvest of the secret jealous thought sown. See the harvest of the illicit pornography sown in that field of the flesh. See the discord, the dissensions. Imagine the harvest of the corruption that comes from sowing to the flesh. God cannot be mocked. There is a principle of the harvest: "Sow a thought, reap a deed; sow a deed, reap a habit; sow a habit, reap a destiny." If you want to be really happy and content, if you want to be truly and eternally joyful, then the great secret of Christian godliness is to sow not to the flesh but to the Spirit. Each little thought and deed mounts up and builds toward a harvest. Sow instead to the Spirit, with regular Bible study and a devotional prayer life. Sow to the Spirit by letting God's Word be sown in your life through the preaching of the gospel. Sow to the Spirit by committed service among God's people. Sow to the Spirit by forgiving, loving, and telling others about Jesus. As you do, you will look forward to a harvest of eternity, as the harvest field of the Spirit is packed with a bountiful fruit.

Doing Good

He applies the principle of the harvest to our active doing good: "Let us not grow weary of doing good, for in due season we will reap, if we do not give up. So then, as we have opportunity, let us do good to everyone, and especially to those who are of the household of faith" (vv. 9–10). Philanthropic activity in the church and in the wider community is something we can grow tired of, so it is necessary to constantly find motivation to keep active in "doing good." Here Paul provides that motivation.

Why continue to give sacrificially? Why continue to serve faithfully? Why not give up when the winds of circumstances blow hard against us, or when criticism comes, or more simply when our favorite TV show is on that evening? What makes us use our spare time toward looking after the poor, reaching out with the gospel to our neighbor, or serving in a certain ministry? Paul says, "In due season we will reap, if we do not give up."

Can you imagine the farmer going out to sow early in the morning and saying to himself, "This is hard work, so I'm going back to bed"? He keeps going because of the harvest. Paul does not say precisely what this harvest is, but it is related to the harvest of the fruit of the Spirit—the love, joy, and peace—and the harvest reward that comes in eternity. When we faithfully do good in church or community, there is always a harvest of some kind. There is the harvest of dearly loved ones coming to faith in Jesus. There is the harvest of a healthy community loving and caring for each other. There is the harvest of civil society being influenced by Christian salt and light to become more conducive to human flourishing. There is, ultimately, the harvest of glory with Christ forever.

Perhaps you feel weary. Perhaps you have served hard throughout this year and you are seeing very little harvest. Paul is saying, "Don't become weary; we are talking about the basic principle of sowing and reaping, the principle of harvest." If you sow wild oats, you reap wild destruction. If you sow God's Word, you reap a bountiful harvest. Of course it takes time; we cannot expect to sow a seed and see a harvest immediately. But in due time a harvest is coming.

It is a great warning to all of us, who are tempted to sow toward the flesh. Do not be deceived: God cannot be mocked. We cannot thumb our nose at him; we cannot disparage him as if he does not see or know. God has set in reality a deliberate policy of harvest. It is his way. It is the principle of the harvest. Just as we sow at a certain time and reap at another appropriate time, our activities and actions, our sowing to the flesh or to the Spirit, our deeds and our beliefs, the attitudes of our heart as well as the deeds of our life—all these things will produce a harvest.

Sometimes the Bible can seem a bit theoretical. When we view some great, rich man prospering at the expense of all his underlings whom he mistreats, it is easy to think that God is mocked. God is not mocked. The delay is just an expression of his principle of harvest.

We are all farmers sowing into one field or another. We have the field of the flesh, on the one hand; we have the field of the Spirit, on the other. You can sow toward the fruit of joy in this life by sowing love and peace, Bible reading and prayer, and faith and godliness, or you can sow toward the flesh.

Paul is not suddenly saying that we are saved by what we do. He has told them that we are not. But our deeds still matter. Our deeds are an expression of our true faith in Christ; our works are a sign of Christ's work in us. There is fruit. We, as Christians, have two fields before us, the flesh and the Spirit, and how we sow will make all the difference.

Perhaps you are someone who, unknown to others, has been sowing to the flesh, and you are hoping that no one will notice. But you are beginning to realize that God is not deceived. You are beginning to taste the bitter fruit of sowing to the flesh. Your children do not wish to spend holidays with you. Your wife is cold toward you. Your husband struggles to smile at you. Imagine what the harvest of that rotting flesh will be in all eternity. Imagine the ages upon ages of nothing but unending corruption, death, and destruction. If you have any doubt as to whether this is real, or practical, simply look at the harvest. It is a basic principle of reality set in stone, unalterable, that what we sow we will also reap.

Conversely, you might be feeling discouraged because, although you've been sowing to the Spirit, you see no harvest. Don't be like a child who expects that as soon as a seed is sown, a plant will appear the next day. It takes time. Each seed sown will produce a crop but at the appropriate time. Imagine what that will be in eternity. Imagine the little bit of fruit you taste now as a result of your sowing to the Spirit magnified many times over and constantly growing and sweetening for all eternity, the harvest that we will reap in due time if we do not give up.

It is easy to think that the Bible is very theoretical, but actually the Bible is like a seed that is sown, and the harvest is coming.

Epilogue:
The Gospel Underlined

See with what large letters I am writing to you with my own hand. It is those who want to make a good showing in the flesh who would force you to be circumcised, and only in order that they may not be persecuted for the cross of Christ. For even those who are circumcised do not themselves keep the law, but they desire to have you circumcised that they may boast in your flesh. But far be it from me to boast except in the cross of our Lord Jesus Christ, by which the world has been crucified to me, and I to the world. For neither circumcision counts for anything, nor uncircumcision, but a new creation. And as for all who walk by this rule, peace and mercy be upon them, and upon the Israel of God. From now on let no one cause me trouble, for I bear on my body the marks of Jesus. The grace of our Lord Jesus Christ be with your spirit, brothers. Amen.

GALATIANS 6:11-18

"Sorry" may be the hardest word to say, but "good-bye" comes close. Especially when you care for people, you are worried about them, and you long to be there to help. That's what Paul was going through here, saying good-bye to the churches of the Galatians at the end of a letter where he has poured out his heart about matters not of secondary or passing importance, but about issues to do with the very heart of the gospel and of eternal consequence. He has said to them that they have been moving away from the gospel, and he has called them back to that one true gospel of Jesus Christ. Now, he commits them to the grace of God, wishes them well, and says good-bye.

He not only summarizes the message he has been preaching, but he also underlines it and puts it in bold. So, when Paul says, "See with what large letters I am writing to you with my own hand" (v. 11), Paul is doing the ancient equivalent of underlining, or using the bold font on an e-mail. These last few words (his good-bye) are in ALL CAPS.

Paul had the practice of ending his letters with a sample of his own writing as a proof that the letter came directly from him (see 1 Cor. 16:21; Col. 4:18; 2 Thess. 3:17), but only here in Galatians is this sample of his writing specifically said to be with "large letters." Sometimes people have thought that this was because Paul had bad handwriting, an opinion with which those of us with poor penmanship certainly empathize. Others have wondered whether Paul wrote with such large letters because his eyesight was poor. These are possibilities, but it seems more likely that Paul is deliberately employing a visual technique for emphasizing how important these final few sentences are. The words are very large so that those in the congregations who are having the letter read to them (rather than the one doing the reading) also get that he has written this part with large letters.

How do you say good-bye to those you care about, who cause you worry, that you walk with so that you can help them keep on the straight and narrow? What you do is say to them, "If you forget everything else I've said, remember this." That's what Paul is doing here. This is the most important thing he has written in the whole letter. It is in bold. It is underlined. It is ALL CAPS. It is with such large letters of the apostle. In summary, he says that *legalism is attractive because it is popular, whereas biblical Christianity is always cross-shaped or cruciform.*

Paul is drawing a clear contrast between legalism, which is attractive because it appeals to the flesh, that is, what is popular to our sinful nature and the gospel of grace and peace, which is always cross shaped. Legalism is about the flesh; Christianity is about the cross.

This is the central and most important point of the book of Galatians, but it is also emphasized throughout the Bible. For instance, in the very heart of Mark's Gospel, where Peter confesses that Jesus is the Christ but is then rebuked for saying that Christ must not die on a cross, we find the same thing (Mark 8:27–33). It is the very heart of the temptation of Jesus to ascend the Messiah's throne, the kingly throne of David, without suffering, without the cross. Christianity without the cross is satanic, it is legalistic, and it is popular because it appeals to our flesh. It claims to offer us God without having to die to ourselves and take up our cross and follow Jesus. Legalism is attractive because it is popular, whereas biblical Christianity is always cross shaped or cruciform.

The Appeal of Legalism

Legalism is appealing because it goes easy on our flesh, our sinful nature: "It is those who want to make a good showing in the flesh who would force you to be circumcised, and only in order that they may not be persecuted for the cross of Christ. For even those who are circumcised do not themselves keep the law, but they desire to have you circumcised that they may boast in your flesh" (vv. 12–13). I want you to notice four things about this side.

1) *Galatians is not really about circumcision but about what circumcision means.* Paul says this explicitly in verse 15: "For neither circumcision counts for anything, nor uncircumcision, but a new creation." Paul is not writing this letter to stop the Galatians from doing ritual Judaistic ceremonies; he is writing to show them that neither circumcised nor uncircumcised is the point. The point is being born again. The point is the new creation. This is of such great importance that Paul not only underlines it with large letters, but he also says that this is the *rule*: "And as for all who walk by this rule, peace and mercy be upon them" (v. 16). This is the central principle of gospel Christianity.

The ancient commentator Jerome was wrong to say that the message of Galatians is just about ritual food rules and circumcision. Paul explicitly says that is not what it's about; it is about being born again. The reason he is talking about circumcision is that the false teachers were trying to get the Galatians to be circumcised, *and*, he says in verse 12, the reason why they are trying to get them to be circumcised is that they want to look good outwardly, or literally, "in the flesh."

2) *Circumcision in this context means an attempt to make a good impression outwardly.* If I can be justified before God by doing something, then it is pleasing to my flesh and makes a good impression. If, on the other hand, as the Bible teaches, there is nothing good in me, and there is nothing I can do in my own power to escape from God's wrath, it does not please my flesh. It humbles me. Only if I let the Spirit do that work of humbling in me can I hear "blessed are the meek, blessed are the poor in Spirit, blessed are those who hunger and thirst for righteousness."

It is a fundamental distinction. Paul is not just speculating about the motives of the false teachers without warrant; nor has he been granted a sort of apostolic X-ray vision, like Superman, to see what they were really thinking and feeling inside. He is just teaching the gospel in this context. The reason why any legalistic message is appealing—anything that says "do this" or "do that"—is that it makes the flesh look good. There will always be a market for that kind of teaching because it is the nature of our human condition.

3) *The appeal to make a good impression outwardly has an added bonus: it helps you avoid persecution for the cross of Christ.* This held appeal in Galatia because it had the effect of avoiding persecution. Getting circumcised would render the Galatian Christians still part of the Jewish community, and therefore they would not be persecuted by other Jews, or by the Romans, perhaps, for Judaism was a grandfathered religion within the pluralism of the ancient Roman Empire.

The same thing is happening today. What makes legalistic messages appealing? Ceremonial and "you've just got to do good things" messages are appealing, in essence, because they offer the same message as any other religion. That's appealing because it stops us from sticking out as those who say that Jesus is the only way to the Father. In many ways, ancient Roman pluralism was like modern global pluralism. Preach Christ crucified, believe that, and pretty soon you get into trouble. If you smash together Hanukkah and "Jingle Bells" and everything else because everyone is trying to be good, then you're fine; but preach Christ crucified and pretty soon you're going to get into trouble.

4) *The whole legalistic thing is a sham*: "For even those who are circumcised do not themselves keep the law" (v. 13). Do this and you'll be saved, but do you? No, you don't. You tithe of your cumin and herbs, but you neglect the weightier matters of justice and mercy. You make your phylacteries wide and your prayer shawls long, but you won't lift a finger to help others escape the judgment of the law and put their faith in Christ crucified (see Matt. 23:1–12). Whether it is issues of global justice, basic neighbor love, or even driving without road rage, we all know that we don't keep the law, however appealing to our flesh might be the idea that we would. So legalism is a sham.

5) Paul says in ALL CAPS that *legalism is attractive because it is popular.* He wants us to get that this is a constant tendency of human religion, of Christianity to degenerate into legalism, of Christianity without the cross. Paul is writing not against circumcision per se but

against how circumcision was being used to self-justify, to avoid persecution for the cross of Christ, and to show us that legalistic techniques to justify ourselves don't work because none of us keep the rules.

So in his good-bye to the Galatians this is the first part that he wants to emphasize. He wants to draw them away from the attraction of a wrong understanding of Christianity, so prevalent then, so frequently prevalent throughout church history—so common today—by showing that this legalism is attractive because it is popular to the flesh, the sinful nature, and it doesn't really work. It just produces hypocrites.

Shaped Like the Cross

Biblical Christianity is always cross shaped or cruciform. This is the second half of the passage from verse 14 to the end, it reads: "Far be it from me to boast except in the cross of our Lord Jesus Christ, by which the world has been crucified to me, and I to the world. For neither circumcision counts for anything, nor uncircumcision, but a new creation. And as for all who walk by this rule, peace and mercy be upon them, and upon the Israel of God. From now on let no one cause me trouble, for I bear on my body the marks of Jesus. The grace of our Lord Jesus Christ be with your spirit, brothers. Amen" (vv. 14–18).

I know of no power in the world but the gospel of Jesus Christ that brings a new creation. I have no hope for the future of the world, or the church, but the gospel of Jesus Christ. Anyone I have seen transformed to a new creation has been made so through the cross of Jesus Christ. The flesh does not like this. It is deeply humbling. Our selfish self is crucified as we put our trust in Christ alone, but as we do, the Holy Spirit makes us new. The gospel is the power for a new creation, and the gospel renews the church too.

We must embrace this truth *personally* (vv. 11, 17). We have already seen the way that Paul puts his name on the line by writing in extra-large letters to emphasize the point. He's not going to boast in anything else but the cross of Jesus Christ. Those of us who have influence—we all have a sphere of influence—from family to work to friends—those who write books or blogs, those who get interviewed or teach, put in ALL CAPS this message. Make it personal. Put your name on the line. Say, "This is my name boasting in nothing else but the cross of Jesus Christ."

You must make it personal if the church is going to be renewed, not in the sense of its being about you but of your putting your name on the line for Jesus. It is about him, not about you. You must embrace it personally not just in name but also in body (v. 17). The medieval church vainly speculated about how these stigmata or marks, as it is translated, were psychosomatic creations of fevered and focused attention in some spiritual sense, but what Paul has in mind is something far more real. He offers to them the marks on his body of the beatings that he experienced for preaching Christ crucified.

I suspect few reading this have been physically beaten up for the gospel, but that is what Paul is talking about, and what some Christians risk still today around the world. Even if we do not risk physical abuse for Christ, we do risk verbal abuse. We risk being socially marginalized, not getting the career promotion, having others sneer about us for being "one of those gospel people." When that happens, be like Paul and say, "Let no one cause me any more trouble, for I bear the marks of Christ." In other words, it is a sweet thing to realize that our sufferings are for Christ's sake, and it enables us to bear them. Martin Luther, who knew a thing or two about suffering for the gospel, in a wonderful passage expresses this principle:

> When we consider the sufferings we receive only so far as we ourselves
> are involved in them, they become not only troubling but intolerable.
> But when the second person "Thy" is added to them, so that we can
> say (2 Cor. 1:5): "We share abundantly in Thy sufferings, O Christ,"
> and as the psalm says (44:22), "For Thy sake we are slain all day
> long," then our sufferings become not only easy but actually sweet, in
> accordance with the saying (Matt. 11:30): "My burden is light, and
> My yoke is easy."[1]

We must embrace it *personally*, this gospel of the cross that leads to the new creation by the Spirit.

We must also embrace it *decisively*: it is through the cross of Jesus Christ that "the world has been crucified to me, and I to the world" (v. 14). That means the world is dead to us and we to the world; it means

---

[1]Martin Luther, *Lectures on Galatians*, Luther's Works, ed. Jaroslav Jan Pelikan (St. Louis, MO: Concordia, 1963), 134.

that it is over. No more hankering over the nicer sports car, bigger job, or more impressive ministry we could have had if we had just compromised and gone with what the world wanted. It is crucified, dead, over, fatally and finally, *decisively* done with.

Personally and decisively—but why? Why embrace the cross, why die to the self? What's the rationale for that? Is it just masochistic or people manipulating us to do things that are bad for us but good for them? No, it is personal, decisive, and also purposeful: "And as for all who walk by this rule, peace and mercy be upon them, and upon the Israel of God" (v. 16). And, "The grace of our Lord Jesus Christ be with your spirit, brothers" (v. 18). There is a purpose to this, a distinct gain—peace and mercy through the grace of Jesus. It is the gospel of grace and peace. That is the summary of his message in ALL CAPS—grace alone by faith alone in Jesus alone (his cross), which is the only way to have peace with God.

No more guilt. No more internal voice constantly, emotionally, wondering whether you have done enough, or done the right thing, or worked hard enough, or whether that thing you did years ago is hanging over your head like Damocles's sword. No more skeleton in the cupboard waiting to come out and mess everything up so that you go through the world with your head down, just waiting for the other shoe to fall.

All peace, but not because you *feel* peace. Paul is talking about the marks on his body. He didn't feel peace always; he had conflict with others. Paul is contrasting legalistic teaching with gospel teaching. There are times of great conflict between the true teachers of the gospel and the false. Our peace is not peace inside, or peace with other people, but the ultimate, cosmic peace with God. From that place of stability and eternal confidence, you can peacefully sail through the biggest storms.

Grace and peace in bold, in ALL CAPS—see what large letters Paul is writing this. A new creation is the only the thing that counts, the cross of Christ through faith alone that leads to us being made new and to the church being renewed. It is the hope for the entire universe. Grace and peace—don't forget it. If you forget everything else, remember this: legalism is appealing because it attracts our sinful human flesh, whereas biblical Christianity is all about the cross through which we are a new creation. "The grace of our Lord Jesus Christ be with your spirit, brothers. Amen."

General Index

Scripture Index